HEMINGWAY
IN ITALY
AND
OTHER
ESSAYS

HEMINGWAY IN ITALY AND OTHER ESSAYS

Edited by
ROBERT W. LEWIS

PRAEGER

New York
Westport, Connecticut
London

Library of Congress Cataloging-in-Publication Data

Hemingway in Italy and other essays / edited by Robert W. Lewis.
    p. cm.
    Includes bibliographical references.
    ISBN 0-275-92916-7
    1. Hemingway, Ernest, 1899–1961—Criticism and interpretation.
  2. Hemingway, Ernest, 1899–1961—Knowledge—Italy. 3. Italy in
literature. I. Lewis, Robert W. (Robert William), 1930– .
PS3515.E37Z61794   1990
813'.54—dc20   89-48747

Library of Congress Catalog Card Number: 89–48747
ISBN: 0-275-92916-7

First published in 1990

Praeger Publishers, One Madison Avenue, New York, NY 10010
An imprint of Greenwood Publishing Group, Inc.

Printed in the United States of America

The paper used in this book complies with the
Permanent Paper Standard issued by the National
Information Standards Organization (Z39.48-1984).

10 9 8 7 6 5 4 3 2 1

Ai nostri amici italiani

Contents

Introduction

Robert W. Lewis

The title of this collection of essays about Ernest Hemingway and his writings derives from the fact that they were among the 50 presentations at the Second International Conference of the Hemingway Society convened in Lignano Sabbiadoro, Province of Udine, Republic of Italy, in June 1986. The place was near his beloved Venice and the area where he had served as a Red Cross volunteer in World War I. Hemingway had often commented on the countries to which he was most attracted, in which he was most "at home." Along with some of his contemporaries who also had an unusual sensitivity to *place* (like D. H. Lawrence, James Joyce, and William Faulkner), Hemingway had strong antipathies and strong attachments to certain landscapes and the people of them. He loved northern Michigan, Spain, Cuba and its waters, and the American high west.

As to Italy, it had a prominent place in his life and in his heart. His World War I experiences, including severe wounding, became inspirations for two novels and a number of short stories. But even when living in and writing about other countries, he remembered the Italy of his youth and of many subsequent sojourns in and around Venice. For instance, in a draft of the poetic last chapter of *Death in the Afternoon* about bullfighting in Spain, he had written of his love for the north of Italy "from Milan to Brescia, to Verona, to Vicenza . . . to Mestre, up to Treviso, all around the Venetian plain and then up to Barca di Cadore, all of the Dolomites . . . I cared about. . . . . I loved Northern Italy like a fool, truly, the way I had loved northern Michigan." (This quotation appears in context in Donald Junkins' chapter on *Death in the Afternoon*.)

Of course, the individual authors here have written from an indirect experience. Theirs are the critics' and scholars' perspectives who see and understand through Hemingway's eyes and imagination, whether his focus was on Italy or elsewhere. And in some instances the Italian connections are incidental, as in James Brasch's chapter on the lengthy correspondence between Hemingway and Bernard Berenson who lived much of his life in Italy but whom Hemingway never met, there or elsewhere. The point is that for Hemingway the artist Italy was a rich feast for his imagination. We who follow sample courses in the banquet.

In turn, Hemingway's work is very popular in Italy, in both English and Italian. Numerous critical works have been published in Italy (Dario Esposito's "Chronological Bibligraphy of Italian Criticism of Ernest Hemingway, September 1961–April 1986" contains 634 entries, including nine books), and in my view the best documentary on his life is the one produced by Italian television in 1985, *Sulle tracce di Hemingway (In the Footsteps of Hemingway),* a copy of which is in the Hemingway collection in the John F. Kennedy Library.

American literature is still relatively youthful. The first book on Herman Melville, Raymond Weaver's (1921), did not appear until a century after Melville's birth. Ten years later (1931), Hemingway had already published enough notable fiction to ensure his own place in literary history. But apart from reviews very little had been written about Hemingway's work until the 1950s. Much of that criticism has been remarkably hardy, and it still (justly) influences commentary. But the current commentary on Hemingway, the man and his work, has entered new fields, and this collection illustrates the point. Contemporary readings are built on and emerge from a larger grid than was available just a generation ago. These essays illustrate the pluralism and richness of current Hemingway research and criticism. Indeed, the sections of the book that follow, although presented to suggest relationships, might have been arranged in other combinations, but these sections well reflect the focus of the book on reconsiderations of Hemingway's understanding of and treatment of women; his relations to and responses from other writers; the blossoming of textual and critical studies enhanced by the availability of the extensive Hemingway collection in the John F. Kennedy Library; as well as analyses of Hemingway's fiction set in Italy.

Some misconceptions of Hemingway's craft have long plagued criticism about his writing. From the earliest criticism of the 1920s he has been perceived as a hard-boiled epitome of machismo, pointing to the title for his second collectoon of short stories, *Men without Women* to illustrate his failure to present women as sympathetic and fully drawn characters. The feminist movement of the 1960s and 1970s emphatically confirmed the initial criticism that Hemingway's women were either bitches or romantic fantasies but never admirable, sentient, complex creatures in their own right. For a male critic or reader to have a serious interest in Hemingway was a sign of arrested development; for a female critic to have a similar interest was hardly conceivable.

But times change. Even before the publication of the posthumous *Garden of Eden* with its two remarkable women characters, a reassessment of Hemingway's sexual politics had well begun. Both men and women critics, newly aware and willing, were perceiving interesting complexities and nuances in his portrayals of women. Some of these critics were enabled by feminism, but they also found that critical tools from many sources such as textual and stylistic studies could be used to understand Hemingway's works in new and insightful ways.

Linda Miller's chapter is a general introduction to and "reassessment" of Hemingway's women characters. She surveys the women characters of the fiction, the women in Hemingway's life, and his complex responses to them. The other chapters in this section examine two particular characters and a pattern of female characterization.

Peter Hays's analysis of the character and role of Catherine Barkley in *A Farewell to Arms* insightfully persuades us that, far from being a shallow fantasy, she is a courageous existential hero, indeed (to return to an early distinction) the code hero of the novel. In a demonstration of how each part in a well made whole can be revealing, Fern Kory analyzes a minor character from the same novel to substantiate her conclusion that the subtle portrait of Helen Ferguson "reflects the sensitivity towards women of the story's narrator and, finally, its author." Roger Stephenson discovers and traces a remarkable pattern of imagery and diction in *The Sun Also Rises, A Farewell to Arms,* and *For Whom the Bell Tolls,* the three most highly regarded novels. His thesis is that the major women in these novels are presented as whore-like and that the effect of such diction and imagery reveals inadequacies and shortcomings in Hemingway's men. Something of a tour de force, the reading is bound to be provocative and to enlarge the dialogue concerning Hemingway's women.

One endlessly fascinating division of authorial studies is the complex give-and-take relationship that springs up among authors, for no author exists in a vacuum. One's biological and literary lives are filled with rivalries, promotions, fights, and loves. The section of essays on Hemingway's relations to other authors focuses on four very different ones in four very different ways. The lengthy correspondence between Hemingway and his admired elder, the art historian Bernard Berenson, reveals aspects of Hemingway's nature only hinted at elsewhere. James Brasch divines an esthetic sensibility and a longing for a father figure and many other revealing notes on his psychic state in those penultimate years of Hemingway's life (1949–56), and of his correspondence with Berenson.

A very different symbiosis, one that fluctuated radically over the years of their relations, existed between Hemingway and F. Scott Fitzgerald. One part of that well known story of love and hate, mutual admiration and mutual hostility that had been hidden is revealed in Alan Margolies' analysis of the composition of *Tender Is the Night.* He speculates that during the writing of that unusual novel Fitzgerald was drawn to and repelled by elements of Hemingway's life and writing style. The writer who had preceded Hemingway in success and had helped the younger man was lately writing in his shadow.

Yet a different relationship was that of the great Argentine fabulist, Jorge

Luis Borges, in his reading and assessment of Hemingway's work. The views of any major writer about another one are apt to be insightful. In this case, Lawrence Martin so demonstrates as he first summarizes Borges' somewhat idiosyncratic *Introduction to American Literature* and then, picking up on one judgment in it, examines the question, apropos Hemingway, "Is there a connection between the impetus to daring sport and the impetus to creative art?" Apart from the obvious differences between the two activities, Lawrence Martin traces the similarities to conclude that in this regard Hemingway's life was one of integrity.

Eugene Kanjo's article might at first glance seem out of place in this section, and indeed as an analysis of one novel it does not connect Hemingway to one other important writer. Informed by recent critical theory of semiotics and Jacques Derrida, the essay nevertheless is full of cross-references to other writers and literary characters: Tom Jones, Melville's Ishmael, the Red Cross Knight, the Wandering Jew, and Huckleberry Finn among the latter; Nietzsche, Heidegger, Whitman, Eliot, Yeats, Beckett, and Dante among the former, all of these allusions by way of better understanding one work under the complex interwoven fabric of Hemingway's (and our) culture.

The rubric for the third section of this book, Hemingway's texts, may be interpreted in a special sense. All critics deal with texts, of course, but there is a sense in which these four chapters are related, even though they range from the intensely personal in the case of the one by Barry Gross, through poet Donald Junkins' poetical renderings and perceptions of passages in *Death in the Afternoon,* to the scholarly neutrality of Paul Smith's and Michael Reynolds' chapters.

The analysis of "My Old Man" by Michael Reynolds illustrates the maturity of the best current Hemingway scholarship, for it is based not only on a careful reading of this critically neglected story, but also on the scholar's careful tracing of actual events that Hemingway made into fiction. It is a case study of "Memory transformed by imagination" in the first story that Hemginway began and finished in the Paris of his formative years.

Paul Smith's chapter illustrates another scholarly approach to better understanding Hemingway's work, and given the availability of the enormously rich and still growing collection of manuscripts, galleys, letters, and other material in the Hemingway collection of the JFK Library that opened in 1980, gives new insights to the understanding of published work and (as here demonstrated, even some of Hemingway's unpublished work) shows part of the iceberg below the surface. Perhaps the mystery of the omission of "Mons (Three)" will one day be solved. Regardless, its story, here so carefully told, well illustrates the value of textual studies.

Donald Junkins, too, has gone to the vast resources of the JFK collection to discover further how Hemingway's art of omission worked. He also reads both published and unpublished passages from the affective last chapter of *Death in the Afternoon* as prose poems. (Indeed, in his influential anthology *One Hundred*

Modern Poems [1949], Selden Rodman had included as a "poem" two long paragraphs and the beginning of a third from this chapter.) The omitted parts, Donald Junkins concludes, were deleted because they were inappropriate, not because they were not good.

The last chapter here also turns on a textual matter, even though the thesis is not entirely dependent on it. This chapter also illustrates convincingly the maturity of Hemingway scholarship in its frank examination of the sensitive issue of anti-Semitism in "reader response" fashion. A scholarly mode of criticism in a personal essay, combining the convincing trump card of the story of a post–World War II German court case based on a bowdlerized edition of *The Sun Also Rises,* makes for a powerful chapter. Furthermore, this chapter and Eugene Kanjo's on *The Sun Also Rises* reinforce each other in coming at the anti-Semitism in the novel in different but complementary ways.

Hemingway's writing about Italy includes the indisputable masterwork *A Farewell to Arms* and, in an irony of geography if not of career, one of the problematically least valued of his novels, *Across the River and into the Trees.* Italy is also the setting, in whole or in part, for a dozen short stories, and among them some of Hemingway's finest.

In other contexts of this collection, other chapters have also been "Italian"—as, for example, Peter Hays's and Fern Kory's chapters on women characters in *A Farewell to Arms.* But these chapters further extend our understanding of Hemingway's Italian-set fiction with different emphases. Robert Gajdusek's chapter is an intensive reading of one chapter of the novel that is likely to meet resisting readers, but it is nonetheless a thoroughgoing and provocative analysis dealing with persistent themes.

The two chapters on *Across the River and into the Trees* are not likely to be the last essays written on that often derided novel. Indeed, they may well stimulate reconsiderations of it, for in spite of flaws it has values perhaps obscured by readers' preconceptions. Charles Oliver focuses on the characterization of the protagonist Richard Cantwell to read the novel in a different way, seeing it not as a maudlin love story but as a carefully plotted novel in which the focus should be upon death, and the relationships of other characters, principally Alvarito, should be equally important and not overshadowed by the relationship of Renata and Cantwell.

John Paul Russo's chapter could have been placed among those relating Hemingway to other writers, but that he limits himself to *Across the River* as he broadens the understanding of the novel by reading it within the tradition of the European Venetian novel—not Hemingway's relation to one writer but to a wide-ranging group of writers and other artists. He patiently explains how once again many readers underestimated the range and intelligence of Hemingway's knowledge of that tradition and how it fed his fertile imagination. Art is about art, and John Paul Russo argues convincingly and in great detail for a historical reading of this novel.

The last two chapters demonstrate effectively the maturity and diversity of

Hemingway studies, again building on a considerable body of criticism, utilizing revelations from manuscripts and galleys, and reaching out to other disciplines such as psychology and aesthetics. Frank Scafella's chapter avoids the pitfalls of the biographical fallacies that have plagued Hemingway studies, but nevertheless he leads us through the writing of "A Way You'll Never Be" to a thorough understanding of its nature and to a rejection of psychobiographical readings of this and other related stories. Erik Nakjavani's chapter complements Frank Scafella's and includes analyses of those other related stories: "Chapter XI" (from *In Our Time*), "Now I Lay Me," and "In Another Country." Inspired by the brilliant insights regarding images and consciousness in Gaston Bachelard's *The Poetics of Space,* this chapter reveals a pattern in the group of stories that enlarges them as it does our understanding of them.

In diverse ways such as these, Hemingway studies have come of age in our time. And if it were not for some prior author's having preempted the metaphor, I would here invite you to a moveable feast.

I

Hemingway's Women

Hemingway's Women: A Reassessment

Linda Patterson Miller

Ernest Hemingway's heroines are either deadly, like Brett Ashley, or saintly, like Catherine Barkley. At least, Edmund Wilson saw it that way 50 years ago; and today, many critics continue to agree with him. Bernice Kert, for example, stresses the accuracy of Wilson's assessment and how the good heroines reflect Hemingway's fantasies while the bad ones reflect his prejudices (Kert 347; 134). In either case, as Kert and others argue it, Hemingway's female characters are one-dimensional and do not seem real.

This belief that Hemingway's heroines are weak *in* character and weak *as* characters has persisted over time. Do critics condemn Hemingway's heroines because they dislike their characteristics? Or because they dislike Hemingway's supposed male chauvinistic views about women? Or because they dislike the Hemingway that fame erected? Or do they condemn these women on artistic grounds, arguing that weak character delineation makes for stereotypical characters, in this case either passive or predatory ones? Although the important issue to focus on is the artistic one, not the sociological or the biographical one, too many readers of Hemingway impose Hemingway's personas (man, writer, legend) upon his art, thus clouding the issue. Because of the stereotypical views of Hemingway and his art, some readers fail to see Hemingway's art apart from the expected response, primarily that his personal and artistic world was one of machismo. Within such a male-oriented framework, the female characters easily seem too narrowly drawn.

Feminist criticism has helped to foster this view. It, like any other *ism,* too readily imposes a preconditioned, formulaic response on a work. According to the radical feminist formula, men are beasts and women are demeaned by these beasts; men have the power and women lack the power; men have an identity and the freedom to name things, and women lack that identity and freedom.

These women then are confused, isolated, and lost. They have few outlets other than to be adored, be abhorred (with an emphasis on the second syllable), or be downright bitchy. In general, the feminists' major outcry is against a traditional literary canon which promotes a patriarchal worldview. Feminist critics usually feel that this predominantly male view is seldom challenged or shown for what it is—male power masked in the language of idealism and universal truth. Female readers of such literature must learn to think like men if they are to find any personal truths in the works. Judith Fetterley believes that the proper feminist approach and, indeed, the best approach for any reader, is to be a resisting reader. Resist the programmed response by challenging it. Come at the literature from a new critical angle so as to see it fresh. Fetterley admits that she cannot rewrite the literature, but she can name what it shows (Fetterley xxii–xxiii). The act of naming becomes the power which can shake up hardened views and bring the literature to a new light. For many feminist critics, this naming means pointing a finger at male dominance and female subjugation. Fetterley's naming, as related to Hemingway, is that Hemingway projected his real-life hatred of women onto his art. Thus, Frederic Henry in *A Farewell to Arms (AFA)* is actually trying to kill off Catherine throughout the novel (*AFA* 53).

From a feminist perspective, Hemingway's real-life interactions with women do seem suspect. Actually, any lover of Hemingway's art need only look at any of the Hemingway biographies to feel betrayed by the man. The particulars are there. He liked his women to keep their place, and they suffered for it when they did not. Usually the abuse was verbal—more mental than physical. When his women did keep their place, as did (largely) his fourth wife Mary, they suffered just the same, for Hemingway then accused them of weakness. He made strong demands of his women, and he expected them to remain "true," even when he did not. He expected his women to anticipate his needs and to meet his needs, and he faulted them for trying to gain independence. Martha Gellhorn, Hemingway's third wife and a recognized writer on her own, remained determined throughout her several years with Hemingway to stand up to him. It was not belligerence or mean-spiritedness on her part, although that was what Hemingway would later call it. Hemingway did not like domineering women, yet he admired strong women. It was sometimes hard for Hemingway's women to find a comfortable middle ground.

Hemingway did have a strong romantic streak which sometimes verged toward the sentimental; and beneath all the swagger, which intensified as he got older and came to love the "Papa" role, there was sensitivity and tenderness. Hemingway's first wife Hadley recognized that Hemingway's outer toughness was merely a mask for his inner fears. He was deeply sensitive and vulnerable in relationships, she said, and his insecurity, which he tried to disguise, sometimes made him lash out at others (Sokoloff 58). During the 1930s and thereafter, he gained a reputation for his undue harshness to his friends, if not also to his wives. Mary Hemingway believed that, with a man as "complicated and contradictory" as Hemingway, tension and unhappiness were inevitable. Hemingway drove women "to bitchery," she said, and she questioned why so many hung on as long as they did (Kert 414–16). She certainly questioned this of herself as she increasingly assumed a subservient role and allowed herself to be demeaned. She sometimes seemed to rationalize that she so acted in the service of art.

Some never try to explain or justify what Hemingway did in real life because it is incidental to the art. Or some, like Mary Hemingway, try to justify what he did in real life, particularly the inevitable cruelties to others, in the name of Art. This is the "higher-law" argument, which sees art as transcendent and transformative. Hemingway used this argument himself. Take the pain, Hemingway would say to Fitzgerald (28 May 1934) in the *Letters (L),* and *use* it for your art. An artist must first and foremost be an artist, at whatever cost to his humanity (*L* 408).

It was as an artist, and not a man, that Hemingway declared his main criteria for his art. It must be true, not sentimental, decorative, or merely tasteful. He adhered to one of the basic tenets of modernist art. As Paul Klee expressed it, the intention of modernist art was "not to reflect the visible, but to make visible" (Read 8). The emphasis on the verb "to make" is important here. In *A Moveable Feast (AMF)*, Hemingway said that writing was "wonderful to do" after he had learned "to break down" his writing, to "get rid of all facility and try to make instead of describe" (*AMF* 156). So as "to make visible" rather than "to reflect" human experience, Hemingway developed the theory of omission to strengthen his writing. "You could omit anything if you knew that you omitted and the omitted part would strengthen the story and make people feel something more than they understood" (*AMF* 75). Essentially, Hemingway wanted to see people and experiences as they were, not as he thought they were or as he wanted them to be. He tried to explain this to his parents, who were outraged by what they saw as the crudity and immorality of his stories. "I'm trying in all my stories to get the feeling of the actual life across—not to just depict life—or critize it—but to actually make it alive," he wrote his father on March 20, 1925. "So that when you have read something by me you actually experience the thing. You can't do this without putting in the bad and the ugly as well as what is beautiful. Because if it is all beautiful you can't believe in it. Things aren't that way. It is only by showing both sides—3 dimensions and if possible 4 that you can write the way I want to" (*L* 153). Hemingway's letter about the actual life mentions those two extremes which many critics feel characterize Hemingway's heroines. Such heroines who are either bad and ugly, or good and beautiful, do not seem actual because they lack complexity.

If some of the misdirected criticism of Hemingway's heroines has to do with certain prejudices regarding a perceived machismo world (those sociological and biographical issues), some of it also has to do with the art itself, or with what I see as a misreading of the text. That is, some readers do not read between the lines to feel more than they understand. Some readers miss the underlying emotional complexity which inheres in Hemingway's art and in his heroines. These readers fail to allow for Hemingway's whittled style. This limitation seems especially true with the novels, more often criticized than the stories for their weak heroines. Many of the women in Hemingway's short stories are true, which is not to say that the women in the novels are not. Hemingway's terse style lent itself well to the short story; yet the same stylistic principles apply to both the novels and the stories. Seven-eighths (by his iceberg ratio) of the character development in all of Hemingway's fiction is not on the page. What some see as a problem in the novels, as related to this style and to the women, is that the novels' overall lengths tend to overwhelm or diminish the women, who are given little to say. Such sketchy treatment is interpreted by some as a weakness of character.

This misguided perception about Hemingway's heroines also has something to do with setting as well as narrative form. Most of Hemingway's best novels build around war or the direct effects of war, a milieu in which situations and human behavior are distorted and intensified, sometimes to the point of hysteria. In *A Farewell to Arms* as well as *For Whom the Bell Tolls (FWBT)*, the male/female characters are thrown together because of extraordinary circumstances, and they cling together with a kind of hopeless desperation as these circumstances threaten to separate and destroy them. If the reader tries to imagine these romances and these characters apart from the context of war, the romances and the characters might not seem real. The women especially, such as Catherine Barkley, too easily become labeled or dismissed as stereotypical hysterical women.

Another cause for a misreading of Hemingway's women, especially in the novels, has to do with his theme, particularly his focus on the male/female relationship in its initial stages. Hemingway shows men and women who are *in love,* rather than in a relationship which has matured over time, which has been tested and which is steady. This "being-in-love" aspect of his theme, similar to the war setting, also makes for a certain distortion of character, one which makes it especially easy to label the women as one-dimensional or exaggerated or silly. In an excised portion of *The Sun Also Rises (TSAR)*, Jake Barnes described well the effect that being in love can have on one's perceptions of the world. "The thing I would like to make whoever reads this believe, however incredible," he states, "is that such a passion and longing could exist in me for Brett Ashley that I would sometimes feel that it would tear me to pieces." He describes how his worldview would become distorted whenever he "had just left Brett." "I felt all of my world taken away, that it was all gone, even the shapes of things were changed, the trees and the houses and the fountains. . . . Brett Ashley could do that to me" (Wagner 243).

Hemingway was probably at his best in capturing men and women in love—the headiness of it, the intensity of feeling that distorts everything else. This is what he shows in his three best novels, *The Sun Also Rises, A Farewell to*

Arms, and *For Whom the Bell Tolls.* He also shows finally how that headiness—call it romance—cannot be sustained in any persistent and certain form. If he can be faulted for romanticizing women and romance itself, he can be faulted too for debunking the romance and showing the coarser side of things.

One of Hemingway's repeated themes has to do with this conflict between the romantic and the real—life as one would like it to be and life as it is. It is often Hemingway's women, more than the men, who see the complexities of life and of male-female relationships. Like the men, they yearn for the romance of life and all of its promise, but they also see this romance less idealistically. That is, they see the romantic view for what it is, a kind of pretense in the face of things that are. Both sexes feel helpless in the face of life and of themselves, but the women are more willing to make themselves vulnerable. To the degree that these women suffer and are willing to confront suffering, they are alive. Hemingway's women are not silly, nor are they glib. This was what Fitzgerald said of Catherine Barkley: She seemed "too glib." Essentially, Fitzgerald believed that Hemingway had made Catherine too one-dimensional. "Don't try to make her make sense," he said, "she probably didn't!" (Letter to Hemingway, June 1929, in Fitzgerald 227). Fitzgerald was right in advising Hemingway that Catherine did not have to make sense. Indeed, she should not make sense. People who are real usually do not "make sense" in any formulaic way, and it is Catherine's very complications that make her true. Although Catherine is often singled out as one of Hemingway's weakest women characters—too passive and bland, she is a viable and well-rounded character who represents characteristics that other of Hemingway's females share.

Catherine exhibits early on in the novel a lucid sense of self and of her world, and one of the repeated motifs of her first dialogues with Frederic are the words "to know." Her lover has just been blown to bits in the war, and she scorns her previously romantic view of the war and of life. She wishes she had " 'married him or anything,' " and she believes that " 'He could have had anything he wanted' had she 'known. . . . I know all about it now,' " Catherine says. " 'But then he wanted to go to war and I didn't know. . . . I didn't know about anything then' " (*AFA* 19). When Frederic pretends to be her dead lover, she realizes soon enough that it is "a rotten game" they play. Frederic responds: "Do you always know what people think?" (*AFA* 31). If Catherine's knowledge is hard-earned and edgy, she is nonetheless willing to hold up the past to the scrutiny of the present. Her dialogue throughout reveals her no-nonsense approach to life, her ability to cut through the romance of life and to see it as it is. Catherine is not unlike other of Hemingway's strong women characters who are willing to take risks and get involved in life, despite its complications.

If Catherine is feminine, courageous, and whole enough to take the risks in a relationship that Frederic resists, the same is also true of Maria in *For Whom the Bell Tolls.* She, like Catherine, has endured a shattering experience, also related to war. She opens herself nonetheless to a relationship with Robert

Jordan. Some see this giving of oneself to a man as negative—the essential feminist position about passivity in the face of male dominance; but it may also be positive, that complete opening up of self which is necessary for any solid and honest relationship. In both novels, the love relationships allow both partners to give of themselves and to become whole.

Problems set in, however, when lovers in such relationships attempt to protect that wholeness in the face of that which tries to undermine it. Catherine and Frederic try to escape life by running away together to Switzerland, but this cloistered environment finally offers no protection. Life gets them there as well. Essentially, Hemingway reveals through the male female relationships in his works that relationships, to be viable, cannot thrive on escapism. This escapism takes two forms. The first is an attempt to keep the relationship superficial—undemanding, fun, exciting, romantic. The second is an attempt to wall-in the relationship. Keep it permanent. Keep it secure. Keep it safe. Hemingway recognized that the security promised by the idea of marriage can be more destructive than constructive. Over time, the security becomes too sure, and it undermines the relationship of the vitality.

Carlos Baker argues that if Hemingway did see women as either good or bad, so did most of the English and American writers who preceded him (1952, 109–11). None of them were part of the consciousness-raising generation. I do not believe, however, that Hemingway did put his women into strict categories. Hemingway the man and Hemingway the writer were too intricate for that kind of black-and-white vision. Even if Hemingway's fictional world was more male than female oriented, in the larger sense it was an androgynous world of passion and disorder and of each individual's fight against loneliness and his or her search for order and a sense of place. If Frederic Henry cries in the night, so does Catherine Barkley, and so do we all. There are universal truths in Hemingway's works, contrary to the extreme feminist view which says that these truths have little to do with women.

Fitzgerald told Hemingway that he was not always "listening to women" in his writing because Hemingway was sometimes listening only to himself. Fitzgerald believed this difference resulted in Hemingway's "own mind beating out facilely a sort of sense that isn't really interesting . . . nor really much except a sort of literary exercise" (1980, 227). In Hemingway's fiction overall, however, he did listen to women and he allowed them the strength to be very much themselves—complicated and contradictory as they may be, as we all are. By and large the women in his fiction are feminine, intuitive, realistic, direct, quiet, and principled. They tend to be risk takers even as they try to order life so as to make some sense out of it and make it manageable. Throughout, they do not take life and themselves so seriously that they lack a sense of humor. Their viable wit allows them to assume an ironic stance to life, even as they involve themselves in it. Catherine Barkley's laughter rings out pure and free as she watches the forces of nature and circumstance conspire to threaten her and Frederic's escape to Switzerland. Her laughter puts everything into perspective as Frederic pulls on the oars of the boat, exhausted, and as the wind turns inside out the umbrella which was to be their sail. Overall, Hemingway's women have a good sense of balance, which keeps them on an even keel, even in the rougher waters.

References

Baker, Carlos. *Hemingway: The Writer as Artist.* Princeton, NJ: Princeton UP, 1952.

Fetterley, Judith. *The Resisting Reader: A Feminist Approach to American Fiction.* Bloomington: Indiana UP, 1978.

Fitzgerald, F. Scott. *Correspondence of F. Scott Fitzgerald.* ed. Matthew J. Bruccoli and Margaret M. Duggan. New York: Random House, 1980.

Hemingway, Ernest. *A Farewell to Arms.* New York: Scribner, 1929.

―――. *A Moveable Feast.* New York: Scribner, 1964.

―――. *Ernest Hemingway: Selected Letters 1917–1961.* ed. Carlos Baker. New York: Scribner, 1981.

Kert, Bernice. *The Hemingway Women.* New York: Norton, 1983.

Read, Herbert. *A Concise History of Modern Painting.* New York: Praeger, 1959.

Sokoloff, Alice Hunt. *Hadley: The First Mrs. Hemingway.* New York: Dodd, Mead, 1973.

Wagner, Linda W. " 'Proud and Friendly and Gently': Women in Hemingway's Early Fiction." *Ernest Hemingway: The Papers of a Writer.* ed. Bernard Oldsey. New York: Garland, 1981. 239–47.

2

Ministrant Barkley in
A Farewell to Arms

Peter L. Hays

The female protagonist of Ernest Hemingway's *A Farewell to Arms (AFA)* has received mixed reviews from critics over the years, being seen as compliant, lacking any strong sense of self by some, and heroic by others. One can easily find a dozen critics split equally. Edmund Wilson, in 1941, leads the list of detractors, speaking of Catherine's "abject devotion" (238) to Lt. Henry. Leslie Fiedler described Hemingway's women characters in 1966 as "mindless, soft, subservient; painless devices for extracting seed without human engagement" (318). Philip Young characterized Catherine as "idealized past the fondest belief of most people, and even the more realistic wishes of some, compliant" (1966, 91). Wendy Martin sees her thus: "Catherine Barkley is the subservient, compliant companion par excellence: as nurse-mistress to Frederic Henry, she is passive femininity incarnate" (1971, 236). The most rabid anti-Hemingway comments come from Judith Fetterley, who says that *A Farewell to Arms* displays hostility toward women and that Catherine's "death is the logical consequence of the cumulative hostilities Frederic feels toward her" (1978, 49, 62). And most recently, in 1984, Millicent Bell described Catherine as "a sort of inflated rubber woman available at will to the onanistic dreamer," Frederic Henry (114).

In contrast to these damning appraisals, Delbert Wylder sees Catherine as the heroine of *A Farewell to Arms* (1969, 87), Jackson Benson describes her as the one who teaches Frederic Henry to love (1969, 106, 112), Deborah Fisher praises her as "the strongest and smartest" of Hemingway's loving women (1974, 35), and Michael Reynolds, like Wylder, elevates Catherine to the novel's main role (1976, 254, 257). Roger Whitlow calls her devotion noble (1984, 22), and Joyce Wexler, whose reading is very close to my own, says that Catherine, when acceding to Frederic's open-mouth kiss (1981, 27), "is not responding to the power of Frederic's lips but to her own resolution to resume her life in spite of her loss. She devises a kind of therapy for herself by pretending to love Frederic in place of her fiancé'' (Wexler 114). Wexler continues:

Far from being a blind romantic, she is a shellshocked victim of the war who chooses love as a method of rechanneling self-destructive feelings of guilt and remorse. (114)

Just as Frederic joins the Italian army because he is in Italy, Catherine chooses to love him because he is there. (115)

She insists that love depends on the will to love. (117)

I believe that Catherine is not the hero in the sense of being the protagonist— she is absent for long passages—but that she is the code hero of this novel: the embodiment of admirable qualities and Henry's tutor in committing to life and love.

Certain details of the relationship between Catherine and Henry,[1] have been well discussed, but let me briefly review them. The priest tells Frederic that "When you love you wish to do things for. You wish to sacrifice for. You wish to serve'' (AFA 72). Frederic makes it obvious that heretofore he has not loved:

"Have you ever loved any one?'' [Catherine asks.]
"No,'' . . . [Frederic replies]. (AFA 19)

"I don't love.'' (AFA 72)

He also makes it clear that his initial interest in Catherine is sexual only; he is seeking no commitment:

[Catherine:] "You did say you loved me, didn't you?''
[Frederic:] "Yes,'' I lied. "I love you.'' I had not said it before. . . . I thought she was probably a little crazy. It was all right if she was. I did not care what I was getting into. . . . I knew I did not love Catherine Barkley nor had any idea of loving her. This was a game. (AFA 30)

A number of critics see Catherine as teaching Frederic to love.[2] Certainly, after her appearance in the hospital in Milan, he repeatedly confesses his love:

When I saw her I was in love with her. Everything turned over inside of me. (AFA 91)

God knows I had not wanted to fall in love with her. . . . But God knows I had. (AFA 93)[3]

Moreover, we see him fulfilling the priest's definition of love: doing for, serving. He accompanies Cat on her rounds, carrying bedpans for her (AFA 113), and though it may be argued that in doing so he reduces the time she has to spend with other patients and so increases her time with him, still, it is a service. In Lausanne[4] Frederic reverses roles, nursing Catherine as she had done for him in Milan, even donning a hospital gown as he administers anesthetic from a gas cylinder. But he also serves her in providing a love object, a focus for her self-prescribed romance therapy that cures her unstable mental state and does bring her happiness (short-lived, but certainly longer than Francis Macomber enjoys).

Does it?

When he meets her, Catherine is, in Frederic's opinion and her own, crazy (see *AFA* 30, 31, 116, 139, 154, 300). Both Norman Grebstein (1973, 123) and Wexler (1981, 114) attribute her neuroses to guilt over having denied sexual relations to her now-dead fiancé, much like Nina Leeds in Eugene O'Neill's *Strange Interlude*. Certainly such feelings of guilt may contribute to her instability, but she had also been nursing for about a year and a half,[5] first in France on the incredibly bloody western front, and then in Italy. As we now know, nurses, too, can suffer battle fatigue, particularly when the losses they see daily are compounded by close, personal ones. In addition, Catherine is in a strange country where she does not speak the language and is cloistered: " 'The Italians didn't want women so near the front. So we're all on very special behavior. We don't go out' " (*AFA* 25). She and Ferguson are two British nurses serving in Italy. Through Hemingway's selection of detail, we see no British males at the British hospital in Gorizia, although British ambulance units are mentioned, and few English-speaking males at all at the American hospital in Milan: Besides Frederic, there are three other patients and Mr. Meyers (whether vice-consul McAdams and the opera singers Simmons and Saunders ever visit is never specified). If she wishes to start her social life over with a male who speaks her own language, her choices are limited, as Hemingway said of himself and his romance with Agnes von Kurowsky: "I know now that the paucity of Americans doubtless had a great deal to do with it" (Griffin 117). Frederic Henry may not be much, but he doesn't have any competition, especially since Catherine makes her commitment to him in Gorizia at their second meeting:

I kissed her hard and held her tight and tried to open her lips; they were closed tight. I was still angry and as I held her suddenly she shivered. I held her close against me and could feel her heart beating and her lips opened and her head went back against my hand and then she was crying on my shoulder.
    "Oh, darling," she said. "You will be good to me, won't you?"
    What the hell, I thought. I stroked her hair and patted her shoulder. She was crying.
    "You will, won't you?" She looked up at me. "Because we're going to have a strange life." (*AFA* 27)

Frederic is obviously still on the make, but just as apparent is Catherine's surrender to the situation and commitment to a long-term relationship, apparent

14

HEMINGWAY IN ITALY AND OTHER ESSAYS

in her last comment. As Fetterley says, anticipating Wexler, "It is Catherine who creates the involvement between herself and Frederic" (Fetterley 59).

Initially, Catherine's surrender is an act of will, not one of romance. It is a commitment, in several senses. As Ken Kesey later did in *One Flew over the Cuckoo's Nest,* also punning on McMurphy's commitment to both the mental hospital and the welfare of his fellow inmates, so Hemingway has Catherine commit herself, not just to a man, but once more to life and love and the possibilities of new pain involved. In that regard, she is like all of his heroes who attempt to achieve something regardless of the odds. She is like Pilar in *For Whom the Bell Tolls* who aligns herself with Robert Jordan and who pushes Maria into his sleeping bag, despite seeing death in his palm; she commits herself to the cause. And like all romantic relationships that last till the death of one of the couple, this one survives through effort, at first, all Catherine's. She nurses Frederic; she, again in two senses of the word, cares for him. She bathes him, feeds him, gives him an enema, takes him on outings and makes love to him. Except for the last item, the list might be those things a mother does for a child. As Bell says, "in the isolation of his hospital bed . . . like a baby in a bassinet, he is totally passive, tended and comforted by female caretakers. . . . The ministering of Catherine, who looks after all his needs, including sexual, . . . is more maternal than connubial." (1984, 114).

As both Reynolds (1976, 252–57) and Donaldson note (1977, 155–57), Frederic at first is the passive accepter of services, Catherine the donor. Carlos Baker said of her that "she half-mothers, half-mistresses Frederick [sic] Henry. . . . Where she is, home is" (1972, 112). In her maternal way, she does endow each site they occupy with a sense of home and security: the hospital room in Milan, the rented room in Montreux, even the red plush hotel room in Milan. It is unusual for a patient, even one of months' duration, to refer to his place of treatment as a home, but so Frederic repeatedly does (see *AFA* 117, 118, 142, 153, 249). On a wider scale, it should be noted that it is Catherine who picks both Montreux and Lausanne as their homes in Switzerland (*AFA* 208, 307). But her efficacy is not limited only to traditional feminine roles.

As Robert Lewis noted, "Catherine, who orders some drinks, has assumed the active, male role" (1965, 49), and Hemingway indicates her authority in several subtle ways and just as deftly undercuts Frederic's. First, Frederic is portrayed as something considerably less than brave, mature, and thoroughly macho:

It made me feel very young to have the dark come after dusk and then remain. It was like being put to bed after supper. (*AFA* 68)

I had the feeling of a boy who thinks of what is happening at a certain hour at the schoolhouse from which he has played truant. (*AFA* 245)

The war seemed as far away as the football games of some one else's college. (*AFA* 291)

Before his operation, Frederic asks Catherine to be on duty that night so that they may again make love, not realizing the seriousness of the surgery or of his postoperative state. Nor is he aware of the danger in enlisting in the Italian army just because he happens to be in Rome when Italy enters the war in 1915. He also insists that he will not talk under the anesthetic. Catherine replies: "Now you're bragging, darling. You know you don't need to brag. . . . you sleep like a little boy with your arm around the pillow." (*AFA* 104). She corrects him similarly later when he drinks a water glass one-third full of cognac: "That was very big. . . . I know brandy is for heroes. But you shouldn't exaggerate" (*AFA* 140).

Also, he is jealous of her dead fiancé and insecure (*AFA* 115–16), and when Ferguson makes a scene at Stresa, Frederic is too naive to recognize her envy:

[Frederic:] "I don't think she wants what we have."
[Catherine:] "You don't know much, darling, for such a wise boy." (*AFA* 257)

Nor is Henry exceptionally competent as a soldier. He is chagrined to learn after his return from leave that "it evidently made no difference whether I was there to look after things or not" (*AFA* 16), as well as being aware that he does not deserve the silver medal awarded him by the Italian government:

[Rinaldi:] "Did you do any heroic act?"
[Frederic:] "No. . . . I was blown up while we were eating cheese." (*AFA* 63)

And while one cannot easily see any alternative he might have attempted, he does not carry out his orders to evacuate the vehicles he commands, as he himself acknowledges: "all I had to do was to get to Pordenone with three ambulances. I had failed at that" (*AFA* 212).[6]

In contrast to these examples of immaturity or ineptness on Frederic's part, Hemingway indicates Catherine's maturity and leadership. When the lovers separate in Milan, Frederic stands in the street in the pouring rain, while Catherine, in the carriage, "pointed in toward the archway." Frederic finally has the intelligence to realize that "she meant for me to get in out of the rain" (*AFA* 158). When they first meet, Catherine is carrying "a thin rattan stick like a toy riding-crop, bound in leather. . . . 'It belonged to a boy who was killed last year. . . . They sent me the little stick. His mother sent it to me. They returned it with his things' " (*AFA* 18–19). The stick's origin is the object carried by one of the models for Catherine, Elsie Jessup, who also lost a fiancé in France. Bernice Kert describes it as a walking stick (1983, 61); I think Carlos Baker is more correct in calling it a swagger stick (1969, 54).[7]

The English did employ cavalry at the Battle of the Somme in 1916, where Catherine's finacé was "blown up," but Hemingway describes the object as "like a toy riding-crop," not very serviceable in battle; moreover, why would the boy's mother consider a riding crop a suitable memento? A swagger stick is more likely, given both Hemingway's description of it and the habits of British officers. A swagger stick is a miniature scepter, a symbol of authority; it is also a strange gift from a mother-in-law to be, unless perhaps she wished to demonstrate—swagger stick or riding crop—that Catherine had the upper hand, the whip hand, in the relationship with her son, as she also does with Frederic Henry.

As Reynolds (1976, 296) and Oldsey (1979, 18–19, 25) have informed us, among the titles Hemingway considered for *A Farewell to Arms* were several based on Flaubert's *L'Education sentimentale:* "Education of the Flesh," "The Carnal Education," "The Sentimental Education of Frederick [sic] Henry," and "The Sentimental Education." If the priest had added "to feel for others," along with "serve" and "sacrifice," then we could see how successful Catherine has been. She does cause Frederic to sacrifice for others, to serve others, and to feel for others. Benson, Reynolds, and Donaldson have all painted Frederic as the less admirable of the two, more passive, the acceptor of services, and less decent. As Reynolds says, "He [Henry] has done little that was heroic, nothing admirable or particularly virtuous. . . . Surviving is the only virtue permitted him" (1976, 60). "If the reader accepts Catherine as the heroine of the novel, it is because Frederic is always aware of her sacrifice and her death" (1976, 254). "By the end of the novel, it is Catherine who dominates the action; Frederic has been reduced in stature while Catherine has gained" (1976, 257).

I don't want to emphasize here the cruelty of the world as it kills the good and separates lovers. I do want to emphasize the role of Catherine Barkley as ministrant, mentor, and teacher. She maturely decides to make a commitment, to love someone who she knows does not love her, and to take full responsibility for her actions throughout, including the pregnancy that occurs. In the dance of their relationship, Catherine leads, and leads so subtly that Frederic never perceives her guidance as more than concern for him. By her example and devotion, she does cause Frederic Henry to fall in love with her. He tells her, "Now if you aren't with me I haven't a thing in the world" (*AFA* 257; see also 116, 169, 262, 293, 298).[8] In Earl Rovit's terms, Catherine is the tutor, Frederic the tyro; thus she is the Hemingway hero, defining her own course of life insofar as is possible, and teaching others—and here, the lesson is love.

Notes

1. Most critics tend to refer to the lovers as Catherine and Henry, she by her first name, he by his first-name sounding last. Sheridan Baker has commented on the softness of Henry's names (1967, 66), and the addition of the title "lieutenant" to it does very little to give it stature, particularly as we know how little authority Lt. Henry possesses. Michael Reynolds also discusses Henry's names, including their various possible sources—Frederic Stendhal, whose real name was Marie Henri Beyle and who

provided a model for Hemingway in *The Charterhouse of Parma;* Frederic Moreau of Flaubert's *L'Education sentimentale;* Henry Fleming of Crane's *The Red Badge of Courage;* and an acquaintance named Barklie Henry (1976, 158–59). And Scott Donaldson comments on the frequency with which Henry is not addressed by name but by such terms of affection (and possibly belittlement) as "good boy," "nice boy," "sick boy," "little puppy," "silly boy," and "baby" (1977, 153). Certainly Baker and Donaldson are correct in pointing to the sense of juvenility and callowness that Hemingway establishes by giving the lieutenant two soft-sounding names, both given names, so that even when formally addressed, the male protagonist does not sound as if he has achieved adulthood.

An ordinary couple would be called Fred and Catherine. Donaldson is right. Catherine does not call her lover Fred, nor do most others in the novel, either (Ettore, on p. 123, seems to be the only one). In addition to undercutting Frederic's authority, Henry's lack of a common first name may also be a way of distancing us from him, of not allowing us to feel too close to him, while maintaining our sympathy for Catherine.

Although her name is attributed to her presumed Scottish background or to Barklie Henry, let me raise two questions. Catherine is a Scots on pages 115 and 126 of the novel, but she is English on pages 21, 66, and 240. The references on 66 and 240 may be generalized ones: Rinaldi and the porter and his wife may, as many Europeans did, say that anyone who speaks English is English. But on page 21 Ferguson is saying of herself that she is Scottish, not English, that she does not like the English as a rule, but that she does like Catherine, who, it is implied, is English. Even Rinaldi acknowledges the distinction, calling Ferguson Scotch here, and Barkley English thereafter. Was Hemingway undecided as to Catherine's nationality and imperfect in revision? Finally, might Catherine be named for Bishop Berkeley? The British pronunciations of the names would be alike, and Berkeley's immaterialist philosophy that things exist only in the mind *(esse is percipi)* is adapted by Catherine's action in her relationship with Frederic: she believes in their love and so creates it, as Wexler said (1981, 117).

2. Among them, Rovit, Balbert, Smith, Wexler, and Benson.

3. Other declarations can be found on pp. 104, 116, 169, 232, 257, 262, 293, and 298 of *A Farewell to Arms.*

4. Bernice Kert asserts that Catherine owes her Scottish origins to Duff Twysden, her appearance to Agnes von Kurowsky, her difficult Caesarian to Pauline, and that "her name Catherine and its abbreviation, Cat, came from Ernest's nickname for Hadley—Feathercat, shortened to Kat or Cat" (1983, 218–19). It was Hadley who had attempted to bring Hemingway's manuscripts to Lausanne so that he might show them to Lincoln Steffens in 1922, only to have them stolen from her train compartment. It was a tremendous loss for the young writer—all his work to that date gone, except for "Up in Michigan" and "My Old Man." Its effect on Hadley was like a death. As Hemingway described it to Carlos Baker, "I had never seen anyone hurt by a thing other than death or unbearable suffering, except Hadley when she told me about the things being gone" (1969, 103). Perhaps the traumatic associations of that loss with Lausanne caused him to pick that Swiss city as the site of Frederic Henry's losses.

5. Frederic and Catherine meet in the spring of 1917; he's wounded shortly thereafter, recuperates during the summer, and returns to active duty in late October of 1917, just in time to participate in the retreat from Caporetto. Catherine has been a V.A.D. "since the end of 'fifteen" (*AFA* 20); she joined the service along with her fiancé.

6. A man who might have served Hemingway as a possible source for Lt. Henry did

get his three ambulances through by taking back roads when the main roads were blocked by evacuees and by skirting Udine (Cecchin 62–63).

7. Both are drawing on the memory of Agnes von Kurowsky who, when interviewed by Michael Reynolds, called it a cane (1976, 174). If it was a cane Elsie Jessup carried, Hemingway, who was there and knew her, obviously changed it for the novel.

8. Given the criticism of the fictional Catherine by so many critics, it is worth noting that Jeffrey Meyers, in his recent biography, praised the real Mary Hemingway for doing what Catherine was condemned for: "Mary . . . gave Hemingway almost everything he wanted and had failed to get from Martha . . . Mary adored him, was sexually responsive . . . Mary understood his emotional needs and made a conscious effort to please him. . . . Mary ministered to his ego and his libido" (1985, 394). Perhaps she had read and understood *A Farewell to Arms*.

References

Baker, Carlos. *Ernest Hemingway: A Life Story*. New York: Scribner, 1969.

——. *Hemingway: The Writer as Artist*. Princeton: Princeton UP, 1972.

Baker, Sheridan. *Ernest Hemingway: An Introduction and Interpretation*. New York: Holt, Rinehart and Winston, 1967.

Balbert, Peter. "From Hemingway to Lawrence to Mailer: Survival and Sexual Identity in *Farewell to Arms*." *Hemingway Review* 3 no. 1 (1983): 30–43.

Bell, Millicent. "*A Farewell to Arms*: Pseudobiography and the Personal Metaphor." *Ernest Hemingway: The Writer in Context*. Ed. James Nagel. Madison: U of Wisconsin P, 1984. 107–28.

Benson, Jackson J. *Hemingway: The Writer's Art of Self-Defense*. Minneapolis: U of Minnesota P, 1969.

Cecchin, Giovanni. *Hemingway, G. M. Trevelyan e il Friuli: Alle Origini di Addio alle armi*. Lignano Sabbiadoro, Italy: Comune di Lignano Sabbiadoro, 1986.

Donaldson, Scott. *By Force of Will: The Life and Art of Ernest Hemingway*. New York: Viking, 1977.

Fetterley, Judith. "*A Farewell to Arms*: Hemingway's 'Resentful Cryptogram.' " *The Resisting Reader*. Bloomington: Indiana UP, 1978. 46–71.

Fiedler, Leslie. *Love and Death in the American Novel*. New York: Stein and Day, 1966.

Fisher, Deborah. "Genuine Heroines Hemingway Style." *Lost Generation Journal* 2 (Spring–Summer 1974): 35–36.

Grebstein, Sheldon Norman. *Hemingway's Craft*. Carbondale: Southern Illinois UP, 1973.

Griffin, Peter. *Along with Youth: Hemingway, the Early Years*. New York: Oxford UP, 1985.

Hemingway, Ernest. *A Farewell to Arms*. 1929. New York: Scribner, 1957.

Kert, Bernice. *The Hemingway Women*. New York: Norton, 1983.

Lewis, Robert W., Jr. *Hemingway on Love*. Austin: U of Texas P, 1965.

Martin, Wendy. "Seduced and Abandoned in the New World: The Image of Woman in American Fiction." *Woman in Sexist Society*. Ed. Vivian Gornick and Barbara K. Moran. New York: Basic Books, 1971. 226–39.

Meyers, Jeffrey. *Hemingway: A Biography*. New York: Harper & Row, 1985.

Oldsey, Bernard. *Hemingway's Hidden Craft: The Writing of* A Farewell to Arms.
    University Park: Pennsylvania State UP, 1979.

Reynolds, Michael S. *Hemingway's First War*. Princeton: Princeton UP, 1976.

Wexler, Joyce. "E.R.A. for Hemingway: A Feminist Defense of *A Farewell to Arms.*"
    Georgia Review 35 (1981): 111–23.

Whitlow, Roger. *Cassandra's Daughters*. Westport, CT.: Greenwood Press, 1984.

Wilson, Edmund. "Hemingway: Gauge of Morale." *The Wound and the Bow*. Cam-
    bridge, MA: Houghton Mifflin, 1941. 214–42.

Wylder, Delbert E. *Hemingway's Heroes*. Albuquerque: U of New Mexico P, 1969.

Young, Philip. *Ernest Hemingway: A Reconsideration*. University Park: Pennsylvania
    State UP, 1966.

3

A Second Look at Helen Ferguson in *A Farewell to Arms*

Fern Kory

Much of the critical discussion of Hemingway's fictional women relies on analysis of biographical details of his relationships with actual women.[1] But even in more textually oriented analyses, *A Farewell to Arms (AFA)* has been the subject of feminist attack, notably in Judith Fetterley's *Resisting Reader* where she calls it one version among many of "the drama of men's power over women" (xiii). It has also been defended, most convincingly for me in Joyce Wexler's "E.R.A. for Hemingway: A Feminist Defense of *A Farewell to Arms*." These discussions of Hemingway's treatment of women focus on Catherine Barkley, which is sensible and appropriate, though apparently not conducive to resolving the controversy over Hemingway's attitudes towards women.[2] In this chapter, I would also like to take a textual approach toward this subject, but focus my attention on Frederic Henry's presentation of one minor female character in the novel. He takes a second look at Helen ("Fergy") Ferguson in his narration of the story, and, if we do the same, I think that we too will see what a complex, interesting, and realistically portrayed character she is. Certainly her presentation also reflects the sensitivity towards women of the story's narrator and, finally, its author.

In a scene central to an understanding of Frederic Henry's attitude towards Ferguson, he recalls that stage of his love affair with Catherine Barkley which took place while he was in the hospital in Milan where Catherine, accompanied by her friend Helen Ferguson, has joined him:

I slept in the daytime and we wrote notes during the day when we were awake and sent them by Ferguson. Ferguson was a fine girl. I never learned anything about her except that she had a brother in the Fifty-Second Division and a brother in Mesopotamia and she was very good to Catherine Barkley. (*AFA* 108)

Even a superficial reading of Ferguson's role in the novel indicates that the services she rendered the young couple merit at least the compliment that she was a "fine girl." What's more intriguing is the direction that Frederic Henry's thoughts take following this restrained bit of enthusiasm. At this point, less than halfway through the telling of his story, Frederic Henry pauses to reflect on how little he knows about Helen Ferguson, the "other" English (Scottish) nurse in *A Farewell to Arms*. The fact that she has brothers involved in the war may go a long way towards explaining Ferguson's involvement in nursing, but, finally, it's not much to know about a person. Beyond this, the belief that she was "good to Catherine Barkley" seems to represent all that Frederic Henry *consciously* noted about Ferguson at the time of the novel's action. This seems to be something which the circumstance of his retelling makes him realize afresh and, perhaps, more thoroughly and appreciatively. He now seems to regret, or at least to be surprised, that he "never," not then or since, "learned anything about her." It seems possible that Frederic now feels that he ought to know more about such an important person, one so involved with the most formative person and relationship of his life.

This new awareness of Helen Ferguson as a person with her own story is part of a thread of evidence that the narrator of this story is more alert to such concerns than the hero of it was. It is important to remember that this account is narrated by Frederic Henry after the fact.[3] We are reminded of this when Frederic Henry speaks from the authority of his new understanding of the experience, as he does when he comments about the priest: "He had always known what I did not know and what, when I learned it, I was always able to forget. But I did not know that then, although I learned it later" (*AFA* 14). But it is easy to forget that the novel's narrator is the older survivor of these events because Frederic Henry, like the narrator of Hemingway's "In Another Country," is usually "trying to remember what it was like for his younger self, what it was like inside the experience. . . . which he re-experiences with great clarity of detail." As James Steinke goes on to point out, in "In Another Country" the intention of this narrative point of view is "for us to realize that the full impact of things was not getting through to [the young American]" (1985, 35). Still, a difference between the two narrators is that "the young American simply has not lived through as much experience as . . . Frederic Henry" (1985, 37).

I would agree with Joyce Wexler that for *A Farewell to Arms* "the meaning of the novel is actually embedded in the process of Frederic's remembering" and, further, that "Catherine is clearly presented as a forerunner of the kind of person Frederic has become by the time he narrates the story of his wartime experiences" (1981, 112–13). The Frederic Henry who narrates shows that he has learned from his relationship with Catherine. By the end of *A Farewell to Arms* he has reached the point of experience and can aspire to the resulting maturity that Catherine demonstrates from quite early in the novel.[4] By the time Frederic tells his story, he too has lost a loved one; however, because

Catherine learned from her loss, he has less to regret, though perhaps more to mourn, than Catherine had when she lost her fiancé.

The new maturity that results from Frederic's experience, which is largely seen in an increased sensitivity to others, leads him to consider that he doesn't know much about Ferguson, as we've seen. He then immediately begins to recall incidents from his acquaintance with Ferguson which not only exemplify Ferguson's protective "goodness" to Catherine, but which also provide evidence that there was, as there always is with *real* people, something more to be known about her. He remembers one particular conversation:

> "Will you come to our wedding, Fergy?" I said to her once.
> "You'll never get married."
> "We will."
> "No you won't."
> "Why not?"
> "You'll fight before you'll marry."
> "We never fight."
> "You've time yet."
> "We don't fight."
> "You'll die then. Fight or die. That's what people do. They don't marry."
> I reached for her hand. "Don't take hold of me," she said. "I'm not crying. Maybe you'll be all right you two. But watch out you don't get her in trouble. You get her in trouble and I'll kill you."
> "I won't get her in trouble."
> "Well watch out then. I hope you'll be all right. You have a good time." (*AFA* 108)

The emotional mixture of protectiveness, and, especially, bitterness, in the details of Ferguson's cynical philosophy of relationships, hints that these emotions come from some experience beyond, or, more likely, previous to the present situation. Known details of Catherine's past, such as her intense emotional and mental reaction to the death of her fiancé, can be used to explain some of the fears that Ferguson expresses for her friend's future happiness. Where, however, does Ferguson get the idea that fights (in the absence of death) always prevent marriage? Her attitude is not explicable by reference to any other details revealed in the novel, though it foreshadows Catherine's explanation to Frederic that people "love each other and they misunderstand on purpose and they fight and then suddenly they aren't the same one" (*AFA* 139). Both Catherine's and Ferguson's fears obviously come from their life experiences. The strength of Ferguson's emotions indicates that the experience is probably quite personal. But it's also important that Ferguson hopes that her experience will not apply to Catherine and Frederic's relationship.

Frederic Henry's recognition of and response to Ferguson's obvious distress ("I reached for her hand"), one of the few examples of sympathetic personal interaction between them, and Ferguson's rejection of it ("Don't take hold of me . . . I'm not crying") should be noted. Frederic obviously feels sorry for

Ferguson, not for himself or Catherine as he would if he believed that Ferguson's dire predictions applied to them. Ferguson's rejection of his sympathy is characteristic.

In the lines that follow, Frederic Henry tells Ferguson, as he's already told us, that she's a "fine girl." She tells him not to try to "flatter" her. She calls him "lucky" because his head doesn't make him "crazy," and asks him to let Catherine off night duty for a while. She says that she would "respect [him] for it" (AFA 109) though she doesn't believe that he will do it. Ferguson does not exhibit a very high opinion of the selflessness of this "young man." A certain amount of suspicion is appropriate considering what she's seen of Frederic's behavior at this stage in his development, though he proves her unjust in this instance. As his impulse to comfort Ferguson indicates, Frederic is not completely insensitive to the needs of others, though his sensitivity is under-developed.

This is emphasized in the scene that follows. Ferguson leaves with a note for Catherine from Frederic, and then Frederic "rang the bell and in a little while Miss Gage came in" (AFA 109). The very few critical comments that touch on Ferguson, or "Catherine's friend," tend to refer to her as perceptive,[5] as a character who sees through Frederic's ends and means. But she's not the only minor character, nor the only woman in the novel to do so. Nurse Gage sees Frederic's immaturity clearly when Frederic ingenuously says to her: "Don't you think Miss Barkley ought to go off night duty for a while? She looks awfully tired. Why does she stay on so long?" In response, "Miss Gage looked at me," Frederic recalls (AFA 110). She tells him: "I'm a friend of yours . . . You don't have to talk to me like that." He persists but she won't play along with this charade by pretending she doesn't know about him and Catherine; she says "Don't be silly. Was that all you wanted?" Gage then reiterates and demonstrates her friendship and sensitivity to Frederic, who continues to evade her honesty with easy flattery.

> "I'm your friend. Don't forget that."
> "You're awfully damned nice."
> "No. I know who you think is nice. But I'm your friend. How does your leg feel?"
> "Fine."
> "I'll bring some cold mineral water to pour over it. It must itch under the cast. It's hot outside."
> "You're awful nice."
> "Does it itch much?"
> "No. It's fine."
> "I'll fix those sandbags better." She leaned over. "I'm your friend."
> "I know you are."
> "No, you don't. But you will some day." (AFA 110–11)

In this last line, Gage foresees the maturation of both Frederic's values and his perception. I think the fact that Frederic chooses to include this scene in his revision of his experience justifies her faith in the maturing powers of time and experience. At the time, though, Frederic is attractive and nice, but immature and absorbed by his growing love for Catherine: "Catherine Barkley took three nights off night duty and then she came back on again. It was though we met again after each of us had been away on a long journey" (*AFA* 111).

To say that Frederic learned Gage's lesson then is as false as to say that he understood Fergy then or even fully appreciated Catherine's love and bravery then. But Frederic Henry's recollection of Gage's prophecy is evidence that he's seeing a little more clearly now. In the same way, recollecting the small peeks he has had into Ferguson's complexities is obviously a conscious attempt to figure out what he may know about Ferguson. He realizes, as we must also, that he doesn't have much in the way of facts about her, just clues, and he soon abandons the attempt to reconstruct Helen Ferguson out of one intriguingly problematic scene.

Still, close observation of Frederic's sketch of Helen Ferguson reveals the depth of the characterization of even Hemingway's minor characters that makes it so "the more you read it the more there will be" (*A Moveable Feast* 75). In this case, though, what the "more" finally tells us is that we, too, will "never" really know why Ferguson acts as she does. But, following up on a moment of sympathetic curiosity about her does represent a recognition by Frederic Henry of Ferguson's humanity, her right to his sympathy and understanding, as well as a recognition of her human complexity. Once we too recognize this, we can see the value in looking more closely at the qualities that make "Fergy" unique.

Though personal scenes between Ferguson and Frederic Henry are few, her quiet ubiquitousness made Ferguson more than just another one of the "friends of ours" (*AFA* 114) who made Catherine and Frederic's developing relationship possible in the hospital in Milan. In many unobtrusive ways, Ferguson "was very good to Catherine Barkley." She is standing by Catherine when we are introduced to her, when Catherine is, by her own account, "a little crazy" (*AFA* 154). Later she goes to Milan with Catherine and stays with her through the pregnancy until they are found by Frederic Henry in Stresa and he takes Catherine away.

From our point of view, we can also see that Ferguson took an active role in making Catherine's romance possible. Ferguson seems to sense what both the priest and Catherine remark upon, that Frederic is, basically, a "good boy" (*AFA* 31). She encourages the relationship, presumably thinking that it will be therapeutic for Catherine; she's right. When Catherine is less than encouraging to Frederic Henry, as she is when he first calls on her alone, Helen ignores Catherine's request that she stay with them and goes to write some letters (*AFA* 25). Then, when Catherine says she is ill when Frederic comes to call, Ferguson gives him the message and some encouragement to try again:

"Do you think it would be any good to try and see her tomorrow?"
"Yes, I do." (*AFA* 41)

Frederic Henry narrates the facts that allow us to see Ferguson's involvement
in his courtship, but generally does not comment on them except as they affect
his plans at the time. As far as the Frederic Henry of the action of the novel is
concerned, Ferguson is largely just "there," an adjunct to Catherine, sometimes a practical necessity. When she is first introduced, she is seen as merely
Catherine's less attractive friend. This is clear in the men's conversation:

> After a while we said good-night and left. Walking home Rinaldi said, "Miss Barkley
> prefers you to me. That is very clear. But the little Scotch one is very nice."
> "Very," I said. I had not noticed her. "You like her?"
> "No," said Rinaldi. (*AFA* 21)

Later, when they are all three at the hospital in Milan, Frederic Henry recalls
that, "sometimes we could go out to dinner if Ferguson went along" (*AFA*
118) and that when they went to the races "Ferguson went too and Crowell
Rodgers, the boy who had been wounded in the eyes by the explosion of the
shell nose-cap" (*AFA* 127). The neutrality of Frederic Henry's response to
Ferguson is accounted for by the fact that, at the time, "All [he] wanted was
to see Catherine" (*AFA* 117). That he notes the presence of other people at all
has to do with his character, his habit of observation. This is the same trait that
makes him an appropriate narrator for a story such as this, one in which the
narrator sees the past from a new perspective while, at the same time, recalling
and re-feeling the emotions of the past. He captures in his narration "what the
actual things were which produced the emotion that you experienced" (*Death
in the Afternoon* 2).

Because he is so observant, Frederic's recounting of his experience of love
and war during this period does contain intriguing indications of Ferguson's
character and circumstances. There are isolated descriptions of her actions and
reactions which are not ever explicated in the context of Frederic Henry's story.
Most of these clues Frederic Henry noted but did not respond to at the time.
That he puts them in now, when as storyteller he must select the details which
best tell his story, shows that he (and Hemingway) put some value on them.

There are small things. Ferguson, for instance, doesn't have an opinion on
whether or not the horse that they bet on at the track has been dyed a different
color to disguise its identity. More interesting is her reaction to the reduction
of their winnings as a result of the manipulations of various shady characters
who manage to reduce the odds on the horse at the last minute. She thinks that
"it's crooked and disgusting" (*AFA* 130). This contrasts with Catherine's reaction which is: "Of course, . . . if it hadn't been crooked we'd never have
backed him at all. But I would have liked the three thousand lire" (*AFA* 130).
Ferguson comes across here as less realistic, perhaps more traditionally "moral,"

possibly a bit hypocritical. Interestingly, it's Catherine who feels "so much cleaner" later after backing "a horse we've never heard of and that Mr. Meyers won't be backing" (*AFA* 131).

Ferguson's response to the races reminds one of other comments that she makes at more critical points. When Frederic Henry comes back from the front and finds Catherine and Ferguson in Stresa, Ferguson's reaction seems moralistic and judgmental. She says to Catherine that "You're two of the same thing. . . . I'm ashamed of you, Catherine Barkley. You have no shame and no honor and you're as sneaky as he is" (*AFA* 247). Catherine's reaction to these insults shows her ability to see beyond the superficial and the literal to respond instead to the real emotional distress from which they come:

"There, there, Fergy," Catherine comforted her. "I'll be ashamed. Don't cry, Fergy. Don't cry, old Fergy."

"I'm not crying," Ferguson sobbed. "I'm not crying except for the awful thing you've gotten into." She looked at me. "I hate you," she said. "She can't make me not hate you. You dirty sneaking American Italian." Her eyes and nose were red with crying.

Catherine smiled at me.

"Don't you smile at him with your arm around me."

"You're unreasonable, Fergy."

"I know it," Ferguson sobbed. "You mustn't mind me, either of you. I'm so upset. I'm not reasonable. I know it. I want you both to be happy." (*AFA* 247)

Again, it seems clear that it is more than Catherine's situation that is prompting Ferguson's reactions. And again, she takes it back finally, as she did when she told Frederic Henry that people "fight or die"; "They don't marry" (*AFA* 108). Catherine, whatever a superficial reading of her "condition" might prompt one to conclude, is obviously very happy and, whatever her fears for Catherine, Ferguson knows it. It is perfectly clear to Catherine that it is Fergy who needs to be comforted, not she. Ferguson's irrational objections, especially her tearful declaration that she's not crying, and the inappropriate reiteration here and before of the "Italian sneakiness" of Frederic Henry's conduct, would probably be funny if she weren't so obviously upset. The same goes for her next comment to Catherine, who is laughing, that "It's nothing to laugh about. . . . Plenty of them have other wives" (*AFA* 248). Is there a fight with a sneaky married Italian in Ferguson's past? Why does her emotional response take the form of a lament over her spoiled vacation: "I've always wanted to go to the Italian lakes and this is how it is" (*AFA* 248). Frederic Henry doesn't know and neither do we. But it's increasingly apparent that there's something to be known. Ferguson knows and says that she's being unreasonable; however, it's also clear that whatever it is that is making her act this way is powerful.

Frederic Henry's point of view at the time is fairly clear. He sees the less attractive aspects of Ferguson's situation ("Her eyes and nose were red with crying" and, slightly earlier, "Her face was red" [*AFA* 247]). To a certain extent, her crisis does not even hold his attention which is absorbed by Catherine: "As she stood comforting Ferguson, I could see no change in her figure" (*AFA* 247). He is "sick of Fergy" (*AFA* 248).

Catherine's fondness for Ferguson is obvious, but it has its limits, too. Much earlier in the novel, when Catherine is preparing Frederic Henry for surgery, they have a conversation that concerns Ferguson.

> "What do you have to do to get me ready for Valentini?"
> "Not much. But quite unpleasant."
> "I wish you didn't have to do it."
> "I don't. I don't want any one else to touch you. I'm silly. I get furious if they touch you."
> "Even Ferguson?"
> "Especially Ferguson and Gage and the other, what's her name?"
> "Walker?"
> "That's it. They've too many nurses here now. There must be some more patients or they'll send us away. They have four nurses now." (*AFA* 103)

Though the previous conversation is full of affectionate silliness about Frederic Henry's "lovely temperature," Catherine is not just being "silly" here; if she were, she wouldn't explain it. Still, there is some playful exaggeration. She "especially" resents all three of the other nurses. But Frederic doubts the applicability of this jealousy only to Ferguson; probably he realizes that there is some foundation for Catherine's jealousy of his drinking buddy, Miss Gage, who didn't "like" Catherine from the moment that she recognized her as Frederic Henry's "friend" (*AFA* 90). Whether in fun or not, Catherine doesn't exclude her best friend, Ferguson, from this "silly" jealousy, though Frederic suggests that she might.

While no serious jealousy is implied, Catherine's possessiveness here, when taken in conjunction with her next injunctions to Frederic not to "brag" (*AFA* 104) while under anaesthetic, both point to her sense that they are not yet in love in quite the same way, or, rather, that Frederic Henry is still a boy in some ways and does not yet understand what he will come to understand about the potential self-sufficiency of their relationship. He does come to some understanding of it, eventually, and describes their reunion in Stresa in terms of their ability to be alone together. He describes an experience which he has not duplicated since:

> We slept when we were tired and if we woke the other one woke too so one was not alone. Often a man wishes to be alone and a girl wishes to be alone too and if they love each other they are jealous of that in each other, but I can truly say we never felt that. We could feel alone when we were together, alone against the others. It has only happened to me like that once. (*AFA* 249)

Catherine's earlier desire to get away from the others at the race track ("I felt very lonely when they were all there" [*AFA* 132]), though Frederic Henry feels that he is having a good time, indicates that he "did not know that then, although [he] learned it later" (*AFA* 14).

He also learns something about other people through their responses to this all-encompassing love. During the period of the novel's action, Frederic Henry's reactions to Ferguson vary. For the most part, she is almost nothing to him, merely Catherine's friend. He eventually comes to understand Ferguson a little better through Catherine's closer, more mature and perceptive reading of the situation. But he "was sick of Fergy" when she seemed to him to require too much of Catherine's attention in Stresa after he has joined them. This is understandable.

This central homecoming scene is a turning point for Frederic Henry. He has left the war, made his "separate peace" (*AFA* 243). Frederic Henry feels that he's found a saner way to live. His priorities have changed a great deal in a short time. In the beginning, "home" is invoked in his descriptions of his wartime billet ("In the late summer of that year we lived in a house in a village that looked across the river and the plain to the mountains" [*AFA* 3]). After he has been with Catherine, "It did not feel like a homecoming" (*AFA* 163) when he returned to his unit. For Frederic Henry, now "home is where the heart is"; even that awful hotel room eventually "felt like our own home. My room at the hospital had been our own home and this room was our home too in the same way" (*AFA* 153). Because of this, he is resentful of the time which Catherine spends with Ferguson. He says to Catherine: "My life used to be full of everything . . . Now if you aren't with me I haven't a thing in the world." He explains that he's not jealous, but that "I'm just so in love with you that there isn't anything else" (*AFA* 257). Catherine has to ask him:

"Will you be a good boy and be nice to Ferguson?"
"I'm always nice to Ferguson unless she curses me."
"Be nice to her. Think how much we have and she hasn't anything."
"I don't think she wants what we have."
"You don't know much, darling, for such a wise boy."
"I'll be nice to her." (*AFA* 257)

Catherine's answer indicates first that there is something else, even when you're in love; there are other people to be considered. She also shows that she feels that Ferguson both recognizes and values "what [they] have." Frederic Henry believes her.

The outcome of this conversation is that Frederic Henry puts himself out to be nice to Ferguson. She responds by allowing herself to be pleased and, afterwards, by discretely retiring and leaving the lovers alone together. As Frederic describes the scene,

We went downstairs to have lunch with Ferguson. She was very impressed by the hotel and the splendor of the dining-room. We had a good lunch with a couple of bottles of white capri. Count Greffi came into the dining-room and bowed to us. His niece, who looked a little like my grandmother, was with him. I told Catherine and Ferguson about him and Ferguson was very impressed. The hotel was very big and grand and empty but the food was good, the wine was very pleasant and finally the wine made us all feel very well. Catherine had no need to feel any better. She was very happy. Ferguson became quite cheerful. I felt very well myself. After lunch Ferguson went back to her hotel. She was going to lie down for a while after lunch she said. (*AFA* 258)

Frederic Henry's point of view is clear in this description of the scene. He notes Ferguson's responses to his information about the Count, not Catherine's. He obviously addresses himself to both women. The most telling lines here are those which describe their moods and which illustrate their interdependence on one another. Catherine is the least complicated. She was very happy to start with—happy to have Frederic back. Her happiness, as well as the wine, sparks Ferguson's gradual cheerfulness, but Frederic Henry's efforts and, I think, Ferguson's own efforts to be "reasonable" are important and implied. Finally, Frederic Henry feels "very well" himself, the result of the wine, his own efforts, and their success. The euphoria which attends these efforts and their success is the flip side of the "immorality" which "made you disgusted afterward" (*The Sun Also Rises* 149).

This is admittedly a subtle change. Frederic Henry does not "turn over a new leaf" at this point or become selfless, or even wildly sympathetic and concerned with Ferguson's problems. The greatest changes come between the end of the events of the novel and Frederic's later narration of them. Right now, he's got problems of his own. The last appearance of Ferguson's name in the novel is typical in its way of the reactions of Catherine and Frederic Henry throughout the action of the novel.

"Poor Ferguson," Catherine said. "In the morning she'll come to the hotel and find we're gone."
"I'm not worrying so much about that," I said, "as about getting into the Swiss part of the lake before it's daylight and the custom guards see us." (*AFA* 271)

No conclusive or comprehensive view of Ferguson can be gleaned from these incidents and words, just indications that Ferguson is more than just a necessary plot device (the useful and ubiquitous "best friend"). We see that she is far too complicated to be fully revealed obliquely. The story's narrator comes to understand this. The novel's author obviously knows it. The amount and type of information we have about her, as well as Frederic's attitude towards her, all indicate that she is intended to be seen as more than "one of a number of weepy women in the novel who appear to have no way of meeting difficulty other than by crying" as Judith Fetterley characterizes many of the novel's minor female characters ("Poor Mrs. Walker, poor Fergy, poor whores, poor virgins" Fetterley 1978, 55).

Ferguson's life is lived for the most part outside of Frederic Henry's vision, and we get glimpses of only those points at which her life intersects with those which are the main subject of the novel. Frederic Henry realizes this when he says that he "never learned anything about her," when he realizes that Ferguson's story is not told, but that there are indications it would be a very interesting story if it were told. Frederic Henry has thus realized in his fictional "life" and in his narration what Hemingway said he hoped to achieve in his art. In *Death in the Afternoon (DA)* Hemingway wrote that:

> When writing a novel a writer should create living people; people not characters. A *character* is a caricature. If a writer can make people live there may be no great characters in his book, but it is possible that his book will remain as a whole; as an entity; as a novel. (*DA* 191)

Helen Ferguson is not a "great character," but there are indications that she is an interesting person. This is particularly notable in the face of the criticism and the more insidious "common knowledge" which holds that Hemingway "rarely wrote of women with sympathy, and virtually never with subtlety and understanding" (Oates 1984, 5).

Notes

1. The most striking recent application of biographical materials to Hemingway's women is in Mimi Reisel Gladstein's *The Indestructible Woman in Faulkner, Hemingway, and Steinbeck*. Gladstein says that "Information about Hemingway's interactions with [his mother, the woman he first proposed to, and his first wife] . . . provides a basis for understanding the character of many of his female creations. . . . These women provided the archetypes, the primal patterns against which other women were measured" (1986, 53). Gladstein argues her interpretations of Hemingway's various fictional women from the texts, but puts these women in categories which come out of her interpretation of Hemingway's life. In " 'Proud and Friendly and Gently': Women in Hemingway's Early Fiction," Linda Wagner also combines biographical and textual materials, including manuscripts. When she comes to discuss *A Farewell to Arms,* Wagner calls it "a novel about loss. And the loss is that of [Hemingway's] father, not of Catherine or a child" (1981, 69). Both Wagner's and Gladstein's readings seem most compelling to me when they deal with the details of the text.

2. An up-to-date survey of feminist and other critical discussions of Hemingway's women is available in Gladstein (1986). Remarkably, in a book about "indomitable" women (54), Gladstein does not discuss Catherine Barkley except in passing (57–58) or even list *A Farewell to Arms* in her bibliography of primary sources. Linda Wagner's " 'Proud and Friendly and Gently': Women in Hemingway's Early Fiction," while largely sympathetic to Hemingway's portrayals of women, also stops short of endorsing *A Farewell to Arms.* Yet, Wagner's view of earlier Hemingway males as "adolescent, selfish, misdirected" (1981, 69) and as men who "learn from Hemingway's women"

(1981, 64) seems to me to hold as true for *A Farewell to Arms* as it does for many of the stories in *In Our Time*.

3. This important fact has been emphasized in Robert W. Lewis' "The Tough Romance" and Earl Rovit's "Learning to Care." See also Michael Reynolds' discussion of Hemingway's de-emphasis in revision of "Frederic-as-author" in *Hemingway's First War*. This parallels Linda Wagner's discussion of manuscript cuts which made more explicit Jake's role in *The Sun Also Rises* as a narrator who is "too much involved in the people he will tell about" to "remain outside the novel" (1981, 67). In discussing the cuts in the beginning of the novel which made more explicit Brett's role as "bereaved and betrayed war victim," Wagner also comments that "Hemingway may have been hesitant to trust his readers with what he thought were interesting women" after the misreading of Brett who "was to have gained readers' sympathy and admiration, and thereby buttressed the positive elements of Jake Barnes' persona." She considers the possibility that Catherine's "submissiveness and languor" in *A Farewell to Arms* "stemmed from what he thought was lack of appreciation of Brett's 'nobility' " (1981, 66). It seems much more likely to me that Hemingway is doing the same thing again, creating a subtle portrait of an interesting woman.

4. For a fuller discussion of Catherine's emotional development through the course of the novel, see Joyce Wexler (1981).

5. References to Helen Ferguson are few and oblique. In describing what he sees as "the persistent image of the masquerade" in the novel, Earl Rovit says: "as Ferguson expertly perceives when she calls him a 'dirty sneaking American Italian,' he is 'a snake with an Italian uniform: with a cape around [his] neck' " (1970, 35). Generally, Ferguson's name comes up only in plot summary. Judith Fetterley's reference to Ferguson (1978, cited in text), though somewhat wholesale, is the only direct discussion I've encountered of Ferguson as a representative Hemingway woman.

References

Fetterley, Judith. *The Resisting Reader: A Feminist Approach to American Fiction.* Bloomington, IN: Indiana UP, 1978.

Gladstein, Mimi Reisel. *The Indestructible Woman in Faulkner, Hemingway, and Steinbeck.* Studies in Modern Literature 45. Ann Arbor, Michigan: U of Michigan Research P, 1986.

Hemingway, Ernest. *Death in the Afternoon.* New York: Scribner, 1932.

———. *A Farewell to Arms.* 1929. New York: Scribner, 1969.

———. *A Moveable Feast.* New York: Scribner, 1964.

———. *The Sun Also Rises.* New York: Scribner, 1926.

Lewis, Robert W. "The Tough Romance." *Twentieth Century Interpretations of* A Farewell to Arms, ed. Jay Gellens. Englewood Cliffs, NJ: Prentice-Hall, 1970: 41–53.

Oates, Joyce Carol. "Ernest Hemingway: Man's Man? Woman-hater? Our Greatest Writer?" *TV Guide* December 8, 1984.

Reynolds, Michael S. *Hemingway's First War: The Making of* A Farewell to Arms. Princeton, NJ: Princeton UP, 1976.

Rovit, Earl. "Learning to Care." *Twentieth Century Interpretations of* A Farewell to Arms, ed. Jay Gellens. Englewood Cliffs, NJ: Prentice-Hall, 1970: 33–40.

Steinke, James. "Hemingway's 'In Another Country' and 'Now I Lay Me.' " *Hemingway Review* V (Fall 1985): 32–39.

Wagner, Linda. " 'Proud and Friendly and Gently': Women in Hemingway's Early Fiction." *Ernest Hemingway: The Papers of a Writer,* ed. Bernard Oldsey. New York: Garland Publishing, 1981.

Wexler, Joyce. "E.R.A. for Hemingway: A Feminist Defense of *A Farewell to Arms.*" *Georgia Review* 35 (1981): 111–23.

Hemingway's Women: Cats Don't Live in the Mountains

E. Roger Stephenson

Many critics have had much to say over the years regarding Hemingway's fictional women. The standard scheme, of course, divides them into "bitches" and "passive dream girls," Brett Ashley/Margot Macomber and Catherine Barkley/Maria (Whitlow 1984, 10–14). Recently corrective readings have surfaced. His women are seen by some as resourceful, responsive, resilient characters (Miller 1986), or they are compared with their male counterparts in terms of emotional maturity—and they are certainly not found wanting (Steinke 1986). Now that so much biographical information is available, others, notably Bernice Kert (1983), continue the work of relating Hemingway's real-life women to their fictional counterparts.

But something is missing in all this. Many readers get the sense that Hemingway's women are not very important of and by themselves—regardless of how they are categorized or assessed, regardless of their real-life counterparts. However large they bulk in the narratives, they are very difficult to discuss by themselves. For good reason. Hemingway *uses* them to characterize his men. What this says about Hemingway's own view of women is, to be sure, debatable. But an equally important issue is what the perceptions of his protagonists tells us about *them*—not Hemingway. His heroes, I think, present us with a remarkably consistent view of women in *The Sun Also Rises, A Farewell to Arms*, and *For Whom the Bell Tolls*. And that consistent view is rendered with an equally remarkably consistent pattern of diction and imagery. Hemingway's heroes see his heroines, in part, as whores or at least whore-like. The diction and the imagery of the novels demonstrate this. Their need to do so clearly shows their shortcomings and inadequacies.

It's true, of course, that Hemingway often uses characters who are, literally whores. "The Light of the World," in *The Short Stories of Ernest Hemingway*

(SS), after all, was one of his favorite stories. And he used "whore" itself metaphorically, too. His "Poem to Mary (Second Poem)" in *88 Poems (P)* is perhaps the best example *(P* 1979, 107–13). But his major women in these three novels are presented in a curious way. They are not literal whores; they are *presented* as metaphorically whore-like. They are seen and presented as whores by the protagonists because of how they function in the fictional lives of those protagonists—which means they are less than literal but more than metaphoric.

In *The Sun Also Rises (TSAR)*, we meet Brett late in chapter 3. She enters the *bal musette* with a group of homosexuals. But we meet Georgette, the whore, before we see Brett, and, in fact, we see Brett through a subtle transference that Jake presents. He's picked up Georgette because of what he calls "a vague sentimental idea that it would be nice to eat with some one" *(TSAR* 16). He finds the whole thing "dull," later ridicules her for his own amusement. Brett enters; she is "with them" (the homosexuals). Within four paragraphs Georgette is "taken up by them" *(TSAR* 20). They change places, in other words. Brett recognizes her kinship with Georgette. She laughingly objects to Georgette's presence; " 'It's in restraint of trade' " *(TSAR* 22). There can be no mistake about what that "trade" is. We hear later from Braddocks that Georgette had a "corking row" after Jake and Brett leave. Four pages later Brett confesses to making an "awful row" *(TSAR* 32) when she visits Jake. But it's Jake who makes the transference complete. When Brett, that "species of woman" who does "a dirty business at night" arrives, Jake says, "Then I heard Brett's voice. Half asleep I had been sure it was Georgette. I don't know why. She could not have known my address" *(TSAR* 32).

Brett and Georgette are linked at the end of the novel as well as at the beginning. In the final chapter, Jake and Brett are in a taxi: "The driver started up the street. I settled back. Brett moved close to me. We sat close against each other. I put my arm around her and she rested against me comfortably" *(TSAR* 247). Early in chapter 3, Jake had "settled" back in a slow-moving horse cab, Georgette "cuddled" against him as he put his "arm around her" *(TSAR* 15). First and last, Brett is linked—through imagery and diction—with the whore.

Brett's role is recognized by the others in the novel, too. When we meet Mike Campbell, he calls Brett a "piece" or a "lovely piece" six times in two pages. Alice in "The Light of the World" *(SS* 390) and Pilar in *For Whom the Bell Tolls (FWBT* 150) specifically relate the term "piece" to whore. Later Mike and Brett tell Jake about their room: " 'We have got the loveliest hotel,' Mike said. 'I think it's a brothel' " *(TSAR* 83).

There are several indirect references to Brett's role, too. Cohn, of course, calls Jake a "pimp" *(TSAR* 190). The term isn't appropriate unless Brett's role has been clearly delineated. Bill Gorton—in jest—says that some people say Jake is supported by women. And he *is* in some very important ways.

The presentation of Brett as a whore and whore-like in Book I may well have its origin in the New Testament. By now most readers and critics agree that Hemingway knew and used the New Testament in his work. Brett's portrayal owes much to the story of the Samaritan woman as it appears in John (4:4–26). Briefly, Christ is traveling through Samaria, stops at a well to drink, and encounters a woman who has come to draw water. He tells her that those who drink this water will thirst again, whereas those who drink of the water which he can give ("living water") will never thirst again. He gently chastises her for having five husbands and living with a sixth man who is not her husband. Finally, he tells her that with this "living water" she will not have to go to the "mountain" to worship.

Notice that the well in the story is Jacob's well. This might help us understand why Brett tells Jake he has a "biblical name" (*TSAR* 22). Brett, too, has had many men—and will have more. Brett, too, thirsts. She is constantly thirsty, from beginning to end of the novel. Notice that she spends most of her time going up hills in Paris. It is certainly ironic that in *The Sun Also Rises* Jacob's well is dry, or, rather, Jake's accident renders him as good as dry. And it is somewhat pathetic that Brett's thirst is never satisfied.

Brett's role, too, is associated with short hair. When we see her first, when her association is made with Georgette, she has her hair "brushed back like a boy's" (*TSAR* 22). Mike's "piece" has a felt hat pulled low, covering her short hair. At the conclusion, Brett tells Jake that Romero wanted her to grow her hair. It would make her more "womanly." But short hair here does not mean "manly." Romero was "ashamed" (*TSAR* 242) of her with short hair; short hair made her whorish. She would need long hair if they were to marry.

Finally, Brett's role is further clarified by her inability to go to the "mountains." She goes up and down "hills" in Paris in a frantic attempt to find satisfaction. She suggests getting brandy "on the hill" (*TSAR* 61), for example. Later, she stays at the Hotel Montana in Madrid. But she's missing from the idyllic fishing excursion to the Irati River. She's out of place in the world of tranquility and peace that Jake and Bill experience. This world is characterized by order, by natural beauty. It's a world where wine can be drawn from water—despite the clearly ironic cast to the mock religious ceremony (119–23). The wine produces sleep, not the stupor which Brett experiences at San Sabastian at the same time. Here, too, Jake admits that he loved Brett " 'Off and on for a hell of a long time' " (*TSAR* 123). He says he doesn't love her any longer, but he doesn't believe this and neither do we. However, Brett's role for him is very much like Georgette's. Had she accompanied him to the Irati she would have brought the chaos and disorder which characterize her life. That chaos and disorder has a place—in the city below. At this time, Jake needs the peace and order of the mountains, not the excitement generated by the chaotic world of *poules*.

Brett is vital to Jake, of course. She mirrors him in some ways. She's wounded, as he is. Because of this, she can fill his nights with a kind of "niceness" that Georgette suggests. He pays for the privilege, to be sure. If she helps him through the night, he's destined to play the role of "pimp" for her. And the "niceness" she represents is just as illusory as Georgette's is. It's "pretty" to think otherwise, but probably just another "vague sentimental idea."

Brett is seen, then, in whorish terms by Jake and others. It's much more difficult for readers to see Catherine Barkley in *A Farewell to Arms* (AFA) as portrayed in these terms—in part, no doubt, because of our willingness to see the novel in very romantic terms. It's a love story, after all. But Hemingway is quite explicit and direct in his presentation of Catherine as whore-like. The programmatic flatness of chapter 1 points to the dry, sterile world of Frederic Henry's experience. But it's chapter 2 that is especially important in setting the parameters for our understanding and assessment of his behavior.

Before we see Catherine, we hear of whores and whorehouses. Our first glimpse of Frederic Henry is in "the bawdy house, the house for officers" (*AFA* 6). That night in the officers' mess the priest becomes the butt of jokes about himself and the "girls." Chapter 2 ends with a discussion of Frederic's upcoming leave. He gets lots of advice. But his choices seem clear enough. He can go to the Abruzzi, as the priest suggests; there in the mountains the air is clear and dry, the people are good and so is the hunting. Or he can go to the "centres of culture and civilization" (*AFA* 8) where there are girls, where, as the captain's "great success" with finger games demonstrates, "You go away soto-tenente! You come back soto-colonello!" (*AFA* 9). As if to prefigure Frederic's choice—not only for his leave but for the direction of his immediate future—he leaves with the captain: "We go whorehouse before it shuts" (*AFA* 9).

Returning from leave, Frederic answers Rinaldi's questions about those "centres." He says Milan was the best place, the place of "beautiful adventures" and Rinaldi continues: "That was because it was first. Where did you meet her? In the Cova? Where did you go? How did you feel? Tell me everything at once. Did you stay all night?" (*AFA* 11). Not long after this, Frederic dreams of taking Catherine to Milan: "I wished I were in Milan with her. I would like to eat at the Cova and then walk down the Via Manzoni . . . and go to the hotel with Catherine Barkley. Maybe she would" (*AFA* 37). The connection between his leave adventure and his view of Catherine is clear enough. But even before Frederic meets her, the connection between Catherine and the world of whores is made by Rinaldi. He says they have "new girls" at the front and, in the same paragraph, mentions the "beautiful English girls" and Catherine Barkley. Catherine here is lumped with the "new girls" in Rinaldi's presentation of facts. She will become one of those "new girls" for Frederic before long.

Hemingway comes back to Frederic's choice of leave that night in the mess. He had wanted to go to the Abruzzi, he says, but he had gone to no such place. He had not gone to a place that was "clear cold and dry," where you were called "Lord" (*AFA* 13):

I had gone to no such place but to the smoke of cafés and nights when the room whirled
. . . when you knew that that was all there was, and the strange excitement of waking
and not knowing who it was with you, and the world all unreal in the dark and so
exciting that you must resume again unknowing and not caring in the night, sure that
this was all and all and all and not caring. (*AFA* 13)

Abruzzi vs. world of whores? Frederic chose the latter—and he never really
rejects that choice.

This is the context which Hemingway provides for the famous first encounter
between Frederic and Catherine. Frederic has made his choice of worlds. It
remains for him to fulfill the demands of that choice. Catherine speaks of her
loss during this first meeting and makes the connection between sexuality—
specifically, giving herself in sexual intercourse—and hair. She wanted to cut
off her hair after her boyfriend was killed. She had not given herself to him;
somehow, cutting her hair would compensate for that. Hair, then, symbolizes
sexual experience. Most readers have seen this connection. Later, though, we'll
see that short hair gains a special meaning for Catherine (and for Maria in *For
Whom the Bell Tolls*)—a meaning clearly related to Brett Ashley's "womanli-
ness."

The scene in chapter 5 where Frederic makes his pass at Catherine makes
more sense when seen against the whore world backdrop. Catherine becomes a
sort of game for Frederic. He has preconditioned himself to see her as someone
he might meet at the Cova. When he conquers her, he touches her hair, as if
to suggest what she is for him. He *is* a "dog in heat," as Rinaldi points out,
or he would be on such a night in Milan or Rome.

Catherine is perceptive and sensitive enough to know what she is for Frederic, and, perhaps, just lonely and despondent enough not to resent his definition of her. Frederic lies to her early about having told her he loved her. This
may all be "bridge" or "chess" to him, but Catherine isn't taken in by him.
She knows that there is a time for "lies," a time when you *say*, when you
pretend to love. And when you do that, you're "nice" or you're "good."
After Frederic's wounding, after his transfer to Milan, Catherine and Frederic
talk about what is said and when. She asks about his being with other girls:

"You're just mine. That's true and you've never belonged to any one else. But I
don't care if you have. I'm not afraid of them. But don't tell me about them. When a
man stays with a girl when does she say how much it costs?"
"I don't know."
"Of course not. Does she say she loves him? Tell me that. I want to know that."
"Yes. If he wants her to."
"Does he say he loves her? Tell me please. It's important."
"He does if he wants to."
"But you never did? Really?"
"No."

"Not really. Tell me the truth."
"No," I lied. (*AFA* 105)

She knows he lies; she, too, will lie. She'll say whatever he wants her to, do whatever he wishes. She'll be a great "success." At what? Being one of those "girls." When she has lost herself saying what he wants to hear, then she'll be "good":

"But I will. I'll say just what you wish and I'll do what you wish and then you will never want any other girls, will you?" She looked at me very happily. "I'll do what you want and say what you want and then I'll be a great success, won't I?"
"Yes."
"What would you like me to do now that you're all ready?"
"Come to the bed again."
"All right. I'll come."
"Oh, darling, darling, darling," I said.
"You see," she said. "I do anything you want."
"You're so lovely."
"I'm afraid I'm not very good at it yet."
"You're lovely."
"I want what you want. There isn't any me any more. Just what you want."
"You sweet."
"I'm good. Aren't I good? You don't want any other girls, do you?"
"No."
"You see? I'm good. I do what you want." (*AFA* 105–6)

She'll be what he wants, and she certainly knows what that is.

Catherine is most explicit about her role the night Frederic returns to the front. They go to the hotel near the train station, and Frederic does in fact what he dreamed of earlier. There is a small boy with buttons and the elevator "clicks," just as he had imagined. Once there, she feels like a "whore" (*AFA* 152). Frederic is annoyed at this; he doesn't want to "argue now." Catherine overcomes her uneasy feelings and says she's his "good girl again" (*AFA* 152). What "good" means ought to be clear by now.

As if to underscore what Catherine is for Frederic, he calls her "Cat" for the first time following the scene in the hotel room: "How do you feel, Cat?" (*AFA* 156). Hemingway used the term "cat" often, as many Hemingway critics have already suggested. But here, in the context of whorehouses, saying what the customer wants said, so that you do a "good" job—here the name "Cat" is a very meaningful term of endearment, indeed. Cats live in cathouses, after all.

During the retreat from Caporetto, Frederic dreams of Catherine as he dozes off in Piani's car. His associations run from two virgins, to bed, to Catherine. She's his stay against confusion. He thinks of her as an alternative to the work world he experiences, as a refuge—just as the Villa Rossa is designed to be an alternative to combat for the officer near the front. Hemingway wrote an interesting poem in 1922 which might shed some light on Frederic's dreaming:

Riparto d'Assalto

Drummed their boots on the camion floor,
Hob-nailed boots on the camion floor.
Sergeants stiff,
Corporals sore.
Lieutenants thought of a Mestre whore—
Warm and short and sleepy whore,
Cozy, warm and lovely whore:
Damned cold, bitter, rotten ride,
Winding road up the Grappa side.
Arditi on beaches stiff and cold,
Pride of their country stiff and cold,
Bristly faces, dirty hides—
Infantry marches, Arditi rides.
Grey, cold, bitter, sullen ride—
To splintered pines on the Grappa side
At Asalone, where the truck-load died. (*P* 46)

For those lieutenants, so also for this one. For them, as for Frederic, the "whore" is a refuge. Catherine has become a kind of permanent "leave" for Frederic, a permanent "good girl."

In the mountains of Switzerland, Frederic and Catherine are more isolated than anything else. Their isolation is expressed most emphatically through the image of hair. Again, hair has to do with sexuality. Catherine suggests cutting her hair, not this time, however, as a symbolic sexual offering. Now she'll *look* more like Frederic. She'll be more like him; she'll mirror him:

"It might be nice short. Then we'd both be alike. Oh, darling, I want you so much I want to be you too."
"You are. We're the same one."
"I know it. At night we are."
"The nights are grand." (*AFA* 299)

This world can't last, of course. In a sense, Frederic has attempted to take his café world to the mountains, to the Abruzzi. In his rejection of the war world, he's tried to combine the Villa Rossa and the mountains. But the world of "cats" is not the world of cold air, of being called "Lord." Catherine and Frederic must, in other words, come down off the mountain. Once at the hospital, the type of relationship we've seen develop is emphasized again. There's no room for a baby in a "cat's" world. There can be no numbers above two.

Catherine is what Frederic makes her—or, rather, we see her in those terms because Frederic presents her that way. She senses what she must be for him.

In the face of a chaotic, meaningless, destructive world of war and death, Frederic has sought refuge in a world of games, of mirrors, of whores. It is interesting to speculate just how conscious Frederic Henry is of his needs and how those needs have distorted his perception of those around him. But it seems clear that—conscious or not—Frederic resorts to a type of adolescent response to a destructive universe. He must block out that world when he can and create one with which he can deal, a "world all unreal in the dark and so exciting that you must resume again unknowing and not caring in the night." Catherine knows only too well what it takes to be "good" in this world.

The tone of *For Whom the Bell Tolls* is somewhat different—primarily because the first person point of view has been abandoned. We see Robert Jordan's world through his eyes—but only in part. This means, among other things, that there is a clearer distinction between what characters are and what they are perceived to be by Jordan. But Hemingway begins this novel as we've seen him do in the previous two. Early in chapter 1, Robert remembers his last meeting with General Golz. Golz asks about the bridge, then says: "I will not make you any speech. Let us now have a drink. So much talking makes me very thirsty, Comrade Hordan. You have a funny name in Spanish, Comrade Hordown" (*FWBT* 7). Hor-down? Almost immediately Golz asks Robert how many girls he has on the other side of the line:

> "No, there is no time for girls."
> "I do not agree. The more irregular the service, the more irregular the life. You have very irregular service. Also you need a haircut." (*FWBT* 7–8)

Hemingway very explicitly establishes a sequence from "whore" to "girls" to "irregular service" to "hair"—a sequence we've seen before. And he'll return to it throughout the novel.

When Robert meets Maria, he calls her "strange" and notes her hair: "cut short . . . little longer than the fur on a beaver pelt" (*FWBT* 22). Later he watches her: "She moved awkwardly as a colt moves, but with the same grace as of a young animal" (*FWBT* 25). Raphael says she was like a "wet dog" (*FWBT* 28) when she was found. Pablo refers to her in chapter 5 as a "colt of a girl with cropped head and the movement of a foal still wet from its mother" (*FWBT* 64). But notice when the most frequent—and most famous—animal reference is made to Maria. She's a "colt" until the beginning of chapter 7. Then she's a "rabbit" (*FWBT* 69) for the first time. As Catherine is "Cat" first when she feels like a "whore," so Maria is "rabbit" for the first time when she comes to Robert's sleeping robe. Many years ago Arturo Barea pointed out that "rabbit" in Spanish is one of the more vulgar euphemisms for the female sex organ. He also notes that the verb *joder*—and the discussion of "bed" itself which takes place in the novel—would "break a taboo which is only lifted in the case of prostitutes" (Barea 210). Indeed. Notice, too, what

Maria serves Robert the first night: rabbit stew. "Rabbit-pie" was—and is—a fairly common Americanism for prostitute.

It's hard to believe that Hemingway—knowledgeable about Spain and Spanish, scrupulous about diction and the use and placement of detail—was not conscious of what sort of connection he was making. This is especially true since it is now clear he knew what those Spanish terms meant later, as James Brasch has discovered ("Hemingway and Bernard Berenson" 1986). Robert Jordan says, "Yes. I care much for jokes but not in the form of address. It's like a flag" (*FWBT* 66). It is clear what this flag "rabbit" says about his perception of Maria and what her function is for him.

Pilar knows, it seems. When she gets angry at Robert during their visit to El Sordo's camp, she tells Robert to go back to the Republic and take his "piece" with him: "Take thy little cropped-headed whore and go back to the Republic" (*FWBT* 150). She says she meant it when she said "whore." Later, when she has calmed herself, she tries to take it back. But the reinforcement, for the reader, has already occurred. Why would Pilar use terms like this to characterize Maria's role? She's sanctioned the relationship from the start. Perhaps it has to do with Augustin's suggestion that, in Spain, Maria's behavior would usually be considered whore-like (*FWBT* 291). But perhaps Pilar is simply following Robert's lead. Five pages after the "piece" and "whore" references, Pilar asks Robert if a cat has eaten his tongue.

"No cat," Robert Jordan said.
"What animal then?" She laid the girl's head down on the ground.
"No animal," Robert Jordan told her.
"You swallowed it yourself, eh?"
"I guess so," Robert Jordan said.
"And did you like the taste?" Pilar turned now and grinned at him.
"Not much."
"I thought not," Pilar said. "I *thought* not. But I give you back your rabbit. Nor ever did I try to take your rabbit. That's a good name for her. I heard you call her that this morning."
Robert Jordan felt his face redden. (*FWBT* 155–56)

He's embarrassed not only because Pilar has overheard an intimacy but because of what that term means.

As is the case with Catherine Barkley, so also Maria mirrors Robert. He teaches her "where the noses go." She does what he says, says what he wants, responds as he wishes. She is a type of dream for him, he admits, in terms reminiscent of Frederic's dream of Catherine, and he says she's like other visitors to his sleeping robe, Harlow and Garbo. But Robert's most explicit and direct reference to Maria's function occurs in chapter 16. Here, referring to his own cold, wet feet, he asks "Thou canst not dry them with thy hair?" (*FWBT* 203). He's joking, he says, but the reference to Mary Magdalen is clear enough.

Pilar, calling him "our ex-Lord Himself," tells us what Maria is for him: "Must you care for him as a sucking child?" (*FWBT* 203). The answer, of course, is yes. For Robert is a type of adolescent—as Frederic Henry is—in his need to isolate himself from a chaotic, warring world in a hall of mirrors.

How conscious is Robert Jordan of what Maria is for him? Hemingway supplies the imagery and diction, but does Robert understand what Maria is? He speculates on their relationship often enough, and he seems to get closer to consciousness than either Jake or Frederic. Thinking about living his whole life in 70 hours, he considers:

What nonsense, he thought. What rot you get to thinking by yourself. That is *really* nonsense. And maybe it isn't nonsense too. Well, we will see. The last time I slept with a girl was in Madrid. No it wasn't. It was in the Escorial and, except that I woke in the night and thought it was some one else and was excited until I realized who it really was, it was just dragging ashes; except that it was pleasant enough. And the time before that was in Madrid and except for some lying and pretending I did to myself as to identity while things were going on, it was the same or something less. So I am no romatic glorifier of the Spanish Woman nor did I ever think of a casual piece as anything much other than a casual piece in any country. But when I am with Maria I love her so that I feel, literally, as though I would die and I never believed in that nor thought that it could happen. (*FWBT* 166)

Maria isn't a "casual piece," then? He turns to the Golz episode treated earlier for clarification:

This was what Golz had talked about. The longer he was around, the smarter Golz seemed. So this was what he was asking about; the compensation of irregular service. Had Golz had this and was it the urgency and the lack of time and the circumstances that made it? Was this something that happened to every one given comparable circumstances? And did he only think it was something special because it was happening to him? Had Golz slept around in a hurry when he was commanding irregular cavalry in the Red Army and had the combination of the circumstances and the rest of it made the girls seem the way Maria was?

Probably Golz knew all about this too and wanted to make the point that you must make your whole life in the two nights that are given to you; that living as we do now you must concentrate all of that which you should always have into the short time that you can have it.

It was a good system of belief. But he did not believe that Maria had only been made by the circumstances. Unless, of course, she is a reaction from her own circumstances as well as his. Her one circumstance is not so good, he thought. No, not so good. (*FWBT* 168–69)

Indeed, their "circumstances" created their function, their roles. "Irregular service" creates a special type of "girl" who may *seem* more than a "casual piece" but who really is not.

Much later in the narrative, Robert comes back to the notion of "lying" alluded to above. He's talking to Maria the night before the bridge is to be blown: "But this time when he talked about Madrid there was no slipping into make-believe again. Now he was just lying to his girl and to himself to pass the night before battle and he knew it." (*FWBT* 345). "Lying" to his "girl" helps him get through the night before battle—as it had for Frederic Henry. Notice, too, that again "hair" is associated with Maria's function. Robert says she can have it cut in Madrid. Her answer: " 'I would look like thee,' she said and held him close to her. 'And then I never would want to change it' " (*FWBT* 345).

Robert and Maria cannot remain in the mountains. Robert is called "Don" here— as Frederic would have been called "Lord"—and they are, temporarily, safe in this cold, snowy world. The action of the novel demands that the band leave. The imagery and diction of the novel demand that the bond between Maria and Robert be broken. "Rabbits" are for "irregular service." True, Robert speculates on marrying Maria and returning with her to America. But the clearly ironic tone of that speculation (*FWBT*, chapter 13) suggests Robert himself knows that this is impossible—and always would be.

The primary function of the "whore" is clear enough in the three novels. She serves to insulate and isolate the protagonist from a chaotic, threatening world. But "whore" is not without its darker connotations. Images of death and "whore" are often linked in Hemingway's work. In *For Whom the Bell Tolls,* Kashkin smells like death-to-come. Pilar likens that smell to the smell of whores and whorish business (*FWBT* 256). This, of course, echoes Hemingway's "Poem to Mary" mentioned earlier:

> Now sleeps he
> With that old whore Death
> Who, yesterday, denied her thrice.
> Repeat after me
> Now sleeps he
> With that old whore Death
> Who, yesterday, denied her thrice. (*P* 107)

Jake's world dances, Frederic's room whirls, and Robert's earth moves—all three seek a "stay against confusion" in the women they embrace. All three find mirrors of themselves because this is what they demand. Hemingway's men insist on a kind of "fictionalized" world—a world of lying, of dreaming, of gaming—that whores and whore-like women supply. Brett, Catherine, and Maria all effect the type of adolescent ego gratification Hemingway's men seem to crave.

They need other things too, of course. There *are* strong domestic images in *A Farewell to Arms* and *For Whom the Bell Tolls:* there *is* strong ritualistic imagery in *The Sun Also Rises*. But the diction and imagery of whores is also clear, and what that diction and imagery show is one more way that the Hem-

ingway protagonist has found to get through the night, one more way to deal
with the threat of annihilation. Jake, Frederic, Robert—all three profess to love
their women. And they do. Usually, they seem barely conscious of how they
themselves perceive these women or how they present them to us.

Finally, the patterns of imagery and diction discussed here do not *necessarily*
support or contradict other critical approaches to Hemingway's women. In fact,
they imply little about the women themselves; they imply very much about
Hemingway's men. Nor do they tell us much—necessarily—about Hemingway's own understanding of women (or lack of it). They show us, again, that
Hemingway could and did portray his protagonists with remarkable skill and
complexity. But we suspected that all along.

References

Barca, Arturo. "Not Spain but Hemingway." *Hemingway and His Critics.* Ed. Carlos
      Baker. New York: Hill and Wang, 1961. 202–12.
Brasch, James. "Hemingway and Bernard Berenson." Address to Second International
      Hemingway Conference. Lignano Sabbiadoro, Italy, 26 June 1986.
Hemingway, Ernest. *88 Poems.* Ed. Nicholas Gerogiannis. New York: Harcourt Brace
      Jovanovich, 1979.
———. *A Farewell to Arms.* New York: Scribner, 1929.
———. *For Whom the Bell Tolls.* New York: Scribner, 1940.
———. *The Short Stories of Ernest Hemingway.* New York: Scribner, 1966.
———. *The Sun Also Rises.* New York: Scribner, 1926.
Kert, Bernice. *The Hemingway Women.* New York: Norton, 1983.
Miller, Linda. "Reassessing the Critics." Address to Second International Hemingway
      Conference. Lignano Sabbiadoro, Italy, 26 June 1986.
New American Bible: Revised New Testament. Grand Rapids, MI: Eerdmans, 1988.
Steinke, James. "Catherine's Quiet Revolution in *A Farewell to Arms.*" Address to
      Second International Hemingway Conference. Lignano Sabbiadoro, Italy, 26 June
      1986.
Whitlow, Roger. *Cassandra's Daughters: The Women in Hemingway.* Westport, CT:
      Greenwood Press, 1984.

II

Hemingway's Relations to Other Writers

"Christ, I Wish I Could Paint": The Correspondence between Ernest Hemingway and Bernard Berenson

James D. Brasch

Hemingway's lonely life in Cuba has been generally ignored by biographers. Even Baker's biography (1969) treated almost two decades of Hemingway's life with the scantest references, and even today it remains by and large a mystery. Baker's edition of only a small portion of the letters (1981) filled in some of the details, but the letters to Hemingway are, of course, omitted, and many of them are in locations not readily accessible to scholars or the interested public. Recently some details have emerged. Hemingway's support of Dr. Fidel Castro and the Cuban revolution (Fuentes 1984) and his close association with José Luis Herrera Sotolongo (Brasch 1986) reveal the Cuban resident as more involved in Cuban affairs than earlier commentary would suggest. Most touching perhaps was his long-standing correspondence with Bernard Berenson, an authority on Renaissance art, who served Hemingway as a surrogate father with whom he occasionally differed, but whose approval Hemingway desperately needed. The correspondence, which began in 1949 and ended in 1956 shortly before Berenson's death, reveals not only a great deal about Hemingway's Cuban years, but suggests another reason for the depression that preceded his death.

With a tone hovering somewhere between blasphemy and devotion reminiscent of e. e. cummings' young boy reflecting on the "defunct" Buffalo Bill ("Jesus/ he was a handsome man") Hemingway's exclamation to Berenson positioned him somewhere between the almost religious confidence that he could "make a scene" as well as any painter and the unsettling knowledge that critics and biographers had not noticed the parallel. "Christ, I wish I could paint" (EH to BB, 11 Aug. 1953; at sea) was not an idle crumb tossed to Bernard

Berenson, the world authority on Italian Renaissance art, but a passionate plea that someone would understand what he was trying to do. At times the humorous, tender, and affectionate tone that Hemingway used to address the aging Berenson suggests that Hemingway may have found the father he never had. At this stage in his life, biographers had bothered him unmercifully, and he was more aware than ever that they didn't have the slightest clue about the relationship between his art and his life. Perhaps the art critic would understand, or, at least, serve as a surrogate "father confessor." "Biographies at 53 are shit," Hemingway wrote to Berenson in 1953. "They [the biographers] don't know. You are too proud to tell them. And they could not understand" (EH to BB, 17 Feb. 1953). But Hemingway obviously felt that Berenson would understand. Berenson's rather cruel rebuke of Hemingway when he refused to grant him a private audience was a serious blow to his ego at a time when he was desperately looking for someone to give meaning to his life. Miró and Cézanne had sufficed during one phase of his career, but a respected art critic who might be able to recognize that Hemingway could "make a scene" like any other painter might be the answer to his lonely paternal search of the 1950s. Ironically, Berenson's reputation as an art critic is unraveling as his dubious relationship with Joseph Duveen is gradually emerging. (See, for example, *Connoisseur*, October, 1986, "The Berenson Scandal," pp. 126–38; and Colin Simpson, *Artful Partners: Bernard Berenson and Joseph Duveen*, New York: Macmillan, 1986.) But the Berenson that Hemingway knew during the later years was a connoisseur without equal.

Nevertheless, few understood why Hemingway included Berenson among those whom he said deserved the Nobel Prize for literature more than he did. When asked for his reaction after the award was announced in 1954, Hemingway said that he would have been happier if Bernard Berenson, the art critic "who had devoted a lifetime to the most lucid and best writing on painting that has been produced" had been honored instead of him (Baker 1969, 527). For all of his loathing of the critics and biographers, his highest admiration remained for the analytical perceptions of the art critic who had taught the world how to look at Renaissance art. Little wonder, then, that as Mary continued her gentle flirtatious correspondence with Bernard Berenson, her husband, as she said, "edged her out" (Mary Welsh Hemingway 1976, 231). If he couldn't paint, he at least wanted to talk to someone who knew what painting was all about.

This, of course, was nothing new. Although he was starved for intellectual companionship in Cuba (EH to BB, 20 Mar. 1953), he counted many artists among his friends, and his library contained almost 200 volumes on painters and art—including seven volumes by and about Berenson (see Appendix II). As Hemingway and Berenson exchanged opinions on such painters as Velázquez and El Greco, Miró and Cézanne, Hemingway admitted that he envied painters such as Picasso (EH to BB, 2 Mar. 1956) who could even sell their failures, unlike writers. According to Hemingway, painters were greater than writers to start with (EH to BB, 13 Sept. 1952). In the twilight of his life, "Christ, I wish I could paint," constituted not only admiration for the work of the accomplished connoisseur of Renaissance art and his admiration for many of his friends, but also an indication of the direction and intention of his own career.

Although Hemingway was aware of Berenson's reputation in the art world as early as 1928 (Meyers 1986, 429), the correspondence between them did not begin until August 25, 1949. It continued until August 24, 1957, only a few months before Berenson died. Hemingway wrote 31 letters to Berenson of which 18 are omitted from Baker's edition of the *Letters* (1981). Hemingway's letters are part of the Berenson collection housed at his former villa, "I Tatti," located between Fiesole and Settignano, just north of Florence, Italy.[1] The friendship resulted from a visit that Mary paid to the elder critic at his home in the company of several friends. Several of Hemingway's letters contain post-scripts or other notes from Mary to Berenson. Baker eliminated Mary's contri-bution to the correspondence. It is a serious omission because Mary's mild flirtations encouraged Berenson's breezy compliments which helped sustain the trialogue. To document Hemingway's obvious assumption that their correspon-dence would eventually be published, a complete record of the correspondence must include a carefully typed letter by Mary to Berenson late in the association that clarifies the origin, the context, and the rationale for their correspondence. The letter certainly reads like a directive to future editors.

In addition to recording that she first met Berenson in the company of the Australian journalist, Alan Moorhead and his wife, Mary Hemingway included several anecdotes that were later retold in her autobiography and that establish the warmth of her relationship to Berenson (MH to BB 21 Aug. 1957 and *How It Was* 310). The typewritten letter is included in the Ernest Hemingway file at "I Tatti," and its placement and tone certainly suggest that it was carefully prepared as an adjunct to Hemingway's letter to Berenson of March 6, 1953, in which he wrote:

Imagine when we are both dead as snakeshit and they publish the famous Berenson-Hemingstein letters. Can I advise you about God as Claudel did to Gide? Cannot we take each other to task about something? That is what the French really love. Do we have to rompre? All friendships in French end with this.

At this point in his life (1953) Hemingway evidently assumed that his corre-spondence would be published. The fact that he signed marginalia in the critical volumes in his library at Finca Vigía also justifies this assumption, as does his habit of carefully dating every letter sent to Berenson.

The two men disagreed on very little, but the letters of these unlikely corre-spondents in their villas in out-of-the-way places revealed two strangely simi-lar spirits lamenting the state of art in the modern world. Both men had a passion for knowledge as the foundation of art. The cultivation of connoisseurship was the raison d'être of Berenson's entire life; Hemingway's passion for knowledge and accuracy in such subjects as horse racing and marlin fishing is now well documented. In addition, both men projected a charismatic presence when they entered a room; both were capable of flirtations and affairs; both were most successful in the company of women; both complained that journalists ruled the world; and both raised serious questions about the meaning of life and the utility of their own careers. They read and celebrated each other's books (see Appendixes II and III) and, perhaps most important, both men saw and celebrated nature as if it were a work of art.

Bernard Berenson's biographer tells the story of a day in which Berenson took a friend, Iris Origo, walking above the valley of the river Sieve:

Suddenly, B.B. stopped and, looking as fixedly as a pointer who had sighted his bird, said, "Look," pointing to a farmhouse below us, with cypresses and behind it a little dove-cot, "Look a Poussin." It was the first time it had occurred to me to look at landscape in terms of art. (Secrest 13)

The incident reveals Hemingway's affinity for Berenson. Hemingway's pronouncements on his ability to "make" a scene in the manner of Cézanne are now well known. Both men shared a great admiration for landscape painting and especially for Paul Cézanne.

Hemingway and Berenson never managed a genuine *rompre* although they did compare notes on many places, people, attitudes, and manners, and during their correspondence they revealed many of their mutual insecurities. They never met. Several times they were very close, and Berenson pleaded repeatedly for a visit from the Hemingways. He was aware that he had a short time to live, and since he had already enjoyed the company of Mary, he was anxious to see her again. "Caress Mary for me" (BB to EH, 15 March 1953) was one of his warmest requests as he signed his *BB* to a letter which addressed Hemingway in "full Jovian splendor" (BB to EH, 22 June 1953).

Perhaps the closest the two friends ever came to a genuine *rompre* occurred when the Hemingways planned a visit to Florence while they were staying in Venice on their way back to Cuba after the disastrous African safari in 1954. The 89-year-old Berenson had many reservations about meeting Hemingway in person, as revealed by his diary entry for March 25, 1954:

Ernest Hemingway is impending, and I look forward with a certain dread to seeing and knowing him in the flesh. Hitherto we have only corresponded. His letters seemed written when he was not quite sober, rambling and affectionate. I fear he may turn out too animal, too overwhelmingly masculine, too Bohemian. He may expect me to drink and guzzle with him, and write me down as a muff. I know him only through his writing, which I admire greatly here and again, but seldom a whole book. What can he know of the real me? Has he seriously read anything I have written? Has he been taken by the myth? Has his present wife, whom I led through my garden some years ago, given him ideas about me? What, I wonder, does he expect? I dread arranged meetings,

I prefer to meet people unexpectedly, casually, with no responsible feeling that I must see them again, or encounter resentment. (Berenson 1963, 339)

The following day, March 26, 1954, Berenson wrote Hemingway in Venice, welcomed him back to Italy, and insisted that he looked "forward with keen zeal to seeing [him] in the flesh." As the letter continued, however, Berenson lamented the crowded calendar that always plagued him in the summer. So many visitors expected to stay for a meal. They would, however, be able to go for a long walk, but unfortunately there was no room for them to stay at "I Tatti." Berenson concluded: "I mention this dolesome fact which will prevent my seeing you both *alone* as much as I should wish. (BB to EH, 26 March 1954; Berenson's emphasis). Hemingway took the letter as a rebuke. He used a long catalogue of his injuries suffered in the two air crashes as an excuse for putting off the trip to Florence, but he was obviously offended by Berenson's reluctance to see them alone. They would come down, he replied, some time when so many of his admirers were not around. The letter from Berenson had clearly offended Hemingway, and they never managed to regain their former intimacy. Berenson's lack of compassion and understanding for his injured friend, whose obituary had been flashed around the world after the two air crashes, was no doubt caused by the self-doubt and recrimination which Berenson suffered throughout most of his later life. The deterioration of Hemingway's mind and composure was evident in the frayed handwriting of the first letter he wrote to Berenson nine days after the crash (EH to BB, 22 January 1954). The letter also included a grizzly photograph of Hemingway's badly burned left hand. Still apparently disappointed that they had not met, Berenson reminded Hemingway at Christmas in 1954: "Don't forget you are mortal" (BB to EH, 22 December 1954).

More important for the correspondence than this failure to meet at a very difficult time in Hemingway's life was the intimacy and cordiality which both men instinctively felt for each other. Carlos Baker included 13 of Hemingway's letters in his collection, and in his biography he makes a number of references to Hemingway's letters to Berenson, but essentially he used them to document Hemingway's location on certain dates. He makes no references to Berenson's letters to Hemingway. His statement that Hemingway "elbowed his way into the correspondence" (Baker 1981, 667) completely ignores the mutual sincerity, compassion, and admiration that dominates the communications of these two famous men. Completely lacking in Baker's references to the eight-year correspondence are the expressions of humor, warmth, encouragement, language, and learning which dominated their exchanges. Baker's "macho" image of Hemingway left little room for sophisticated conversation with a man like Berenson or compassion for Hemingway's earlier loss of his real father by suicide.

Hemingway wrote to Berenson for the same reason that he wrote to Malcolm Cowley and Arthur Mizener: He was lonely and bored in Cuba. But the personal dimension that reaches beyond these other exchanges is what makes this correspondence so significant. Hemingway constantly asks Berenson to write and let him know that he is well. His tenderness to Berenson as when he details his love for Mary (EH to BB, 20 March 1953), was frequently echoed in his honest concern for the old man's health and even his love of the Italian landscape. For example, he asked Berenson to "Remember [him] to any big slow oxen and to all cypress trees, all bends in the road, and to any hill you meet" (EH to BB, 6 March 1953). There is never any question that they were addressing each other in the familiar *"tu,"* but on one occasion Hemingway defined his understanding of their linguistic intimacy: "you alone, you only, you who I love, you who I see again, you with who I share a tribal secret" (EH to BB, 2 February 1954).

   Hemingway's intimacy was also flavored with a delicate humor. Writing about his son, Patrick, for example, and some of the difficulties of parenthood, he wrote to this world authority on Italian Renaissance art that Patrick was "sort of an angel; not Botticelli angel" but "Northern Cheyenne Indian angel where they have very good angels too" (EH to BB, 18 September 1955). On another occasion while praising the natural beauty of Cuba, Hemingway wrote in the same tone:

   Lately we have had the curious juxtaposition of Venus, Jupiter, Mars and Mercury in the sky. I have never seen Venus so wonderful in my life and no one will again for a long time. Then, now, all the migratory birds are coming through and there are ten pairs of mocking birds nested here on the place. I play Bach on the phonograph to one and he learns it very well. (EH to BB, 20 March 1953)

   When Berenson, with wobbly fingers, asked Hemingway to pray for him, Hemingway replied that he had already taken care of that. Not only had "a nonbelieving ⅛ Northern Cheyenne . . . pray[ed] for a Jew," in Chartres, Burgos, Segovia, and two minor places, but he apologized for not having prayed yet at "the home office, Santiago de Compostella" (EH to BB, 11 August 1953). Later Hemingway admitted that he prayed for Berenson whenever he was in trouble (EH to BB, 4 October 1955). He had signed off a letter to Berenson with the reflection:

   I prayed for you all the time on the [African safari] whenever I would wake up in the night. I doubt whether it has any practical value but it is pleasant and healthy to do. I quit praying for myself in Spain in the war because it seemed too egotistical with everyone having it so bad. But now I pray for you, for Mary, for my grand-daughter. You were probably joking when you said to pray for you. But I don't think it could do any harm. The prayers of sinners, I believe, are especially potent. (EH to BB, 4 May 1953)

   The subject of death and what would happen to them in the next world was a constant undercurrent of the correspondence. After Berenson had reminded

Hemingway, "Don't forget that you are mortal" (BB to EH, 22 December 1954), Hemingway advised Berenson that when he died he was not to tell Dante, if he saw him of their little joke about expecting to meet in an afterlife (EH to BB, 10 June 1953). "Pity the poor people who believe in any other life," Hemingway, labeling himself as "El Profundo," had written to Berenson a few months earlier. "If they really had any such dirty trick we will be together and have a fine time. You classify and I will make a running comment and we'll disturb the circles. Poor Dante. Maybe we can find him a job as concierge" (EH to BB, 17 February 1953). The witty and tender tones of the letters to Berenson were another of Hemingway's secrets and characterized none of his other sustained correspondence with the possible exception of the letters to his children. The tenderness suggests again that Hemingway was seeking not only the approval, but also the affection of a father.

The joke of the sinner sending secret letters to the saint was expanded in their continued discussion of the Hemingway he-man image as compared to the esthete. Berenson returned to the contrast time and again. It probably was the reason that they never met. Berenson focused constantly on the public image of Hemingway and seemed not to recognize the lonely man behind the hard-drinking, hard-whoring, and hard-fighting sporting man, apparently without recognizing the tenderness and compassion in his correspondent's letters. Perhaps, he mused to Hemingway, he himself had never lived. He wondered if Hemingway would put him down as a "muff." Berenson seemed to question the worth of his entire life in his letters to Hemingway (BB to EH, 22 June 1953). He seemed especially depressed in the light of Hemingway's image. He had rarely played "the beast with two backs" but had to admit that compared to Santayana, he had led an adventurous and colorful life (BB to EH, 29 March 1953).

Santayana paid frequent visits to their exchanges. Santayana, also an immigrant Jew, had arrived in America from Avila, Spain. Berenson had originally immigrated with his family to the United States from Lithuania. Santayana, however, had preceded Berenson to Harvard by one year, and as a result Berenson always seemed on the defensive about Santayana, although in other contexts, when Harvard was not being considered, he would joke about him. Berenson felt that Santayana wrote beautifully and occasionally there was a good thought (BB to EH, 29 March 1953). He had to admit, however, that the chief reason he wrote beautifully was that "he had never lived" (BB to EH, 15 March 1953). Hemingway was evidently reading Santayana at the time—there were five volumes by Santayana in Hemingway's library—and was less compassionate than Berenson. In addition to dismissing Santayana as "a chickenshit philosopher" who died unloving and unloved, "except by nuns" (EH to BB, 10 June 1953), on one occasion he reflected at some length:

If there is any point that I would try to make it is that if you come from Avila there is no mystery about Avila. I never knew Saint Teresa because she was before my time.

If we had been contemporaries, I am quite sure we would have been good friends. The same with Juan de la Cruz. Quevedo I feel I know better than my brother. Santayana to me is a different business. Because he comes from a walled town he thinks that makes a difference. It makes no difference in the heart. Anyone who has lived in a walled town knows how much human shit there is on the ramparts and under the towers. We know who fought for it and helped build it and who did not. . . . You know that what ruined, and what made Spain, was the Inquisition. They missed Santayana's family and he became a beautifully writing apologist for it. This is very unjust but you be patient with me too. (EH to BB, 21 March 1953)

(Berenson constantly asked Hemingway to be patient with his almost illegible handwriting.) The day before, however, Hemingway had promised that if Berenson insisted, he would try to envy Santayana as a "spiritual exercise."

This sort of talk, however, always brought on bouts of self-doubt for Berenson when he was confronted by the public image of Hemingway. This European dandy, brother-in-law of Bertrand Russell and all of the free-thinking that went with that circle, who openly lived for many years with a mistress married to another man, and associated with Oscar Wilde, confided his deepest sexual doubts and fears to Hemingway:

What is life? Is it exercising to the utmost all . . . one's animal functions? That seems to be what the likes of you seem to write about, do write about and picture that it is LIFE. Then poor ME has not lived at all. I have loved much, but fucked little (although exquisitely and ecstatically as you sip a priceless liqueur). I have never been drunk and do not like a drink except of wines too expensive for my pocket. I never fought nor bled. In short I have never been a he man. Would you write me down as a muff! Not if you knew me I hope. And bluff, Don Ernesto. Where is man to be? (BB to EH, 15 March 1953)

Hemingway's reply to this self-doubt was a compassionate and very different reply than might be expected from the public image of Hemingway which Berenson had insisted on addressing:

Please don't get mixed up about LIFE. That is only a picture magazine. I always joke and much of it is gallow's humor. You must truly know that no matter how stupid people act, in order not to argue with fools, any writer that you respect at all, or that has given you pleasure, can think a little bit (EH to BB, 20 March 1953).

Later, Hemingway wrote that Berenson should consider him as his "pup" because Hemingway had been educated by his "god-damned beautifully worked out lovely books" (EH to BB, 2 February 1954). Berenson was amazed that the famous writer would denigrate himself to an art historian. In his own insecurities, Berenson seemed incapable of recognizing Hemingway's longing for an authoritative father.

Hemingway appreciated the beauty in Berenson's books but admitted, "I cannot write beautifully but I can write with great accuracy (sometimes; I hope) and the accuracy makes a sort of beauty" (EH to BB, 20 March 1953). "You have done a good job," he wrote encouragingly to Berenson, "and left things in order" (EH to BB, 21 March 1953). Hemingway especially envied Berenson's managed and ordered library. Since his own had been looted and pilfered (EH to BB, 4 October 1955) he felt Berenson was better off: "you are always better off than me because you have more books. Thank God for books" (EH to BB, 24 September 1954).

Writing and reading in fact made up a good portion of their correspondence. Hemingway warmed to the subject as he wrote to the learned art critic. His language bridged the gap between writing and painting. Whether Hemingway sensed Berenson's antipathy to more recent art is not always clear. Berenson claimed to have lost interest in painting "after Matisse" (Secrest 1979, 219). Little was written, however, about specific painters, but Hemingway took pains to define his writing in visual terms. He could "make country" he wrote on two occasions (EH to BB, 20 March 1953; 27 May 1953) but that this was very difficult. Another time, he admitted that he could "make" people because he had "a perfect ear" (EH to BB, 20 March 1953). He felt an "obligation," he insisted, to write fiction, however, because that was the way that he could "invent" in such a way that he would create fiction that was "truer than things can be true" (EH to BB, 24 September 1954). As he had written to Malcolm Cowley on a number of occasions, Hemingway repeated to Berenson that fiction writers were only liars who steal from others. What they don't steal they invent (EH to BB, 24 September 1954). And he returned to the lying metaphor several times not only to analyze his own methods, but also to bolster the elder writer's genre of writing as he denigrates his own:

Writers of fiction are only super-liars who if they know enough and are disciplined can make their lies truer than the truth. If you have fought and diced and served at court and gone to the wars and know navigation, sea-manship, the bad world and the great world and the different countries and other things then you have good knowledge to lie out of. That is all a writer of fiction is. (EH to BB, 14 October 1952)

Berenson had been complaining about how difficult it was to get started on a new book that he had been planning for some time although he wondered if his work was not all a terrible waste of time. Hemingway rejoins with, "don't write silly stuff about wasting your life. It was in doing what you had to do that you learned what it is worth while to say now. . . . You [should] start to write the book now" (EII to BB, 14 October 1952).

Hemingway had had his own problems when he started writing as he frankly wrote to Berenson:

I had found the paragraph almost impossible. The chapter, I knew was beyond me. And the writing of a whole novel seemed like an assault on the Himalayas. But I knew

I had to do it so I wrote one. When I wrote as a kid it seemed so easy but when I had started trying to make country that you could walk back into and to learn what it was in speech that your ear actually retained and to try to move people emotionally with the landscape without being descriptive then writing got harder and harder to do. It still is damned hard and it is only the un-avaidable [sic] awkwardnesses that show. Peple [sic] think that is your style. And other poor bastards copy the awkwardnesses and think that is the secret. (EH to BB, 27 May 1953)

The dialogue on writing had started over Berenson's admiration for *The Old Man and the Sea*. Berenson admired Hemingway because he felt that he wrote from "within" about "the creative spasm" (BB to EH, 17 September 1954) while he, of course, only dealt with the end product. Berenson had endeared himself to Hemingway early in their correspondence by comparing the style of *The Old Man and the Sea* to that of Homer and by saying that he much preferred Hemingway's old fisherman to Herman Melville's Ahab (BB to EH, 6 September 1952). Hemingway responded by writing that *Moby-Dick* was good "journalism" which resulted only in a "forced rhetorical epic" (EH to BB, 13 September 1952). He compliments "the only critic I respect" and then pays tribute to the knowledge which is behind *The Old Man and the Sea* and which the great connoisseur should appreciate:

There isn't any symbolism (mis-spelled). The sea is the sea. The old man is an old man. The boy is a boy and the fish is a fish. The sharks are all sharks—no better and no worse. All the symbolism that people say is shit. What goes beyond is what you see beyond when you know. A writer should know too much. (EH to BB, 13 September 1952)

The thought, if not the diction, seems borrowed from Henry James's "The Art of Fiction." If Berenson recognized the language of his old friend from Cambridge with whom he had spent many hours, he did not report it to Hemingway.

Hemingway was so delighted with his correspondent's praise, however, that he could not resist asking him for a blurb to be printed on the book jacket. After Hemingway sent the galleys to him, Berenson sent the following statement to the London publishers of *The Old Man and the Sea:*

Hemingway's Old Man and the Sea is an idyll of the sea as sea, as un-Byronic and un-Melvillian as Homer himself and communicated in a prose as calm and compelling as Homer's verse. No real artist symbolizes or allegorizes—and Hemingway is a real artist—but every real work of art exhales symbols and allegories. So does this short but not small masterpiece. Bernard Berenson. (Cable to Rupert Belleville, Whites, London, 9 September 1952)

Hemingway probably felt that a testimonial from someone with Berenson's stature could be used to hold off the critics and Hemingway bashers who had sneered at *Across the River and into the Trees. The Old Man and the Sea,* however, needed no help from Berenson. His comment, nevertheless, did appear in Scribner's advertisement for *The Old Man and the Sea,* above similar accolades from Cyril Connolly, Malcolm Cowley, Carlos Baker, and Somerset Maugham. (See, for example, The New York *Times,* November 10, 1952, p. 23.) In appreciation, Hemingway sent a highly annotated copy of the ad to Berenson with a notation at the top: "File under: Where Do We Go From Here? EH."

Hemingway also wrote Berenson many anecdotes about writing *The Sun Also Rises* and *A Farewell to Arms.* Hemingway wrote to him as a worldly-wise sage and reassured Berenson that no writer really reveals himself in writing. Berenson was, nevertheless, filled with self-doubt, not only about his writing but about the entire meaning of his life. He saw the life of the connoisseur, especially as revealed in his writings, as one of waste. Just as Berenson insisted on constantly addressing the public image of Hemingway, so Hemingway constantly addressed the public image of Berenson. Neither seemed to recognize or at least admit that they were writing to someone who in his private life was more insecure and troubled than the public image which was manufactured. Perhaps they recognized the dichotomy, and in spite of much frankness, each respected the loneliness and privacy of the other. Their affection for each other was constantly apparent and may have been augmented by this mutual recognition. In a rare burst of affection Hemingway admitted that Berenson was one of his heroes.

As the two correspondents grew closer together, they exchanged impressions and prejudices not only about Santayana, as already mentioned, but about many figures who reveal the breadth and depth of their common interest. Among them: Koestler (BB to EH, 10 October 1952 and EH to BB, 14 October 1952); Malraux—a liar—Hemingway's contempt began during the Spanish Civil War—Berenson liked and admired him (EH to BB, 12 January 1953, 17 February 1953 and 6 March 1953; BB to EH, 25 February 1953); D. H. Lawrence (EH to BB, 14 October 1952 and 4 October 1955); Gertrude and Leo Stein—Gertrude hated Berenson (EH to BB, 4 May 1953); Joyce (EH to BB, 14 October 1952, 4 October 1955 and 10 April 1956); Thomas Wolfe (BB to EH, 25 November 1952); Lillian Ross—"like being good friends with a circular saw" (EH to BB, 24 January 1953); Sherwood Anderson—Hemingway did not trust "anyone with a Southern accent" (EH to BB, 24 January 1953); Dante (EH to BB, 17 February 1953); Henry James—"I was wounded badly before Henry James received O.M. for his patriotic sentiments" (EH to BB, 20, 21 March 1953, 4 October 1955); Unamuno (EH to BB, 20, 21 March 1953); Thomas Mann—Hemingway liked *Buddenbrooks* (EH to BB, 18 September 1955); Pound who wrote "U.T." [Unknown Tongue] (EH to BB, 24 October 1955 and 20, 21 October 1953); Faulkner—"When I get tired sometimes I imitate Faulkner a little bit just to show him how it should be done. It is like loosening up with a five finger exercise" (EH to BB, 24 October 1955 and BB to EH, 2 November 1955); Joan Miró (EH to BB, 4 October 1953); Mary McCarthy (EH to BB, 9 July 1955); Rosamund Lehman (EH to BB, 27 May 1953 and 4 April 1954); and El Greco (EH to BB, 10 June 1953). This listing is by no means complete, but simply suggestive of the content, tone, and direction of their exchanges.

One is constantly wondering how much Hemingway knew about Berenson. Did he know that Berenson was an intimate of Henry James as a student at Harvard and later a good friend of his brother, William? Did he know that Berenson's wife/mistress, Mary Costello, was a good friend of Whitman? These puzzles increase as the correspondence continues and intensify the unfortunate fact that the two men never met.

One of the aspects of Hemingway that intrigued Berenson most was Hemingway's legendary success with women. As a product of that liberal British circle that included Oscar Wilde and Bertrand Russell, Berenson was constantly asking for details about the sexual exploits of many of the visitors who sought him out at "I Tatti." It was Mary's visit there in 1948 that had started the correspondence in the first place, and Berenson was always looking for juicy details. Sexual innuendo was frequently just beneath the surface of their communications and often surfaced. Mary Hemingway recalled how in their first and only meeting Berenson had startled her. She had been sent into the garden to tell him tea was served:

"What number are you?" asked Mr. B.

"Sir? Do you number your guests?"

"Wife," said he, excusing my density, and when I told him "number four" he asked how it was Ernest had managed to get through so many wives.

"I have no simple answer for that, sir," said I as we moved up toward the house. "Of course, Ernest is a man of tremendous energy and exuberance."

"Does he demonstrate those characteristics in bed?" the renowned art expert asked in the most casual tones, totally flummoxing me. I was relieved to turn him over to the other guests and Lucy [Moorehead], noticing my strawberry-red face, giggled knowingly. (Mary Welsh Hemingway 1976, 230)

In a similar vein, Berenson's biographer, Meryle Secrest, records a meeting between Martha Gellhorn, Hemingway's third wife, and the aging, but still amorous, Berenson:

"He used to stay in a hotel in Rome to which I'd be invited for dinner; there were practically pink-shaded lamps," Martha Gellhorn remembers. "I am an exceedingly unswoony lady, and at a given moment, he'd sit next to me on the sofa and I'd say, 'Nothing doing. Keep your little hands to yourself.' " (Secrest 1979, 12)

When Berenson was almost 90, he asked Hemingway to caress Mary for him (BB to EH, 15 March 1953) and wrote that Hemingway's description of a German/Indonesian houseguest [probably Herta Klausser; see Baker 1969, 508] "warmed his cold balls" (BB to EH, 15 March 1953). Undoubtedly, a father-son relationship was not the only explanation for the two correspondents' interest in each other.

Because of Berenson's long association with Martha Gellhorn, it was not long before Hemingway was asked "when in genial mood, all passion spent" to write Berenson about his third wife (BB to EH, 21 May 1953). Hemingway responded immediately but didn't send the letter until about a month later when he was in France. Basically Hemingway is kind and gentle towards Martha, a woman over whom he had spent a great amount of spirit in a waste of shame, but his comments reveal that there was a great deal of bitterness remaining between them. Martha's correspondence to Berenson makes it quite clear that after they had separated, she was terrified of accidentally bumping into Hemingway. Whether she would meet Berenson at the Hotel Europa would depend on "how Ernest-free the Venetian waterways" were (MG to BB, 26 April 1954). Not always overly generous, Hemingway resorted to Spanish slang for his former wife: "Miss Martha was a conejo and I was well deceived" (EH to BB, 10 June 1953).

Hemingway appears to have been most terrified, however, of her ambition. It led to innumerable arguments and jealousies that he was later amused by, but that obviously left them incompatible. Hemingway had mixed feelings about writing to Berenson about his third wife. He knew that the honesty would be difficult, and he also felt she had made a fool out of him and so the problem was truly complicated:

B.B. you asked me to write you about Miss Martha. So I started dutifully and had a wonderful time writing what you should never write. But then I realized that no one, no matter how truthful they think they are writing, can write truthfully in the round about a personal thing. Also having lived much of my life in France, Italy, Spain and here [Cuba] I have the Latin's hatred of being a fool and the Latin contempt for a fool. When the fool was yourself the contempt increases. (EH to BB, 27 May 1953)

Hemingway's analysis of Martha for Berenson tells as much about him as it does about Martha. His recollections also tell us a great deal about his theories about the relationship between fact and fiction. If he had trouble remembering many of the details, how could a biographer capture the reality? His reminiscences of Martha read much like his letters to Mizener about Fitzgerald; Hemingway is the real topic. Hemingway admitted to Berenson that he was frightened of ambitious women, and as a result he avoided them. Martha's ambition troubled him, and so he recognized that although he was in love with her, he didn't really like her very much. In spite of his reservations, he recognized her generosity and devotion to a cause. The causes she espoused were not always the highest in Hemingway's ranking. For example, he wrote to Berenson that even though she read and spoke French very well, the only French books she ever read were by Colette. The only reason that she read them was because

Colette had been the mistress of Henri du Juvenal, and since she had been the mistress of young Bertrand de Juvenal, her reasons for indulging in such reading were questionable. The differences in their tastes in reading had been a considerable source of difficulty. Hemingway admitted that as a reader he corrupted easily, and as a result he picked up Martha's passion for detective fiction which became their substitute for thinking. Not only did she not love good books, but she did not care about pictures or good music. Little wonder that this student of Cézanne and Bach, among many other mentors, found himself married to a woman whom he loved but didn't like.

Probably the strangest difference between them was their different attitude toward war. Hemingway's contempt for her beautiful uniforms and tailored dresses that would show up even the highest generals in a war zone was scathing. He thought that she had never seen a man killed in battle, and as a result, she not only loved war and all of its trappings, its glamour and the attention a beautiful girl receives when she moves around 2 million men who have left their women behind, but she also loved the money she made from the whole nasty business of war: "she probably made more tax-free money writing about our dead and about atrocities than any female author made since Harriet Beecher Stowe wrote Uncle Tom's Cabin" (EH to BB, 27 May 1953). She was also capable of making him feel like a "damned fool and a shit" for leaving his wife and children. He used alcohol as an anaesthetic and sunk so low, he repeated to Berenson, that he even read detective stories.

Hemingway went on to a more generous assessment of their relationship, especially commenting on Martha's graciousness toward his children, but the entire tone of the long letter (EH to BB, 27 May 1953), which no doubt titillated Berenson, reveals the chasm between Hemingway and his third wife which was filled with enmity, bitterness, and despair.

A typical confrontation, for example, occurred during the invasion of Normandy. Hemingway was flown over to France by the RAF, but Martha had to go by boat (EH to BB, 19 August 1956). She was not amused. Martha had insisted that he pack two pin-stripe suits, a blue serge suit and several tweed jackets, an approach to haberdashery that evidently clouded or began many of their bitter quarrels. Hemingway had asked her if they were going on an invasion or to "some ball room banana festival." But he took the clothes "to be a good boy." Not only were his clothes in need of improvement, but she tried to rid him of his middlewestern accent (EH to BB, 19 August 1956) so that he would fit in better with the social set in England where Hemingway always felt out of place. He also admitted to Berenson that "after Martha" he frequently used the reading of detective fiction as a substitute for thinking (EH to BB, 27 May 1953). His library indeed still has vast amounts of the genre, and his son Patrick told me that his father returned from World War II carrying everything ever written by Georges Simenon.

Hemingway was quick to admit that although he found Martha difficult, he was also bad for her (EH to BB, 27 May 1953). Berenson assured Hemingway that Martha always spoke well of him both as a worker and as a novelist. He omits what she said about him as a man. After Hemingway's rather frank letter, Berenson assured him that he had seen Martha only once in two or three years (BB to EH, 10 October 1952) and, of course, never admitted to his meeting her at a hotel at any time.

Hemingway's reputation and rather free talk about loose women struck a sympathetic and responsive chord in Berenson. Martha's ghosts were well gone by the time Hemingway visited the Hotel Florida in Madrid with his fourth wife (EH to BB, 11 August 1953), but Hemingway returned again and again to the subject of Martha during his correspondence with Berenson. By 1956 he was both horrified and relieved that his third marriage had not ended more disastrously than it did. The words of Martha still plagued his reminiscences: "We were giants and could have had the world at our feet." To which Hemingway could only add: "Good God! Perhaps it would be best if Mary McCarthy, Malraux and Martha were all hanged—upside down" (EH to BB, 10 April 1956).

Berenson's letters were filled with the recognition that he had a short time to live. Gradually the same feeling overtook Hemingway as he admitted in 1957 that he had seen "many people [that] year [who] made it easier to think of leaving this world than [he] believed it would ever be" (EH to BB, 30 April 1957). In fact, he wrote that dying was "simpler than going to the bathroom" (EH to BB, 9 April 1954). The two writers shared a diminishing view of the world, and in all of their sexual banter, recalling of old times, and reminiscences about comfortable and meaningful artists and landscapes, they both recognized that the world they once loved was now used up and mutilated. In spite of Hemingway's filial gesture to Berenson that he was writing to "divert [him] with funny letters" (EH to BB, 4 October 1955), the ultimate tone of their correspondence was captured in one of Hemingway's reminiscences:

Maybe because you have complicated blood, as I have, you would understand this. One time when I was out at the Wind River reservation a very old Indian spoke to me and said, "You Indian Boy?" I said, "Sure." He said, "Cheyenne?" I said, "Sure." He said, "Long time ago good. Now no good." (EH to BB, 22 March 1953)

A good measure of what Hemingway wrote to Berenson has been noted before. What is especially significant in addition to the fact that Hemingway counted among his close friends one of the world's greatest art critics is the tone of wit, humor, compassion, delight, and honest affection that dominated this eight-year correspondence. More and more the intimate glimpse of Hemingway in the turtleneck sweater captured by Joseph Karsh, who said that he never met a person more insecure than Ernest Hemingway, is replacing the rather macho personality created by Maxwell Perkins and Carlos Baker and perpetuated by many others.

It is unfortunate that all of the correspondence (see Appendix I) was not included in Carlos Baker's edition of Hemingway's letters. Even then, however, Berenson's contribution would be lacking. Since Berenson's letters are rapidly deteriorating because of the poor quality of the paper on which they were written, and in spite of the fact that they are carefully preserved in the John F. Kennedy Library in Boston, the extent of this rare expression of mutual love and admiration will probably never be completely known. Those letters by Hemingway not included in Baker's edition of the letters are virtually inaccessible at Villa "I Tatti." This brief overview of the content has been an attempt to record one of Hemingway's most intimate relationships during the final years of his life. Many harsh notes have been uttered about this troubled time of his life, but the difficulties and loneliness of those final years in Cuba were perhaps best recorded in Hemingway's rambling letters to Bernard Berenson. The portrait of Hemingway staring at that blank white wall in front of his typewriter or at the gathering smog over his beloved Havana is best captured by Berenson's recent biographer, Meryle Secrest:

If Hemingway's letters are ever published, they will demonstrate that the legend of Hemingway does an injustice to the reality of the man. His letters to Berenson are a delight, full of wit, anecdote, and imaginative invention. They are rambling and discursive, with much parenthetical exclamation and explanation, and are, in fact, so spontaneous that they will banish forever the image of Hemingway as an anguished writer painfully producing a sentence every third day. They are indomitable and life-enhancing letters, full of whimsical reminiscence and unguarded insights into himself, written in a labored hand, like a child learning to write. They show a wistful, tender, and loving man, transparently insecure, and one diametrically opposite to the almost ludicrous ultramasculine image offered to the world. (1979, 376)

The problems of their public images dominated the correspondence and caused a constant tension and separation in their communication, but Berenson's delight in their exchange was no less positive than Hemingway's love of the connoisseur from "I Tatti" who signed one of his last letters with the telling recognition of a proud father: "My best to Mary and your magnificent self" (BB to EH, 2 November 1955).

APPENDIX I
Log of the Ernest Hemingway/Bernard Berenson Correspondence

25 August 1949 - 24 August 1957

DATE	LETTER	DATELINE	PRESENT LOCATION
25 Aug. 49	EH (M) to BB	FV, Cuba	"I Tatti"; Baker, 666.
14 Nov. 49	MH to BB	FV, Cuba	"I Tatti"
26 Dec. 50	BB to EH	Settignano	KL
31 Dec. 50	EH to BB	FV, Cuba	"I Tatti"
6 Sept. 52	BB to EH	Vallombrosa/ Settignano	KL
13 Sept. 52	EH (M) to BB	FV, Cuba	"I Tatti"; Baker, 780.
21 Sept. 52	BB to EH	Vallombrosa/ Settignano	KL
27 Sept. 52	Cable: BB to R. Belleville	Vallombrosa	KL
2 Oct. 52 (included several newspaper clippings and reviews)	EH to BB	FV, Cuba	"I Tatti", Baker, 784.
10 Oct. 52	BB to EH	Settignano	KL
14 Oct. 52 (included newspaper clippings)	EH to BB	FV, Cuba	"I Tatti"; Baker, 788.
11 Nov. 52	BB to EH	Rome	KL
25 Nov. 52	BB to EH	Rome	KL
4 Dec. 52	BB to EH		?
24 Jan. 53	EH to BB	FV, Cuba	"I Tatti"; Baker, 801.
12 Feb. 53	BB to EH		?
17 Feb. 53	EH to BB	FV, Cuba	"I Tatti"; Baker, 803.
28 Feb. 53	BB to EH	Settignano	KL
6 Mar. 53	EH to BB	FV, Cuba	"I Tatti"
15 Mar. 53	BB to EH	Settignano	KL
20-22 Mar. 53	EH to BB	FV, Cuba	"I Tatti"; Baker, 808.
29 Mar. 53	BB to EH	?	KL
13 Apr. 53	EH to BB	FV, Cuba	"I Tatti"
22 Apr. 53	BB to EH	Settignano	KL
4 May 53	EH to BB	Ruar del Rio, Cuba	"I Tatti"
21 May 53	BB to EH	Messanio	KL
27 May 53 (sent 10 June 53)	EH to BB	FV, Cuba	"I Tatti"
10 June 53	EH to BB	FV, Cuba	"I Tatti"
22 June 53	BB to EH	Naples	KL
11 Aug. 53	EH to BB	at sea	"I Tatti"; Baker, 823.
15 Sept. 53	EH to BB	Kenya/Tanganika border	"I Tatti"; Baker, 825
29 Sept. 53	BB to EH	Masera	KL
31 Sept. 53	BB to EH	?	KL
15 Nov. 53	EH to BB	Kenya	"I Tatti"
22 Nov. 53	BB to EH	Rome	KL
23 Jan. 54	Cable: BB to EH	?	?

2 Feb. 54	EH to BB	Kenya	"I Tatti"; Baker, 827.
26 Mar. 54	BB to EH	Settignano	KL
29 Mar. 54	EH to BB	Venice	"I Tatti"
3 Apr. 54	BB to EH	Settignano	KL
4 Apr. 54	EH to BB	Venice	"I Tatti"
6 Apr. 54	BB to EH	Settignano	KL
9 Apr. 54 (sent 1 May 54)	EH to BB	Venice	"I Tatti"
1 May 54	EH to BB	Venice	"I Tatti"
29 Aug. 54	EH to BB	FV, Cuba	"I Tatti"
11 Sept. 54	BB to EH	Vallombrosa	KL
4 Sept. 54	EH to BB	?	See BB, 17 Sept 54.
17 Sept. 54	BB to EH	Settignano	KL
24 Sept. 55	EH to BB	FV, Cuba	"I Tatti"; Baker, 836.
22 Dec. 54	BB to EH	Settignano	KL
9 July 55 (sent 10 Apr. 56)	EH to BB	Key West	"I Tatti"
18 Sept. 55	EH to BB	FV, Cuba	"I Tatti"; Baker, 846.
29 Sept. 55	BB to EH	Venice	KL
4 Oct. 55	EH to BB	FV, Cuba	"I Tatti"
19 Oct. 55	BB to EH	Venice	KL
24 Oct. 55	EH to BB	FV, Cuba	"I Tatti"; Baker, 847.
2 Nov. 55	BB to EH	Settignano	KL
21 Dec. 55	BB to EH	Settignano	KL
2 Mar. 56	EH to BB	FV, Cuba	"I Tatti"
8 Aug. 56	BB to EH	Settignano	KL
19 Aug. 56	EH to BB	Paris	"I Tatti"
30 Apr. 57	EH to BB	FV, Cuba	"I Tatti"
21 Aug. 57	MH to BB	FV, Cuba	"I Tatti"
24 Aug. 57	EH to BB	FV, Cuba	"I Tatti"

Key: FV, Cuba — Finca Vigía, San Francisco de Paula, Cuba.
    "I Tatti" — via di Vincigliata 26, 50135 Florence, Italy.
    (M) — Postscripts by Mary Hemingway, none of which were included in Baker's edition of the letters.
    KL — Hemingway Collection, John F. Kennedy Library, Columbia Point, Boston, Mass.

APPENDIX II
Books in Hemingway's Library by or about Bernard Berenson

Berenson, Bernard. *Aesthetics and History in the Visual Arts*. New York: Pantheon, 1948.

————. *The Italian Painters of the Renaissance*. London: Oxford, 1948.

————. *Italian Pictures of the Renaissance: A List of the Principal Artists and Their Works, with an Index of Places*. Oxford: Clarendon, 1932.

————. *Rumor and Reflection*. New York: Simon and Schuster, 1952.

————. *Seeing and Knowing*. New York: Macmillan, 1954.

————. *Sketch for a Self-Portrait*. New York: Pantheon, 1949.

Mostyn-Owen, William. *Bibliografia di Bernard Berenson*. Milan: Electra, 1955.

Source: James D. Brasch and Joseph Sigman, *Hemingway's Library: A Composite Record* (New York: Garland Press, 1981).

APPENDIX III
Books in Berenson's Library by or about Ernest Hemingway

Cowley, Malcolm, ed. *Hemingway*. The Viking Portable Library. New York: The Viking Press, 1944.

Eastman, Max. *Great Companions*. London: Museum Press Ltd., 1959. "The Great and Small Ernest Hemingway," pp. 32–58.

Hemingway, Ernest. *Across the River and into the Trees*. London: Jonathan Cape, 1950.

———. *The Essential Hemingway*. London: Jonathan Cape, 1947.

———. *A Farewell to Arms*. New York: Charles Scribner's Sons, 1929.

———. *The Old Man and the Sea*. New York: Charles Scribner's Sons, 1952. (Card in envelope attached: "Dear Ber. B. Hope that you are well and this won't bore you. Mary sends her love. Maybe we'll all learn how to write some time. It shouldn't be difficult if there was time enough. Your friend and admirer, E. Hemingway.")

———. *To Have and Have Not*. London: Jonathan Cape, 1937.

New Republic. 40th Anniversary Issue. 131:21, Nov. 22, 1954. "Italy—1927" by Ernest Hemingway.

Wilson, Edmund. *The Wound and the Bow*. Cambridge, Mass.: Houghton Mifflin Company, 1941. "Hemingway—Gauge of Morale," pp. 214–242.

Source: "I Tatti."

Note

1. I am indebted to the late Cecil Anrep for permission to read Hemingway's letters to Berenson and for providing me with copies of the letters, now under the administration of Harvard University. I would also like to thank Dottoressa Fiorella Geoffredi-Superbi who graciously assisted my reexamination of the letters including the many articles attached to the original letters. My thanks also to the staff of Villa "I Tatti," now the Harvard University Center for Renaissance Studies, for giving me access during July 1986 to the correspondence between Martha Gellhorn and Bernard Berenson and Berenson's books by Hemingway.

References

Baker, Carlos. *Ernest Hemingway: A Life Story*. New York: Scribner, 1969.

———. *Ernest Hemingway: Selected Letters, 1917–1961*. New York: Scribner, 1981.

Berenson, Bernard. *Sunset and Twilight*. ed. Nicky Mariano. New York: Harcourt, 1963.

Brasch, James D. "Hemingway's Doctor: José Luis Herrera Sotolongo." *Journal of Modern Literature* 13 (1986): 185–210.

Fuentes, Norberto. *Hemingway in Cuba*. Secaucus, NJ: Lyle Stuart, 1984.

Hemingway, Mary Welsh. *How It Was*. New York: Knopf, 1976.

Meyers, Jeffrey. *Hemingway: A Biography*. New York: Harper & Row, 1986.

Secrest, Meryle. *Being Bernard Berenson*. New York: Holt, 1979.

"Particular Rhythms" and Other Influences: Hemingway and *Tender Is the Night*

Alan Margolies

In the March 16, 1928 issue of Princeton's *Daily Princetonian,* novelist F. Scott Fitzgerald, class of 1917, reviewed the March issue of the university's *Nassau Literary Magazine.* Fitzgerald found the issue "dignified" but "unadventurous" (3). For some reason, the last sentence found in Fitzgerald's typed carbon on file at Princeton Library was omitted from the published review. Fitzgerald's original conclusion was: "The issue sets, I believe, a record among American magazines of the year; it contains no imitations of Ernest Hemingway."

Although the statement was meant to be humorous, it is possible that even then Fitzgerald felt drawn himself at times to his friend's style. Some six years later, in his reply to Hemingway's May 28, 1934, evaluation of *Tender Is the Night (TIN)*, Fitzgerald wrote, "I think it is obvious that my respect for your artistic life is absolutely unqualified, that save for a few of the dead or dying old men you are the only man writing fiction in America that I look up to very much. There are pieces and paragraphs of your work that I read over and over—in fact, I stopped myself doing it for a year and a half because I was afraid that your particular rhythms were going to creep in on mine by process of infiltration. Perhaps you will recognize some of your remarks in *Tender,* but I did every damn thing I could to avoid that" (Turnbull, ed. *Letters* 1963, 309).

Fitzgerald was not exaggerating. How much he was wary of reminding the reader of his fellow novelist—and not just what he referred to as Hemingway's "rhythms"—can be seen in the manuscripts of *Tender Is the Night* at Princeton University.

Because of his drinking, because of his wife's illness, because of many other reasons, it took Fitzgerald some nine years to complete this novel. When he first began writing it in 1925, it was about a young male film technician on the French Riviera, Francis Melarky, who kills his mother. After some four drafts, in 1929, it was changed to the story of Lew Kelly, a motion picture director. Finally, in 1932, Fitzgerald started working on the Dick Diver version. It is in this version, specifically those drafts worked on in 1932 and 1933, that we see what Fitzgerald was referring to. Mainly, these are the drafts Matthew J. Bruccoli has labelled the "first holograph draft of the Dick Diver version" (*Composition of "Tender Is the Night"* 1963, 89) and the "first typescript of the Dick Diver version" (161), the latter containing many holograph corrections.

What may be the most obvious similarity to Hemingway's style in these manuscripts occurs at the beginning of Chapter VI of the holograph draft. In this scene, Dick Diver and Rosemary Spears' mother sit in a café in Cannes. They refer to a letter from Rosemary discussing Nicole Diver's insanity. Fitzgerald introduced the scene with lines similar to the latter part of the first paragraph of *A Farewell to Arms,* where Frederic Henry says: "Troops went by the house and down the road and the dust they raised powdered the leaves of the trees. The trunks of the trees too were dusty and the leaves fell early that year and we saw the troops marching along the road and the dust rising and leaves, stirred by the breeze, falling and the soldiers marching and afterward the road bare and white except for the leaves" (1929, 3). In his draft Fitzgerald wrote: "Dick and Mrs. Speers sat in the Cafe des Allies in Cannes. It was August now and all the leaves were dusty and the sparkle of the mica was dulled and dusty on the baked ground."[1] And he followed it with: "A few gusts of a mistral from farther down the coast seeped through the Esteral and rocked the fishing boats in the harbor, pointing their masts here and there at the featureless sky. The waiters sweated working in the shade." That sentence, "It was August now and all the leaves were dusty and the sparkle of the mica was dulled and dusty on the baked ground," especially with its repetition of the word "dusty," bothered Fitzgerald. In the typed copy of this holograph, he wrote "Hemmingway" in the margin and placed parentheses around "and dusty." In the next draft, the carbon of this emended typescript, Fitzgerald deleted the second appearance of "dusty" and made other changes as well that were retained in the published version. Here "dust" is mentioned only once; the leaves are not there; the sweating waiters are gone; and the passage in general has been shortened. The published version reads: "Doctor Richard Diver and Mrs. Elsie Speers sat in the Café des Alliées in August, under cool and dusty trees. The sparkle of the mica was dulled by the baked ground, and a few gusts of mistral from down the coast seeped through the Esteral and rocked the fishing boats in the harbor, pointing the masts here and there at a featureless sky" (1934, 213).

Of course, for the most part it is impossible to determine exactly which, if any, specific work of Hemingway Fitzgerald had in mind when he mentioned his friend and rival in these drafts. For example, here he may also have been thinking of the beginning of "A Clean, Well-Lighted Place," published first in *Scribner's Magazine* in March 1933 and then in *Winner Take Nothing* on October 27 of the same year, the period when Fitzgerald was working on these drafts. Although it begins at night with an old man, the first paragraph does have a café, the street is dusty, and it has two waiters.

The following chapter in the typescript draft takes place some time later in a hotel room. Here Fitzgerald wrote about Dick Diver: "His property looked bright—he took out the French call portfolio and laid it on the desk with the bulging papers and letters." Fitzgerald took his pencil here, placed parentheses around the descriptive phrase "looked bright," and wrote "Hem" above the words. In the corrected carbon, Fitzgerald retained the two words but changed the remainder of the sentence: "His property looked bright—he looked over the bulging papers and letters in his portfolio." In the next draft, the carbon copy for the serial publication of the novel, he deleted the entire sentence along with other sections of the scene, and it did not appear in the novel.

Another example in the holograph occurs in a confrontation in the clinic between Dick and his partner Carl Struppen, renamed Franz Gregorovius in the published version. The conversation is about another patient, a young male homosexual, and about Diver's excessive drinking. The scene begins with Dick talking about Carl's wife, named Catherine in this version, and his patient Nicole, later to become Dick's wife. Referring to his partner's recent vacation, Dick asks "How [w]as Mount Everest?" Carl replies "You're talking now. We could very well have done Mount Everest the rate we were doing. We thought of shifting to Mount Everest. How goes it all?" Dick replies, "It goes." Then Carl asks, "How is Catherine, how is Nicole." Dick asks, "Didn't Catherine meet you?" and Carl replies, "Yes, but I didn't ask her. Catherine's always all right. How about you both." At this point in the manuscript Fitzgerald wrote, "Beware Ernest in this scene," and followed it with Dick's statement, "All right. We had a scene this morning." What was Fitzgerald thinking of? In using the name Catherine, was he concerned that the reader might be reminded of Hemingway's heroine in *A Farewell to Arms*? After all, the only changes that Fitzgerald made on the typed copy of this page, which once again includes the statement "Beware Ernest in this scene," were those of the names of two of his characters. On this typed copy Fitzgerald in pencil twice deleted Carl Struppen's name and pencilled in "Franz" and three times he deleted the name Catherine and wrote over it "Kaethe," the name that appears in the published version.

But it is much more likely that it was the clipped repetitive style in those brief exchanges, especially with the repetition of phrases from one speaker to the next, that made Fitzgerald feel that the reader might be reminded of Hemingway. When published, the dialogue was cut and the staccato effect alleviated, although the word "goes" was still repeated. And at least some of what remains has been replaced with Fitzgerald's more familiar rhythmic style. Here we read, "How was Mount Everest?" asks Dick. Franz replies, "We could very well have done Mount Everest the rate we were doing. We thought of it. How goes it all? How is my Kaethe, how is your Nicole?" And Dick concludes, "All goes smooth domestically. But my God, Franz, we had a rotten scene this morning" (*TIN* 328).

In another conversation at the psychiatric clinic between Dick and Franz, Fitzgerald wrote and then erased "No Hemmingway" in a marginal note beside some four lines of deleted dialogue and some partially obliterated and erased narrative. The notation can also be read "No[!] Hemmingway," since the first word is above the second. Here Franz has criticized Dick for wasting his life and devoting time to writing a simple student textbook. Franz suggests that if his (Franz's) father were alive his father would criticize Dick's work by folding his napkin in a certain way and grunting. Franz says to Dick, " 'You're intensely conceited like all men who are popular with women.' Dick look[s] at him without smiling [and says], 'I'm beginning to think you're a sort of restrained rabbit—' " He then says "I'm going to fold up my napkin like your father and grunt." The remainder of the erased dialogue and narrative includes Dick's sarcastic suggestion that he cure the patient, Nicole Warren, by seducing her. Originally Fitzgerald had him say, "What do you want me to do— seduce her?" Then he deleted "seduce her" in the typescript and wrote in pencil in the margin, "He didn't know what to do with his cigarette and Franz didn't know how to help him but pushed him toward an inadequate . . . " [the word is obliterated, possibly "decision"]. Fitzgerald ended the passage with "Take her out in the" but he never finished the sentence. Finally he deleted and erased all of this, possibly at the same time he erased "No Hemmingway." Then he came up with the speech: "What do you want me to do— take her up in the eidelwiess?" and it (the spelling corrected), with a few other changes in the scene, appears in the novel (*TIN* 182–83). Unfortunately it is not clear what the "No Hemmingway" or "No[!] Hemmingway" referred to. Did the phrase "men who are popular with women" remind Fitzgerald of Hemingway's 1927 title *Men Without Women?* Was the section too overtly sexual? One can only speculate.

Then, further on in this holograph draft, Fitzgerald introduced a scene in Munich with Tommy Costello, later renamed Tommy Barban, with the following incomplete and somewhat vague notation: "Now cheerful cafe scene but remember to avoid Hemmingway, Men on green felt table cloths, Swiss memories somehow draining down." Again it is not clear what the admonition refers to, especially since there are two separate but somewhat parallel holograph sections in the Fitzgerald papers, and one cannot be certain which was written first and which, if either, was written immediately after the warning. One of these holographs starts with a paragraph—one that was cancelled in the next draft—setting the scene: "It was in a green-top table café on the Luggerstrasse, a superior place of the type where men play xx [Fitzgerald would add the name later] shaking their dice on little tapestry mats. The air was full of smoke and beer, the clog of dice, the intensive tone of men at politics, the explosive tone of men at games. There was a recently installed American bar and as Dick stood up to it he noticed the table of two Americans and two Europeans as he correctly guessed, and he knew too that though one of the Americans was doing the talking the man . . . with his back to him was ruling the table.'' The second holograph draft begins differently: "Thomas Costello waiting for Dick in the bar of the (Regina) was old and hard, though he was only thirty five and had courteous manners. He was a ruler and now he was ruling a table, dominated superficially by a man named Hanson. Tommy drank no alcohol, not even wine and beer, while Hanson was out of hand and clowning wildly. Tommy didn't mind. 'Chuck, chuck, chuck!' he would laugh, and when Hanson seemed to him particularly funny he would share a side smile with someone else at table, laugh 'Chuck, chuck, chuck!' belittling Hanson and at the same time encouraging him. He was afraid of nothing—He did not like anybody much or feel their presence with intensity—he was all tuned up for combat.'' And later Fitzgerald wrote: "Courage was his game and he sat at table with an eighth of the area of his skull removed & growing together under his hair, a wound got at polo (explain). Everyone at the table was afraid of him but the weakest busboy could have killed him with a napkin." In all likelihood, Fitzgerald wanted to avoid "the clipped sentences, the ironic understatement, the inventories of drinks" that remind one of Hemingway (*Composition of "Tender Is the Night"* 1963, 120).[2] But Fitzgerald may also have wanted to make certain, if this is the section the warning refers to, that Tommy Barban, who eventually becomes Nicole Diver's lover, did not sound like a character out of one of his friend's novels. In his notes to the novel written earlier, Fitzgerald had determined that Barban would be a "wild man," one who "hates all sham & pretense" one who "fought three years in the French foreign legion in the war and then painted a little and then fought the Riff" (*Composition of "Tender Is the Night"* 1963, 81–82). Was Fitzgerald afraid that he would get too close to what he thought was a character that might be found in a Hemingway novel, such as Count Mippipopolous with his two raised white welts, arrow wounds from Abyssinia? Did Fitzgerald's notation refer to the sense of physical strength and violence communicated here? Or, as Matthew J. Bruccoli has suggested in *Scott and Ernest,* was Tommy Barban partly modeled upon Hemingway? (1978, 122). It is obvious that Fitzgerald was disturbed by the scene because here the typescript copy is heavily emended and retained only a little of what he had originally written. In the published version we read, "As a rule, he drank little; courage was his game and his companions were always a little afraid of him. Recently an eighth of the area of his skull had been removed by a Warsaw surgeon and was knitting under his hair. . . .'' And a few paragraphs later, Fitzgerald wrote: "He did not like any man very much nor feel their presence with much intensity—he was all relaxed for combat; as a fine athlete playing secondary defense in any sport is really resting much of the time, while a lesser man only pretends to rest and is at a continual and self-destroying nervous tension'' (*TIN* 256–57). One can only wonder if this is another one of those passages that Fitzgerald referred to when he wrote Hemingway in that May 28, 1934, letter, "Perhaps you will recognize some of your remarks in *Tender*'' (Turnbull, ed. *Letters* 1963, 309).

And finally, in chapter 7 of the holograph, in an allusion to *A Farewell to Arms,* we see an even more obvious example of Fitzgerald's wariness of reminding the reader of Hemingway. Here the rhythm is Fitzgerald's, but at least one of the ideas is from *A Farewell to Arms.* In the clinic, Dick Diver is talking to a young female patient, an artist, whose psychological problems manifest themselves in an extreme case of eczema. She is a "living agonizing sore" (*TIN* 240). Dick advises her to "[meet] the problems of every day." But he knows that she never will be able to "examine—once more . . .—'the frontiers of consciousness'—that all artists must explore." Fitzgerald then wrote: "It was not for her, ever. It was not for her he knew. She was a fine spun, inbred Virginian who might eventually find rest in some quiet mysticism. The exploration was for peasants with big thighs and thick ankles who could take punishment as they took bread and salt, take it on every inch of flesh until the word pride was distorted and meaningless, like those words honor and glory and sacrifice that Hemingway speaks of as having been made meaningless in the war." After his typist had typed this holograph, Fitzgerald made one pencil emendation in the typescript, adding Hemingway's first name to that last clause. In addition, he placed three question marks directly left in the margin. When published, that last long sentence was cut in half and the second half, including the specific reference to Hemingway, deleted (*TIN* 242). But the remainder, the praise of the peasant class, is still there, probably the residue of one of Hemingway's remarks that Fitzgerald had referred to in that May 28, 1934, letter.

These are the only allusions to Hemingway in the many drafts of the novel at Princeton University. However, the collection is not complete; there may have been other notations similar to these in those drafts that Fitzgerald destroyed. Further, one can but surmise that this is only the tip of the iceberg, that Fitzgerald was constantly wary of Hemingway's influence. What does exist, however, does make more believable his statement to Hemingway that he had stopped rereading the latter's work for more than a year and a half because he was afraid of imitating his style.

Notes

Carol Highsaw of Princeton University assisted me with the research for this chapter.
1. I have retained Fitzgerald's spelling, capitalization, and punctuation here and elsewhere in this chapter.
2. Matthew J. Bruccoli in *The Composition of "Tender Is the Night"* (1963, 118–

20) noted Fitzgerald's mention of Hemingway here as well as in the aforementioned confrontation scene between Diver and Struppen in the clinic and, in addition, discussed Hemingway's influence in these scenes.

References

Bruccoli, Matthew J. *The Composition of "Tender Is the Night": A Study of the Manuscripts*. Pittsburgh: U of Pittsburgh P, 1963.

———. *Scott and Ernest: The Authority of Failure and the Authority of Success*. New York: Random House, 1978.

F. Scott Fitzgerald Papers, Princeton University Library, Princeton, NJ.

Fitzgerald, F. Scott. "F. Scott Fitzgerald Is Bored by Efforts at Realism in 'Lit,' " *The Daily Princetonian* 16 March 1928: 1, 3.

———. *Tender Is the Night*. New York: Scribner, 1934.

Hemingway, Ernest. *A Farewell to Arms*. New York: Scribner, 1929.

Turnbull, Andrew, ed. *The Letters of F. Scott Fitzgerald*. New York: Scribner, 1963.

7

Borges on Hemingway, Hemingway on Hemingway: Craft, Grief, and Sport

Lawrence H. Martin, Jr.

There are a certain few observations by foreign commentators that cast a brilliant light on American life and letters. One thinks first, of course, of Alexis de Tocqueville's *Democracy in America* and of his interpretation of the relationship between literature and the culture and the political economy.[1] It was Tocqueville who proposed in 1835 that "In democracies it is by no means the case that all who cultivate literature have themselves received a literary education" (Tocqueville 1969, 473). In our own century perhaps the most original foreign critic is D. H. Lawrence whose *Studies in Classic American Literature* has become itself a classic and has explained to us why we created both a Fenimore Cooper and his Deerslayer/Leatherstocking character. What Lawrence saw was something in the American grain, some impulse—contrary to Cooper's own genteel Europeanism—to become one's own fictional creation. "Natty was Fenimore's great wish," says Lawrence, adding, "his wish-fulfillment" (Lawrence 1964, 49).

But perhaps an equally important (though less well known) interpretation of American literature is Jorge Luis Borges' *Introducción a la literatura norteamericana*. Brief where Tocqueville is expansive, plain spoken where Lawrence is psychoanalytical, Borges is nonetheless equally as independent in his literary judgments as Lawrence and as provocative as Tocqueville in his proposal of sociological causes and meanings. The American reader, however, schooled in the conventions of the relative merits—one might say the relative gravity—of our authors, will find Borges' opinions eccentric, even quirky, and his categories of writers and movements odd. For example, Transcendentalism is covered in a single chapter in which Emerson gets two paragraphs. A chapter half again as long is devoted to The Detective Story, Science Fiction, and The Far West, supplementing an earlier chapter on The West. Franklin and Cooper as a pair get a chapter, as do Hawthorne and Poe. Whitman and Melville are another chapter-pair. The book ends abruptly with a brief piece on The Oral Poetry of the Indians.

The reader, by now quite disoriented or at least deprived of his prejudices about the hierarchy of American writers, is also faced with Borges' highly personal arrangement of categories for authors and genres. Theater is represented by Eugene O'Neill, Thornton Wilder, William Saroyan, Tennessee Williams, and Arthur Miller—an important quintet, certainly, but hardly a comprehensive gathering. Borges' cast for The Poets is equally selective, as is his coverage of The Novel. From this latter chapter Ernest Hemingway is missing, though Truman Capote is present. Hemingway is also absent from The Expatriates, but Fitzgerald, Pound, and Stein are there, along with Henry James and Henry Miller. The absence of Hemingway from Borges' understanding of "expatriate" is noteworthy, suggesting that his expatriation was not, to Borges, a categorical definition of Hemingway's views or themes.

Hemingway's place in Borges' constellation is among The Narrators, a curious distinction from The Novelists and the writers in other conventional genres. What Borge means by "narrators," and why their craft is distinguished from the identity-by-genre of the novelists, might be deduced from the membership of this specially titled group: In addition to Hemingway, Borges' "narrators" are Crane, Anderson, Dos Passos, and Faulkner, one or two of them Hemingway's acknowledged teachers, another his friend (and later, so characteristically, his enemy), and the last his major direct competitor and predecessor in winning the Nobel Prize.[2] Surprisingly, Borges does not explain the craft of narration itself, except implicitly by commenting on the narrators and their works.

Borges' technique throughout the book is to draw in a few swift, clean strokes the outline of a writer's significance and to offer an epitome of the writer's life. (Apparently, Borges has never adopted the antibiographical ideology of the half-century-old New Criticism.) These biographical glimpses are striking not only for their compression but also for their power to crystallize an idea. Though the ideas are frequently arresting, they are also frequently based on slight historical fact. "Melville," Borges says, generalizing memorably but inaccurately on a few early years, "led the kind of adventurous life of which the sedentary Whitman dreamed" (Borges 1971, 33). Forgotten are the many uneventful years after Melville's active sea service, and forgotten too is Whitman's courageous medical duty in the American Civil War. On Poe, Borges produces this epigrammatic summation: "a man of weak will and one torn by the most contradictory passions, [Poe] professed a cult of reason and lucidity" (Borges 1971, 21). Or, on Thoreau, understatement: "He was fond of solitude" (Borges 1971, 27).

Adapted perhaps from Lucretius, or perhaps from the English seventeenth-century classical imitation (or perhaps invented for the purpose by Borges), this provocative character making has its charms, but it also has its limitations.

Deft, assertive, often insightful, these biographical asides have the sound of authority and, of course, the authority of Borges' name. In a phrase or a sentence, they relate the writer and his art, suggesting causes and consequences and leaving an iconographic picture of the connection between the life and the works.

In the chapter called "The Narrators" Borges pays considerable attention to Hemingway. We learn in a few compact sentences of Hemingway's youth and Michigan upbringing, about his years abroad and his journalism, and about his failures and successes in literature. In one sentence we read of his 1954 Nobel Prize, and in the next we find this: "Overcome by his inability to go on writing, and suffering from insanity, he killed himself in 1961. *It grieved him to have devoted his life to physical adventures rather than the pure and simple exercise of the intelligence*" (Borges 1971, 50, emphasis added). The idea is striking, not so much for its oversimplification of biography as for its implicit thesis that "physical adventures" are the contrary of "pure and simple exercise of the intelligence." And Borges asks not only that we accept the opposition but that we also believe that Hemingway regretted the physical, adventurous part of his life—or even that he "devoted" his life to nonintellectual activity, as if, at the end, Hemingway bitterly understood the unrecoverable waste and misspent energy of a life passed in amusement rather than creation. Even if Borges exaggerates or oversimplifies, he proposes several quite serious questions about Hemingway: What was the relationship of the contemplative and the active in his life? Is there a connection between the impetus to daring sport and the impetus to creative art? What is the meaning of Hemingway's penchant for "physical adventures"? And, indeed, is there a connection between (or a difference between) the physical and the cerebral?

Borges is not the first to raise these questions. The first, perhaps, was Hemingway himself, in the character Kandisky, the Austrian plantation manager in *Green Hills of Africa* (*GHA* 1935). The scene is a set piece in this sporting book studded with literary opinions. At a singularly improbable but historically factual encounter in the East African bush,[3] Hemingway meets an Austrian who knows Hemingway's 1924–25 poetry in the avant-garde journal *Der Querschnitt* and recognizes him as Hemingway *der Dichter* (*GHA* 7). The comic irony of the scene is cleverly underplayed, for Hemingway, as a character in his own prose experiment, has just climbed out of a dusty shooting blind, is accompanied by two African trackers, and carries a rifle—hardly the conventional or romanticized image of the urbane, refined, European man of letters. Kandisky pounces on his literary prey as swiftly as the hunter on his quarry: Virtually his first words, on discovering this displaced specimen of the life of the mind, are "What do you think of Ringelnatz? . . . What do you think of Heinrich Mann?" (*GHA* 7). And on getting the answer that one is "splendid" and the other "no good," confirming his own critical judgment (or his prejudices), he asserts in the spirit of newfound literary brotherhood, "I see we have

many things in common." Only after the matter of high priority, literature and
literary reputation, is dealt with, does Kandisky think to ask the obvious question: "What are you doing here?" The laconic answer: "Shooting." After
satisfying himself that Hemingway the poet is not an ivory hunter—a business,
not a sport—he seems dismayed to learn that the poet is actually hunting kudu.
At this point Kandisky takes the stance that Borges takes: "Why should any
man shoot a kudu? You, an intelligent man, a poet, to shoot kudu" (*GHA* 8).
Hemingway, Kandisky's interlocutor and Kandisky's voice, has posed the central question to himself: Why indeed should an artist hunt, and why especially
should anyone hunt sporting game with no ivory and no commercial value?
Kandisky elaborates, prefiguring even more exactly Borges' criticism of 35
years in the future: "At the end of [a year] you have shot everything and you
are sorry for it. . . . Why do you do it?" (*GHA* 8). Taking up his own persona
again, Hemingway answers simply and bluntly: "I like to do it" (*GHA* 8).

   There is no arguing—so the saying goes—with taste: *chacun à son goût*. If
the poet likes kudu hunting, there is no recourse in argument or persuasion.
Faced with such irrefutable subjectivity, Kandisky can only retreat into literary
chitchat, dropping names—Valéry, Joyce, Sinclair Lewis—whose works he has
not read or whom he knows only indirectly by gossip. Here, in the opening
pages of a book ostensibly about blood sport (but really about so many other
things), Hemingway has established a theme that appears and reappears throughout
Green Hills and, indeed, throughout the author's life and his lifework: the real
act versus the secondhand impression, the thing itself versus its shadowy substitute. In this case, Hemingway the literary character is doing the real thing:
pursuing real game across a real terrain with a real rifle. By contrast, Herr
Kandisky is hunting intangible reputations and opinions, living on the remote
margin of the life of literature. The essential difference is that Hemingway the
poet-hunter actually hunts; Kandisky the enthusiast of writing does not actually
write. Like the celebrated angleworms in the bottle (*GHA* 21), Kandisky is
attempting to derive nourishment from contact, not from what he is able to
produce himself.

   The relationship between sport and art, which Kandisky cannot grasp and
Borges mistakes, is summarized by Hemingway in a reflection on the artist's
and sportsman's problem of time. He says, "The way to hunt is for as long as
you live against as long as there is such and such an animal; just as the way to
paint is as long as there is you and colors and canvas, and to write as long as
you can live and there is pencil and paper or ink or any machine to do it with,
or anything you care to write about, and you feel a fool, and you are a fool,
to do it any other way" (*GHA* 12). The immediate point of the passage is the
approaching rainy season and with it the end of the hunt, but its significance is
far broader. Whether one paints or writes or hunts, he must do what he does
freely and intensely. That Hemingway should have chosen painting and writing
for his analogy to sport is deeply revealing; evidently, he sees them as similar
enterprises, or complementary, or even identical. Later, responding once more

to Kandisky's renewed criticism of "this silliness of kudu," Hemingway says that he likes hunting them as much as he likes going to the great painting collection of the Prado, for "One is not better than the other" but "One is as necessary as the other" (GHA 25).

To the Austrian who believes narrowly that literary talk is "the Heinz Tomato Ketchup on the daily food . . . the best part of life. The life of the mind . . . not killing kudu" (GHA 18–19), the point about equal necessities must be cryptic or even nonsensical. What links sport and art, in Hemingway's mind, is the demand that they both be done "without tricks and without cheating" (GHA 27). To do them well, one must have "talent," "discipline," and "an absolute conscience as unchanging as the standard meter in Paris, to prevent faking" (GHA 27). These descriptions are applied to writers, namely Kipling and Flaubert, but they apply equally well to Hemingway's ritualized notion of doing any act well, whether shooting in Africa or fishing in the Gulf Stream or writing in a good café on the Place St.-Michel.

Furthermore, the artist and the sportsman act alone. The individuality of sport and art attracts Hemingway powerfully, and it is a commonplace to observe that his heroes are independent. He explained his lifelong philosophy of composition (and of independence) in his 1954 Nobel Prize acceptance message, mentioning four times in the one-paragraph address the writer's need to work alone and concluding that the artist must go "far out past where he can go, out where no one can help him" (Baker 1970, 669–70). Years earlier he had said the same thing in Green Hills, and even earlier in Death in the Afternoon, a book which is itself a study of skillful, graceful, and above all individual confrontation with danger and death.

What Hemingway sought, it is well known, was truth—one true sentence, and a fourth and a fifth dimension. To compose true art is to do something basic, to get to the foundation of meaning. Writing, true writing, is therefore basic and elemental. It requires some technical skill—Hemingway is, of course, an innovative, accomplished technician—but moreover it requires a wholehearted commitment of the self, the artistic equivalent of afición—passion, involvement. Writing of this kind focuses intensity so that the writer momentarily lives in his art, not in the ordinary world. "I did not want to leave the river," he says in 1959, thinking of the early 'twenties, "where I could see the trout in the pool, its surface pushing and swelling smooth against the resistance of the log-driven piles of the bridge" (Hemingway, A Moveable Feast 1964, 76). Actually, the writer was at the moment in the Closerie de Lilas in Paris, not on a bridge over a river in Seney, Michigan, but the intense perception of the one overcomes and replaces the other.

So it is also with the kinds of sport that Hemingway loved and practiced, the sports that are not merely amusements or pastimes but, as he said of bullfighting in a 1923 Toronto Star Weekly article, "tragedy" (Hemingway in White, ed. 1967, 90–98). Just as the painting of Cézanne or his own writing reveals truth, so also does the ritualized drama of the ring. The bullfighter is heroic or cowardly, he acts skillfully or incompetently, he lives or dies. By fighting or even by watching the tragedy, one participates in the elemental.

In sport, too, there is the demand of the act well done. Dangerous and intense sports, such as bullfighting, big game hunting, and trophy fishing, demand superb skill and self-control. One must know how to use the sword and to read the wind, to shoot well and to understand the terrain, and to know the life of the great Stream. Technique is important, and the expert succeeds and survives. Furthermore, the sportsman, if he is to practice his craft well, follows an unwritten code of ethics, a code that invariably makes the sport more difficult and challenging, and more dangerous. One does not chase game with motor cars, as Wilson coldly remarks in "The Short Happy Life of Francis Macomber" (Hemingway, *The Short Stories* 1938, 29), and one does not shave the horns of fighting bulls or permit the picador to tire the animal before the fight commences (Hemingway, *The Dangerous Summer* 1985, passim). In other words, dishonesty is as shameful in sport as in art, for both enterprises reveal the character, indeed the soul, of the man.

To face what is difficult tells what the artist (or the bullfighter or hunter) is made of. The Francis Macomber who stands firm for the charge of the buffalo is a hero, though that firmness may have been indirectly the cause of his death. Writing is difficult, Hemingway says again and again in asides in his books such as *Green Hills of Africa, Death in the Afternoon,* and *A Moveable Feast,* in his articles for periodicals, and perhaps most revealingly and directly in his letters to friends and his editor Perkins. What Hemingway rejects, by contrast, is the easy way, what he called "cheating" and "slop" (*GHA* 22–23). In "Shootism versus Sport," a 1934 *Esquire* magazine column resulting from the same safari that produced the reflections on literature in *Green Hills,* Hemingway sets forth a methodology and a code of ethics for the sportsman, telling first how to "murder" a lion unfairly and easily (Hemingway, in White, ed. 1967, 162–66). He concludes, though, that the ethical sportsman shoots "cleanly"—that is, without resorting to tricks or cheating. The column may have been intended as nothing more than what it seems to be, a colorful piece on expertise in African big game hunting; but it contains nonetheless a clear pronouncement on right action in the face of difficulty or danger.

Rightness and competitiveness: these are the shared ingredients of art and sport. In Hemingway, their outcome is on the one hand a life of "physical adventure" (Borges 1971, 50) and on the other a "life of the mind" (*GHA* 18). They are related because they both belong to, or result from, the elemental—sporting adventures belonging to the class of the physically elemental, and artistic creativity belonging to the class of the intellectually elemental. Neither, it could be argued, is whole without the other. In *Green Hills of Africa* and *Death in the Afternoon,* and in other works such as "Banal Story," which bitterly contrasts salon literature to the death of the bullfighter Maera, Hemingway argues that Kandisky's notion of "the life of the mind" is incomplete and even ridiculous. For Hemingway, intellectual activity and physical activity were acts of self-definition and self-assertion. Springing from one source, they were alike in nature, not contradictory.

There is no record in history or biography of Hemingway's regretting to the point of grief the "physical adventures" of his life, or regretting that he had not spent more time and energy in perfecting his craft or merely producing more books. His few regrets are simple and practical: that he allowed his famous generosity to permit others, friends as well as strangers, to assume a relationship that did not exist; that his life had become prematurely the property of scholars and interpreters, who made mistakes; and that—here "remorse" is the better word—he had left Hadley Richardson.

The view asserted by Borges, that Hemingway eventually regretted having had a life of adventure, rather than spending it in the exercise of intellect, can be persuasive only if one accepts the idea that the two activities are opposite and mutually canceling. If they were opposite, then there would be much to regret. But in Hemingway they operated together. It could be argued too (as John Raeburn has)[4] that Hemingway's vigorous life was only an advertisement for himself, a way of making the public personality more important than the literary achievement and, in the process, becoming a "celebrity" and a *"bon vivant"* (Raeburn 1984, 120), suitable for coverage in the society columns. While there is much truth to the claims that Hemingway was aware of his own personality and cultivated an image of himself as a vigorous, virile, rather unintellectual figure, those practices do not nullify the important connection between physical activity, particularly sport, and intellectual endeavor. In Hemingway, there is completeness, wholeness, even comprehensiveness that cannot be dismissed by disparaging remarks about shrewd self-promotion.

As Philip Young says of Hemingway, evaluating the essential meaning of a complex life composed of crosscurrents of high achievement and puzzling eccentricity, "There was always the stubborn honesty and the sense of personal integrity" (Young 1966, 159). In art and in sport, these basic instincts prevailed; and to do one well was not to imply that the other was less significant or less valuable. All activities that were real engagements with life were worthwhile, and all were expressions, however varied, of the same central motivation.

The question, in the end, is not whether Borges' conclusion was right or wrong, but whether the premise was valid. The question is whether Hemingway's art and the "adventurous" aspects of his life were integral, and the answer is that they were. "One is as necessary as the other," Hemingway said (*GHA* 25), and in this phrase he declared that the impetus is one though its expressions are many.

Notes

1. See especially Tocqueville, *Democracy in America,* Vol. 2, Pt. 1, Ch. 13, "Literary Characteristics of Democratic Countries" and Ch. 14, "The Industry of Literature."

2. See Hemingway, *Green Hills of Africa,* 22–23, on Crane. See Carlos Baker, *Ernest Hemingway: A Life Story* on Hemingway's relations with and opinions of Sherwood Anderson, John Dos Passos, and William Faulkner.

3. Kandisky is modeled on one Hans Koritschoner, an Austrian whom Hemingway met in circumstances identical to those of the *Green Hills of Africa* episode. See Carlos Baker, *Ernest Hemingway: A Life Story,* 326.

4. John Raeburn, *Fame Became of Him: Hemingway as Public Writer,* sees Hemingway as a self-made "celebrity" engaged throughout his life in seeking "public reputation." Raeburn mentions, however, that Hemingway is "one of the most significant [novelists] in modern American literature" (1), but that "Hemingway's literary achievement is tangential to understanding [his] public fame" (1).

References

Baker, Carlos. *Ernest Hemingway: A Life Story.* New York: Bantam, 1970.

Borges, Jorge Luis. *An Introduction to American Literature,* edited and translated by L. Clark Keating and Robert O. Evans. Lexington: UP of Kentucky, 1971.

Hemingway, Ernest. "Banal Story," *The Short Stories.* New York: Scribner, 1938.

———. "Bull Fighting a Tragedy," *Toronto Star Weekly,* October 20, 1923. In William White, ed., *By-Line: Ernest Hemingway.* New York: Scribner, 1967.

———. *The Dangerous Summer.* New York: Scribner, 1985.

———. *Death in the Afternoon.* New York: Scribner, 1932.

———. *Green Hills of Africa.* New York: Scribner, 1935.

———. *A Moveable Feast.* New York: Scribner, 1964.

———. "Shootism versus Sport: The Second Tanganyika Letter," *Esquire,* June, 1934.

———. "The Short Happy Life of Francis Macomber," *The Short Stories.* New York: Scribner, 1938.

Lawrence, D. H. *Studies in Classic American Literature.* New York: Viking, 1964.

Raeburn, John. *Fame Became of Him: Hemingway as Public Writer.* Bloomington, IN: Indiana UP, 1984.

de Tocqueville, Alexis. *Democracy in America,* J. P. Mayer, ed. Garden City, NY: Doubleday, 1969.

Young Philip. *Ernest Hemingway: A Reconsideration.* University Park: Pennsylvania State UP, 1966.

8

Signs Are Taken for Nothing in *The Sun Also Rises*

Eugene Kanjo

Signs are taken for wonders. "We would see a sign."
T. S. Eliot, "Gerontion," 1920

There is a subliminal text expounded upon in *The Sun Also Rises* ([*TSAR*] 1926), the epigraph of *Winner Take Nothing* ([*WTN*] 1933): "Unlike all other forms of lutte or combat the conditions are that the winner shall take nothing; neither his ease, nor his pleasure, nor any notions of glory; nor, if he win far enough, shall there be any reward within himself." Written after the novel, it is, in one sense, the novel's wake in which the stories of *Winner Take Nothing* float. In another sense, it is a paradigm of Hemingway's fictional canon. The Sun Rise Edition of *Winner Take Nothing* (1938) omits it, in its place a graphic design, or ideogram, of the sun rising. Thus the sign also rises—the sun icon as a sign of the epigraph, the epigraph as a retrospective sign of the novel, and the novel as a sign of reality. The novel is a message, and the epigraph is a code, like semaphore, that helps us decode or discover the praxis, ideology, or vision that the novel imitates.

The main clause of the epigraph—"the conditions are that the winner shall take nothing"—links the subject "conditions" with a substantive of no substance, the subject complement "nothing." This paradox of comic syntax and diction is intensified when the protagonist is put in the extreme of the present subjunctive ("if he win far enough"), and yet finds pleasure and reward won in action vanishing right before his eyes, like pouring water into a sieve, with himself as the leaky vessel.

To "take nothing" means accepting the nothingness inherent in being when being ceases to exist in its natural state (like a tree or rock) and desires to be historical being (in history rather than in nature). Pushing aside natural being,

historical being thus creates an area of "nothingness within being," the very
desire and anxiety that compel human action. If action works for Tom Jones it
is because he lives at a historical moment when action and speech have significance. In *The Sun Also Rises,* however, the historical moment is dominated
by nihilism, when history is at "the apogee of non-meaning." and so "all
action is absurd" and "all speech is insignificant," and thus the protagonist
"enters into an irremediable idleness, an aimlessness without end" (Descombes 1980, 32–36).

The "winner" might put the case this way: "Now that God is dead, there is
nothing to do and nothing left to say. Truly, all action is a game, and the only
things left are pleasure itself and the rules you make for living in a world
without meaning. Whatever you say about life is bound to be a joke. So be a
minimalist of language and rules." Jake is the novel's chief joker: "That was
morality; things that made you disgusted afterward. No, that must be immorality. That was a large statement. What a lot of bilge I could think up at night"
(TSAR 149). These are the words of a utilitarian hedonist comically recognizing
that he is caught in the grip of nihilism, which is the ideological context of the
novel.

Jake stands to the others in their lived relation to the invisible epigraph, as
Ishmael stands to the crew members reading the visible doubloon. As narrator,
Jake encompasses all views, and yet is himself encompassed. If he is comic,
he is himself an object of his creator's comic mockery.

The fight is fixed (in John Fowles' phrase about plot) when the reader senses
before Jake does that a love tryst between Brett and Robert will take place at
San Sebastian. He's the butt of Hemingway's ironic plotting of the action.
Having been thus duped may have inspired Jake's setting up the Brett/Romero
affair, and so he cuts off his nose to spite his face. Jake suffers doubly, then,
at his own and at Hemingway's hands. And he will suffer further at Brett's
hands in Madrid where she checks his belief in God and mates him to nihilism.
Jake is duped again. Hemingway abandons him at novel's end and, like the
priest at Sam Cardinella's hanging, skips back "on the scaffolding just before
the drop fell," letting Jake twist in the nihilistic wind of the epigraph.

Lost in the funhouse of Paris, self-cast in the role of ardent cutups, the
morbid nihilists "comfort" themselves for having killed God—"What was hol-
iest and most powerful of all that the world has yet owned has bled to death
under our knives" (Nietzsche):

Nietzsche uses nihilism as the name for the historical movement that he was the first to
recognize and that already governed the previous century while defining the century to
come, the movement whose essential interpretation he concentrates in the terse sentence:
"God is dead." That is to say, the "Christian God" has lost his power over beings and
the determination of man. "Christian God" also stands for the "transcendent" in general in its previous meanings—for "ideals" and "norms," "principles" and "rules,"
"ends" and "values," which are set "above" the being, in order to give being as a

whole a purpose, an order, and—as it is succinctly expressed—meaning. (Heidegger 1982, 4)

Without belief in the transcendent, the novel's protagonists suffer from nihilism, the worm within that hollows them out. They are "hollow men" filling the void left in their lives by God's disappearance with the idea of place. They comfort their hollowness by taking refuge in their own tight little island, an Isle de Paris, and live beyond the pale as an enclave of hedonists. Paris offers the consolations of civilization—its great streets and monuments, the river and its bridges, its cafés, and even the cathedral. Although they are discontent with civilization, Europe is still their moveable feast and Jake their Baedeker of desire. When the season's right, he advises Pamplona for the bullfights, the Irati for fishing. When the fiesta ends, the enclave disperses, either to San Sebastian, Madrid, or Paris. Bill will sail to America, which he's been at pains to mock. The paradox of the use of place is that the protagonists must have a place in order to know that they have no place. Place is their center, but within place they are decentered. They act in complicity with place even though place as civilization, with its traditional values, sets itself against them.

Jake and his tribe are caught in the game of the circularity of human action in which nothingness is a parasite of historical being, that is, of being a "winner." Action and thought put into question preceding action and thought (Derrida 1978, 281): sexual viability yields to sexual dysfunction, sexual exuberance gives way to sexual ennui, religious feeling yields to metaphysical misery, belief in God hits the shoals of nihilism, the graceful bullfight ends in gore and death, and the complete angler must bang the head of "a good trout . . . against the timber so that he quivered out straight" (*TSAR* 119).

An extension of the nothingness within is the sense of the nothingness without, a world without uppermost or transcendent value. The Red Cross Knight can fall into the slough of despond with assurance because there is God. The knight's sin is his salvation. Our Parisiens have not outer certitude such as his since sin and salvation are out of business in our time, and so the Christian God, competing with romanticism and nihilism for human souls, comes away with nothing and loses the game.

The Christian God loses to Jake's game of comic reduction, a game in which Jake comically reflects his fast-disappearing religious sensibility. He contemplates the inside of a cathedral: "It was dim and dark and the pillars went high up, and there were people praying, and it smelt of incense, and there were some wonderful big windows" (*TSAR* 96–97). The voice echoes the serious boy Huck whose mask Jake playfully wears. The comic upshot reaches its climax in the last clause as the whole sentence pokes fun at the very awe it proclaims.

When Jake tells us about his praying in the cathedral, Huck again comes to mind. Told he would get whatever he prays for, Huck tries it out: "Once I got a fish-line, but no hooks. It warn't any good to me without hooks. I tried for the hooks three or four times, but somehow I couldn't make it work. By-and-by, one day, I asked Miss Watson to try for me, but she said I was a fool. She never told me why, and I couldn't make it out no way.'' The irony of this passage is lost on the serious innocent, and so we laugh for him.

When Jake prays we laugh with him at his conscious mockery of prayer and of himself. He prays ''for everybody . . . separately for the ones I liked, and lumping all the rest, then I prayed for myself again, and while I was praying for myself I found I was getting sleepy, so I prayed that the bull-fights would be good . . . I wondered if there was anything else I might pray for, and I thought I would like to have some money, so I prayed that I would make a lot of money, and then I started to think how I would make it . . . and as all the time I was kneeling with my forehead on the wood in front of me, and was thinking of myself as praying, I was a little ashamed, and regretted I was such a rotten Catholic, but realized there was nothing I could do about it, at least for a while, and maybe never, but that anyway it was a grand religion, and I only wished I felt religious and maybe I would the next time . . .'' (*TSAR* 97).

But there is no ''next time,'' only the here and now. Mockery ends when his ''forehead on the wood'' brings him back to the reality of his ironic situation—a disbeliever kneeling at prayer. Jake has shifted stylistic gears: He stands outside himself and complains at the emptiness of his religious feelings, in a tone more sentimental than comic, more banal than sad. Would Huck utter such soft-headed thoughts? When he wishes he were religious and had gone to Sunday school to become a better person, we know satirical darts are flying at Twain's behest. Does Hemingway approve of his persona's self-indulgence attempting to pass itself off as tough-mindedness? Twain doggedly will not let Huck be religious, but Hemingway seemingly pines for Jake to be religious.

Outside the cathedral, Jake speaks in a different tone of voice: ''and then I was out in the hot sun on the steps of the cathedral, and the forefingers and the thumb of my right hand were still damp, and I felt them dry in the sun. The sunlight was hot and hard'' (*TSAR* 97). The language of self-mockery and sentimentality give way to haiku-like language, natural or ideographic, that acquires symbolic value. In this sharp, imagistic moment, the sunlight of nothingness evaporates the water of religious feeling. If Hemingway sends Jake into the cathedral full of wonder and sentimentality, he brings him out of it as dry and hard as the sun.

In and out of the cathedral, Jake puts into question the very values that might save him. Brett puts into question the very values she lives by, as in this exchange with the count:

''You see, Mr. Barnes, it is because I have lived very much that now I can enjoy everything so well. Don't you find it like that?''

''Yes, Absolutely.''

''I know,'' said the count. ''That is the secret. You must get to know the values.''

"Doesn't anything ever happen to your values?" Brett asked.

"No. Not any more."

"Never fall in love?"

"Always," said the count. "I am always in love."

"What does that do to your values?"

"That, too, has got a place in my values."

"You haven't any values. You're dead, that's all."

"No, my dear. You're not right. I'm not dead at all." (*TSAR* 60–61)

Unlike Jake in the cathedral, she seeks not the grace of spiritual salvation but the light of human truth. As a figure of death-in-life (like the others in the novel)—that is, one who lives without uppermost values—the count plays the role of alazon to Brett's eiron. Before the dialogue, he had been showing off his arrow wounds, but it is Brett who deals his moral values a death blow, and since Jake assents to the count's philosophy during this stichomythian exchange, he too must bear the brunt of her direct satire.

Style, conceived in terms of signs that "are taken for nothing" rather than "for wonders," is the instrument that describes the novel's praxis, the dramatization of nihilism in the lives of the characters, and that reduces values (humanistic, romantic, or Christian) and those who hold them through the uses of wit and irony.

The above dialogue anticipates Jake's attempt, in the opening section of Chapter XIV (*TSAR* 147–49) to formulate what can be called a set of humanistic values. Jake's mind, muddled with "much too much brandy" and disturbed by Brett and Mike being together in bed in the next room, struggles to put together in this comic context a philosophy to live by, which is itself a pretty comic endeavor: "Perhaps as you went along you did learn something. I did not care what it was all about. All I wanted to know was how to live in it. Maybe if you found out how to live in it you learned from that what it was all about." One of the things you learn in the process of living—"as you went along"— is that "Enjoying living was learning to get your money's worth," a willingness to pay the bill when it came. Life taken as process, finding relative rather than absolute values to live by, is grist to Hemingway's comic mill.

Its counterpart is the absolute value of art. The section opens and closes with Jake reading Turgenieff. "In the oversensitized state of my mind" suggests the creative imagination. Jake's meditation on language and style in general and Turgenieff's book in particular ("I would remember it somewhere, and afterward it would seem as though it had really happened to me. I would always have it") is an affirmation of the experience of art as life's only absolute or transcendent value. Art is the only saving grace in a world of muddled or relative values. Art is absolute but not Christian belief and not romantic readiness.

If Jake gently ridicules Christian belief, he intensely ridicules Robert's romanticism. Robert is as pugnaciously committed to romantic values as he is to knocking people down. The world has been against him as a Jew, and now he thinks of Jake as his main court of appeal for his romantic sensibility, but Jake treats his romanticism to a comic-ironic hearing.

Robert-as-romantic longs to be, using Whitman's phrases, "a simple separate person" who sends forth "fine centrifugal spokes of light" in hopes of connecting with others and nature. His romantic hope contrasts with the morbid nihilism of the others, as well as with Jake's enfeebled sense of the Christian God. Jake "the rotten Catholic," whose Christian light is dim, is bent on turning out Robert's romantic light. In order for the reduction of romanticism to take place, however, Jake must first ridicule Robert the person.

Two forms of rhetoric are employed in doing so, hypotaxis (subordination of phrases and clauses) and parataxis (coordination of phrases and clauses). The result is a series of burlesques. Robert the intellectual student: "In his last year at Princeton he read too much and took to wearing glasses" (*TSAR* 3). The boxer and nice person: "There was a certain inner comfort in knowing he could knock down anybody who was snooty to him, although, being very shy and a thoroughly nice boy, he never fought except in the gym" (*TSAR* 3). The husband beaten to the punch by his wife: "and just when he made up his mind to leave his wife she left him and went off with a miniature painter" (*TSAR* 4). The novelist: "He wrote a novel, and it was really not such a bad novel as the critics later called it, although it was a very poor novel" (*TSAR* 5–6).

After such burlesquing, can there be anything to Jake's, "I rather liked him" (*TSAR* 7)? To Harvey Stone, he's positively effusive about Robert: " 'I like him. . . . I'm fond of him. You don't want to get sore at him' " (*TSAR* 44). Jake often suffers the irony of the anxiety of his role as historical being, in general reducing what he values. He castigates and defends Robert; he tells Brett to go to hell but rushes to her side in Madrid; though he loves her, he plays the pander in fixing her up with Romero; by this act he betrays the bull-fight even though he is its true aficionado. If "Romero's bull-fighting gave real emotion, because he kept the absolute purity of line in his movements" (*TSAR* 168), Jake's behavior indicates an inability to keep a moral purity of line in his actions.

It is interesting that the crypto-biography of Robert, in Chapters I and II, ridicules romanticism to the accompaniment of an anti-Semitism that seems to compromise Jake's character. Each chapter begins with thematically relevant moments of Robert's past, and then concludes with an action in the present, in Paris. Robert "learned boxing painfully and thoroughly to counteract the feeling of inferiority and shyness he had felt on being treated as a Jew at Princeton" (*TSAR* 3). If this information, especially the notion of "inferiority," comes to Jake from either Robert or his classmates, the biographical report, in this instance, clears him of anti-Semitism, though it highlights its existence at Princeton, which should bear the responsibility for anti-Semitism.

But then paratactic and hypotactic tricks are put in the service of an ethnic joke on "Spider Kelly's star pupil": "He was so good that Spider promptly overmatched him and got his nose permanently flattened. This increased Cohn's distaste for boxing, but it gave him a certain satisfaction of some strange sort, and it certainly improved his nose'' (*TSAR* 3). If the former statement takes Jake off the anti-Semitic hook, this one puts him on it. And to say that nobody at military school had made Robert ''race-conscious'' (''No one had ever made him feel he was a Jew'' [*TSAR* 4]) may be intended to be an indirect way of causing readers to think about their own race-consciousness.

Although Jake makes clearly anti-Semitic statements about Robert, he comes to his defense against attack from others. Perhaps Jake's ambivalence comes from his being attracted to Robert's romantic feelings, themselves more vital, though more naive, than the nihilistic attitudes of the other characters. Or perhaps it comes from a suppressed homosexual attraction for Robert, suggested in his outpouring of feeling for him to Harvey Stone, or in going to Robert's room (after Robert has knocked him down) because Robert wants to see him, a scene that is the counterpart of Jake's going to see Brett in Madrid.

If Hemingway mocks Jake's anti-Semitism, doesn't he also mock Robert's violent defense against anti-Semitism, which provides Robert no more satisfaction than the beating he administers Romero? Perhaps Hemingway gets the merry-go-round in motion, like the narrator in the film *La Ronde,* with the desire to put the moral problem of anti-Semitism at the forefront of the action and, though not solving it, exposing it.

Hemingway puts into question both anti-Semitism and romanticism, the latter in terms of Robert's enchantment with W. H. Hudson's *The Purple Land.* Reading it is ''an innocent enough occupation,'' but ''a very sinister book if read too late in life'' (*TSAR* 9). The main device of ridicule is the comic attributive: ''It recounts splendid imaginary amorous adventures of a perfect English gentleman in an intensely romantic land, the scenery of which is very well described'' (*TSAR* 9). The other device is exaggerated analogy: ''For a man to take it at thirty-four as a guide-book to what life holds is about as safe as it would be for a man of the same age to enter Wall Street direct from a French convent, equipped with a complete set of the more practical Horatio Alger books. Cohn, I believe, took every word of 'The Purple Land' as literally as though it had been an R. G. Dun report'' (*TSAR* 9). With comic efficiency, romanticism is reduced to philistinism, the spiritual to the economic, the idealistic to the materialistic.

When Jake deconstructs Hudson's narrative, he implies that his own cannot be taken ''literally.'' Because it is a book of signs, it cannot be taken literally. Yet it is a truer ''guide-book'' because it sees through the romantic to the nihilistic as the true historical context for human action. In arguing against Robert's desire to journey to South America, urging Paris on him instead, Jake is closing the circle Robert would like to escape. At chapter's end, Robert's ''God, what a rotten dream!'' (*TSAR* 12) is the symbolic equivalent of Jake's being ''a rotten Catholic.''

Robert's romantic ''cheerfulness''—his ''personal longings for adventure'' and "boyish sort of cheerfulness that had never been trained out of him" (*TSAR* 45), but Jake and the others will—is unlike the British major's of *A Farewell to Arms (AFA)* who thinks everybody is "cooked," but maintains "a great contrast between his world pessimism and personal cheeriness" (*AFA* 134). Robert, the single-minded idealist, desiring to suit practice to conception (like the romantic Jay Gatsby), unable or unwilling to play this double role, leaves Pamplona and goes "Up to Paris" (*TSAR* 222). What will become of him? Will he move toward nihilism, now that romanticism has been put into question? Or will he assume a new role (perhaps his true role), that of the Wandering Jew denied the sanctuary of both heaven and earth?

In the novel's penultimate chapter (*TSAR* 222), twice Jake says to Bill, "To hell with" Robert, and then twice says, "I feel like hell," (*TSAR* 222) completing the circle begun by Robert's (in the previous chapter) twice saying, "I've been through hell" (*TSAR* 194). Feeling "low as hell," Jake, now a used-up case, is in danger of forsaking historical being by lapsing into natural being.

Belmonte has gone through the process in retiring from the bullring. Returning to it, to "the terrain of human action, envisaged as equivalent to that of history" (Derrida 1978, 32), he hopes to regain his status as historical being: "In bull-fighting they speak of the terrain of the bull and the terrain of the bull-fighter. As long as a bull-fighter stays in his own terrain he is comparatively safe. Each time he enters into the terrain of the bull he is in great danger. Belmonte, in his best days, worked always in the terrain of the bull. This way he gave the sensation of coming tragedy . . . Now Belmonte imposed conditions and insisted that his bulls should not be too large, nor too dangerously armed with horns, and so the element that was necessary to give the sensation of tragedy was not there" (*TSAR* 213–14). Belmonte has really not left natural being behind when he chooses to play the game safely, to stay in his own terrain, and thus cannot be considered the "winner" he once was. To enter the bull's terrain is to experience the tragedy of nothingness and to be willing to risk death.

When Jake enters either Robert's or Brett's terrain, the reader feels a sensation not of coming tragedy but of comedy. Robert has no dangerous horns, just a good punch, and Jake enters his terrain because romanticism tempts him even as he mocks it. With Robert gone to Paris, there's nobody to kick around anymore, and so he settles alone into the terrain of natural being at San Sebastian. When Brett wires him, he goes to her without hesitation because without a role he cannot be a "winner." Although nothingness is a portion of any role, better enter her terrain than no terrain at all. Unlike Robert, however, Brett turns out to be a pretty dangerous bull for Jake.

Before arid Madrid and wet San Sebastian, Jake has taken pleasure in fishing the Irati and going to bullfights, in their way also wet and dry places. Still, the fiesta as Pleasure Fair, a connotative sign of the novel's ideology of nothingness, is itself an analogue of what Jake calls "the false aesthetics of the bull-fighters of the decadent period'' (*TSAR* 215). It is a false Paradise but a true Hell, and it is an ironic paradox that what gives Jake pleasure, "a swell fiesta," also gives him "a wonderful nightmare" and leaves him in a "damn depression" (*TSAR* 222–23). He's depressed because he's at a standstill, an actor without a role to play. He misses the nothingness that gives identity to historical being.

At San Sebastian, Jake creates a prose poem of a seashore experience with a Whitmanian undercurrent:

> Although the tide was going out, there were a few slow rollers. They came like undulations in the water, gathered weight of water, and then broke smoothly on the warm sand. I waded out. The water was cold. As a roller came I dove, swam out under water, and came to the surface with all the chill gone. I swam out to the raft, pulled myself up, and lay on the hot planks. A boy and girl were at the other end. The girl had undone the top strap of her bathing-suit and was browning her back. The boy lay face downward on the raft and talked to her. She laughed at things he said, and turned her brown back in the sun. I lay on the raft in the sun until I was dry. Then I tried several dives. I dove deep once, swimming down to the bottom. I swam with my eyes open and it was green and dark. The raft made a dark shadow. I came out of water beside the raft, pulled up, dove once more, holding it for length, and then swam ashore. I lay on the beach until I was dry. (*TSAR* 235)

In a sense, Jake has drowned in nihilistic seas, but he achieves here resurrection through the creative imagination. Rhythmical and sensuous, static and kinetic, the passage has circular structure. The tide goes out, rollers come in; "undulations" break "smoothly"; the sand is warm, the water cold; Jake swims the surface and the depth of the sea. The poetic heft of "gathered weight of water" displaces the gathered weight of Paris and Pamplona. Unlike the linear movement of Huck's raft—a means of escaping the slavery of reality (and the reality of slavery), of making a run for the freedom of the body and the spirit (and for the body and the spirit of freedom)—the San Sebastian raft simply floats signs of circularity.

Its flotation of signs connotes human limitation. He "dove deep once, swimming down to the bottom," "and it was green and dark" and the "raft made a dark shadow." With the sounding devices of alliteration and assonance, Jake sounds the soundless depths of being and nothingness.

Doubly limited, Jake cannot be like the lovers anymore than he can remove the shadow cast by the raft, which connotes God's hiddenness from human perception. The boy and the girl begin anew the circle of love closed by Jake and Brett. They are models of sexual love—"the young in one another's arms," no country for an impotent man—and Jake is their artist, the artist of the beautiful, who transforms kinetic being into the stasis of art. Without life, no art, but art validates life.

Or does it? Is the gap between life and art too deep to bear? Pressing real flesh is not the same as creating an image of flesh, unless the image in the mind presses deeper into being than flesh itself. For Jake on the raft, art is art, life is life, and the twain shall never meet. But from the separate terrains of art and life, he forges a style that "sees it through." The style is the man, which is to say that the artist is neither natural nor historical being, but imaginative being. Not being a fornicator but being a fabulist is the true, the only transcendence possible in a nihilistic universe. At this moment in San Sebastian, Jake sails out of nature and out of history into a Yeatsian Byzantium where the issue, "the winner shall take nothing," is no longer an issue.

But living in history requires action. Stronger now than he has ever been during the course of the action, Jake goes to Brett. Her telegrams are urgent signs in a cryptic style that she thinks recall him to his true condition, "that the winner shall take nothing." He goes because he can be in or out of history, participate in everyday existence (in this instance as loyal friend) or in states of imaginative creativity (as a maker of fables).

In Madrid, Brett's near-hysteria is seemingly the price you pay when you got plenty of nothing, and nothing is plenty for you. The style is the woman, too, displayed here in a tone of British stiff upper lip as she shapes passion gone awry into a grip on things. (In Chapter XIV, Jake says, "The English talked with inflected phrases" [TSAR 149].) Jake's style plays the chord of long on irony and short on pity in response to her speeches.

Since it is Brett who must explain the urgent telegrams, her lines are memorable, dramatic (TSAR 241–45). "I didn't have a sou to go away and leave Romero." "I couldn't take his money, you know." (Yet when Jake tries to pay her hotel bill, the "bill had been paid.") She doesn't keep Romero because "It isn't the sort of thing one does." "I'm not going to be one of these bitches that ruins children." "You know it makes one feel rather good deciding not to be a bitch." "It's sort of what we have instead of God." Jake's mildly evangelical response, "Some people have God. . . . Quite a lot," leads to her "He never worked very well with me." When Jake replies, "Should we have another Martini?" we are reminded of the count's feeble riposte to Brett. She defeats them both. Jake's comic rhetorical question seems sensible enough for a man at the end of his historical tether.

Her tone of noblesse oblige, though crossed with discontent at having opted for both sexual and spiritual abstinence, signifies the paradox of nihilistic sickness (the "nothingness of will") in contention with an emergent will-to-power. Brett's reference to "children" echoes allusions to children by others. Frances Clyne, wanting no children of her own, declares herself a writer; Cohn, a writer who seems unable to write any longer, has children and never mentions them; and Jake, a writer, says, "The Spanish children are beautiful" (TSAR 237). Brett's call to Jake is not a mating call, but a call to be birds of a feather in a nihilistic nest, barren of children and of God.

The combat between Christian belief and nihilism reaches a comic climax at Botin's, "one of the best restaurants in the world. We had young suckling pig and drank *rioja alta*. Brett did not eat much. She never ate much. I ate a very big meal and drank three bottles of *rioja alta.*" Brett says, "My God! what a meal you've eaten" (*TSAR* 245–46), as though it were a meal to end all meals, like a profane Last Supper. Is Jake Bacchus-Christ, and Brett Judas Iscariot?

In rejecting God, she reveals her will to power over those ("quite a lot") who "have God," over desire (letting Romero go) itself, and over the phallocentric order of things. She abjures servitude to both the transcendent and the sexual. Her nihilism equals "lack"—lack of belief (God excluded from her values) and sexual lack (the female without a phallus, without the power it embodies) (Silverman 1983, 131). Jake's phallic dysfunction constitutes his sexual "lack," which signifies his disempowered will to believe. Gluttony and drunkenness fill the sexual and the spiritual void. Transcendence does not compensate for sexual lack, nor sexuality for transcendent lack. It is a case of lacks one, lacks both.

Sexually viable Brett suffers from having to endure the phallocentric order that de-privileges the female: "My God! the things a woman goes through" (*TSAR* 184). Her role all along has been to demonstrate female equality, even superiority.

She first appears in the company of homosexuals, her hair "brushed back like a boy's" (*TSAR* 22), and Jake notes she "was very much with them" (*TSAR* 20). She participates in their deviant behavior to exhibit her sexual difference and sexual identity. She plays successful sexual games and intellectual games. She defeats the count and Jake. It is she who really "takes" Cohn at San Sebastian: she "rather thought it would be good for him," and he "gets a little dull." It is she who leaves Romero. It is she who rejects God, who "never worked very well," because He is the ground of the phallocentric order she would overcome. If she were to posit God as female, her nihilism might vanish, and she'd even pray in a cathedral. (In Chapter XIV, she goes to church with Jake.) Brett is already god-like, the *riau-riau* dancers wanting "her as an image to dance around" (*TSAR* 155). She thus makes a circle of herself, different from yet identical to Augustine's definition of God as a circle whose center is nowhere and circumference everywhere.

Their final speeches—"Oh, Jake, we could have had such a damned good time together" and "Yes. Isn't it pretty to think so?" (*TSAR* 247)—sound a tristful, sentimental note that actually conceals an ironic paradox. His line emanates from a mind sunk in comic dejection, and he thus fulfills the letter and the spirit of the epigraph. When he says, "Yes," he affirms her regret over their missed pleasure. His rhetorical question is an irony directed not simply at what could have been, but at the loss of the uppermost values that disappeared along with God. He has a double regret, the loss of the sexual and the transcendent. But he misses the essential point of her utterance. While he's busy playing the game of irony and pity, she's in the process of putting her life in perspective.

Her speech comes from a mind making something out of nothing. True, her words signify the sexual life they could have had together. But is sexual desire her true concern? If Jake could regain his sexual power, she wouldn't hesitate to pit her femaleness against his maleness, and defeat him, too, as she has the count (his hedonism), Robert (his romanticism), and Romero (his phallicism). Having defeated them, she "could have had such a damned good time" overcoming (or coming over) Jake's phallus. She's not bent on sexual gratification, but on displacing the male of the species from the catbird seat. She intends to pursue the only form of "lutte or combat" she cares about—the process of transvaluating the phallocentric order. Reversing the negations of the epigraph, she rises above morbid nihilism and romantic love. In her will to difference, she's now in the business of transvaluating while Jake seemingly lingers at the brink of the abyss.

In the taxi, Jake perceives reality in imagistic terms—"It was very hot and bright, and the houses looked sharply white" (*TSAR* 247). The imagery recapitulates the cathedral steps where the hot sun evaporates the holy water on his forefingers and thumb; and San Sebastian where it evaporates the sea water on his back. In Madrid, the sun burns out being, that is, "the houses," making them "sharply white," a sign of nothingness. The risen sun sustains life on earth, but signifies the lack of human purpose, order and meaning in life, and thus stands for the absence of the Christian God.

A complex of signs occurs in the penultimate paragraph: "Ahead was a mounted policeman in khaki directing traffic. He raised his baton. The car slowed suddenly pressing Brett against me" (*TSAR* 247). The "mounted policeman" and his "raised . . . baton" are inverse signs of Jake's lost phallicism, now diminished to the involuntary pressing of Brett against him. The raised baton is also the stick of nothingness that directs the comings and goings of the "lost generation." Just as the risen sun is the natural phenomenon that causes the earth to abide forever, so the raised baton is the metaphysical idea arresting our gaze on being and nothingness.

Brett and Jake, like Paul Klee figures, as much stick as flesh, are a sign of the emptiness of human life in a world without God. Existing in a fable of nothingness, they are Estragon and Vladimir waiting for Godot, who may well be more than a stick. But if Godot is an anagram of *Gott ist tot,* then Brett and Jake, caught in the circle of the taxi, are indeed waiting for nothing.

Yet they achieve partial transcendence. Like Dante, they have to go down in order to go up, descend into Hell before climbing into Purgatory. Unlike Dante, Paradise doesn't appear to be within their reach. But within the human circle, as they sit "close against each other," with his "arm around her and she rested against me comfortably" (*TSAR* 247)—the human touch—they transcend the essential aloneness of human beings in a Godless universe. And Brett transvaluates the traditional role of woman in the phallocentric order of things. And Jake-as-artist puts into question the negativity of the baton, and perceives himself as "set upon" that symbolic stick, upon "a golden bough to sing / To lords and ladies of Byzantium / Of what is past, or passing or to come." "Isn't it pretty to think so?"

References

Derrida, Jacques. *Writing and Difference*. Trans. Alan Bass. Chicago: U of Chicago P, 1978.

Descombes, Vincent. *Modern French Philosophy*. Trans. L. Scott-Fox and J. M. Harding. Cambridge: Cambridge UP, 1980.

Hanneman, Audre. *Ernest Hemingway: A Comprehensive Bibliography*. Princeton: Princeton UP, 1967.

Heidegger, Martin. *Nietzsche*. Trans. Frank A. Capuzzi. San Francisco: Harper & Row, 1982. Vol. 4: *Nihilism*.

Hemingway, Ernest. *The Sun Also Rises*. New York: Scribner, 1926.

Kaufman, Walter, ed. *The Portable Nietzsche*. New York: Viking, 1954.

Silverman, Kaja. *The Subject of Semiotics*. New York: Oxford UP, 1983.

III

Hemingway's Texts

9

Hemingway's "My Old Man": Turf Days in Paris

Michael S. Reynolds

Hemingway, like John Berryman, knew that life was boring and that art should never be. Unfortunately, Hemingway did not always distinguish between life and art. Perhaps no writer does. But the life which he invented has come under such close scrutiny of late that many of his embellished feats have been debunked or deflated. (No big surprise. Where is the man who would care to have his children examine too closely the tales of his youth?) This debunking, however, has carried over to the fiction in ways sometimes irrelevant. To find that his fiction does not match biographical reality is no more meaningful than to discover that the printed train schedule does not coincide with one's experience at the station.

To rise above mere pedantry, the pursuing scholar must enrich either the fiction or our understanding of creative process. The literary historian must recover the fiction's milieu, for all authors assume their audience to know and recognize certain signs, signs that fade in one generation and disappear in the next. (Without recovered knowledge of medieval medicine, our appreciation of Chaucer would be the less.) Equally valuable is the reconstruction of the creative process, the transformation of boring life into abiding fiction. The process is not peculiar to the writer. We all practice it to various degrees, for we are all, as Whitman told us, our own poets, creating fictions out of our own less than exciting lives. To observe this common practice in Hemingway's "My Old Man" may serve as an object lesson.

Perhaps because the story seems a stylistic anomaly in *In Our Time,* "My Old Man" has never received the attention it deserves. It is usually dismissed as bearing the influence of Sherwood Anderson, which it does, but to say that is to miss its significance. In "My Old Man" we find Hemingway trying out, for the first time, themes and techniques which he would later perfect. The

fixed race, which is the heart of the story, reappears as a central metaphor in
A Farewell to Arms. More importantly, this is Hemingway's first story in which
the father disappoints the son. In his Chicago juvenilia, Hemingway wrote several stories in which the son could not please the father or some other figure
whose admiration he sought. After "My Old Man," Hemingway's fictional
fathers seldom meet the expectations of their needy sons. Doctor Henry Adams,
Mr. Krebs, the father in "A Day's Wait," and Nick Adams himself in "Fathers and Sons" manage, one way or another, to disappoint their sons. Frederic Henry assures Catherine Barkley that she will never have to meet his parents. Robert Jordan is severely disappointed by his father's suicide, and Thomas
Hudson feels he has failed his sons.

Equally significant, "My Old Man" is the first Hemingway story to employ
the Huck Finn voice which would resurface periodically in both his fiction and
nonfiction as late as *A Moveable Feast*. To dismiss that voice as Andersonian
is a mistake, for it has little of Anderson's sentimentality and a good deal of
Twain's wise child. In the story Hemingway also tries out a number of techniques which became his stock in trade. Here he invents the narrator who has
inside expertise, specialized knowledge not readily available to the average
reader. Joe Butler may be young, but his knowledge of French and Italian
racetracks and their surrounding environments is detailed, specific, and highly
accurate.

Joe tells us he lives with his father in a pension at Maisons-Lafitte, "where
just about everybody lives except the gang at Chantilly"—everybody, of course,
being the jockeys. Nearby there was "a lake and a swell forest" with rabbits
and magpies to shoot with a slingshot (Hemingway 1953, 195). The 1924 Baedeker guide confirms the "numerous pensions-restaurants" at Maisons, which,
we are told, is "situated near the forest of St-Germain, on the left bank of the
Seine. Many of the financial magnates of Paris have villas here, and there are
several racing stables" (Baedeker 385). Joe Butler is impressed with the French
attitude toward horse racing; he says:

it's got the best race courses in the world. Seems as though that were the thing that
keeps it all going and about the only thing you can figure on is that every day the buses
will be going out to whatever track they're running at, going right out through everything to the track. (Hemingway 1953, 195)

In fact, the Maisons track, located 18 miles from the center of Paris, was one
of several tracks where the Paris racing season was run on an almost daily
basis from March to the end of July. On racing days, special trains were run
directly from Paris to Maisons, cutting what could be a two-hour trip to only
30 minutes (Baedeker 386). In August, when many turf enthusiasts were out
of the city, the Paris tracks closed and the horses followed the crowds to the
summer resorts. Thus Joe Butler is "glad when the horses came back from
Deauville and the summer" (Hemingway 1953, 196).

That Hemingway incorporated accurate detail from the Paris racetracks is hardly surprising, for, as we know from *A Moveable Feast*, he spent enough time handicapping the horses to use that setting with authority. What is not apparent on the surface of "My Old Man" is the degree to which the story is built on disparate but actual events taken from the Paris racing season of 1922. The two central events—the fixed race and the dead jockey—Hemingway did not actually see, but he found them ready-made in newspaper accounts. Despite his claims as a handicapper, Hemingway was out of Paris so frequently in 1922 on various trips that he had less than two months in which he could have been at the track. Much of his insider information he probably got from Evan Shipman, who knew a great deal about trotting horses, and from Harold Stearns, who a year later was writing the handicapping column for the Paris *Tribune* under the name of Peter Pickem. As for Hemingway's ability to spot long-shot winners, his record is less than spectacular. Of the horses he remembers so fondly in *Death in the Afternoon*—Man of War, Exterminator, Epinard, Ksar, Heros XII, Master Bob, and Uncas—only Uncas was a long shot (Hemingway 1932, 5).[1] The others, including Ksar, were always the favorites at odds so short they returned little on a bet. That he includes Ksar in his list of favorites should have raised the question long ago about the fixed race between Ksar and Kircubbin which is at the heart of "My Old Man."

As any serious turf man in 1922 knew, Ksar and Kircubbin were real horses who raced on July 2 at the St. Cloud track, exactly where Hemingway sets his story. But Hemingway's knowledge of the two horses began earlier in the year. Just before he left for the Genoa Conference in April, the Longchamp track opened its season with the Prix des Sablons as its featured race. As the front page *Tribune* headline reported, "KSAR ROMPS HOME IN FEATURE," and the sports section said that Ksar was shaping up as the best horse on the continent (3 April 1922). Ksar's jockey was Frank Bullock, one of the numerous English riders who worked the French circuit. On May 8, just before Hemingway left Paris to go to Italy, Bullock rode Ksar, "France's Wonder Horse," to another impressive victory. On June 5, while Hemingway was in Milan, Frank Bullock "was seriously injured . . . when [his horse] Sainte Ursule . . . fell and rolled on him. Bullock was taken to the jockey's hospital unconscious." The next day Kircubbin, an Irish horse, who had won the important St. Leger, took the Grand Prix de Temps for his third consecutive win on the continent. When Hemingway returned to Paris, two weeks before the Ksar-Kircubbin race, all the racing sheets and turf enthusiasts were convinced that Ksar would be unbeatable in the prestigious Prix du President race.

On July 2, the day of the race, the Paris *Tribune* reported:

Only an accident can prevent Mme Edmond Blanc's thoroughbred [Ksar] from carrying off the 200,000 francs and the precious soup tureen that goes to the winner.

But there will be two or three gamesters up there in front looking for this break and Kircubbin, Flechois, and Adry are the most likely looking battlers. . . .

Trained at Saint-Cloud, Ksar has never appeared in competition before on that course,
while Kircubbin . . . has grabbed off three consecutive victories there.

With J. Childs as his jockey, Ksar went to the starting post a heavy 1 to 2
favorite. In "My Old Man" Hemingway uses the same odds: 5 for 10, which
meant one had to bet two francs to win one. The actual odds on Kircubbin
were 65 to 10—almost exactly what Hemingway makes them in the story (67.5
to 10). The winner's share of the 250,000 franc race was 200,000 francs—the
same sum Hemingway uses in his story (Hemingway 1953, 197). Joe Butler's
father, armed with inside information from Ksar's jockey, knows the fictional
race is fixed; he bets 5000 francs on Kircubbin to win and another 1000 francs
on him to place, just in case the fix goes wrong. In the real race and in Hemingway's fiction, Kircubbin won by a nose at the wire. The only difference
between the real and fictional races was the fix. Kircubbin was a magnificent
horse who needed no aid to win, and there was no suggestion that the race was
fixed.

However, during that 1922 racing season in both Paris and Deauville, there
were a number of suspicious races. Three weeks after the Prix du President
race, the *Tribune* reported that the "rumors circulating at the present time regarding several cases of doping all center on the horses of a particular stable,
and they tend to be consistent. They concern a stable trained at Maisons-Lafitte,
of which one of the veterans recently occupied public opinion by reason of its
extremely contradictory performances" (*Chicago Tribune,* 27 July 1922).
Maisons-Lafitte, of course, was where Butler lived and trained. Four days later
the *London Times* reported that a well-known French trainer had been sus-
pended and fined on charges of doping his horses. Specifically he was charged
with administering a "powerful stimulant" to Arcady who won the Prix Ante-
lope at the Tremblay track one day after the Ksar-Kircubbin race. Later that
season the winner of the Prix de la Theve at the Chantilly track was disqualified
after a saliva test, and three cases of doping were charged during the August
season at Deauville (*London Times,* 17 August and 27 September 1922). Hemingway, who was in Paris from mid-June through early August, was well aware
of the doping charges that circulated, and incorporated them into his story,
which he probably began writing in September of 1922 before he left to cover
the Greco-Turkish war for his Toronto paper.

Hemingway used another element from the 1922 Paris racing season when
he had Butler use 30,000 francs of his winnings to buy Gilford, an Irish-bred
steeplechaser at a claiming plate race. In early May, Hemingway could have
seen the real horse—Guildford—finish fifth in a claiming plate. Just before
Hemingway left for Italy at the end of May 1922, the real Guildford won the
Prix D'Albian race at St. Cloud, paying 144 francs on a 10 franc bet—just the
sort of long shot that Hemingway so admired (*Chicago Tribune,* 22 May 1922).
Two days later Guildford ran second at the Tremblay track. If Hemingway
made any money on the long shot in May, he probably lost it back on Guild-

ford during the remainder of the season, for the horse did not run in the money in June or July. When he began constructing "My Old Man," Hemingway used the name Guildford; he changed the spelling slightly but not out of fear of recognition, for he did not change Kircubbin, and he changed Ksar only slightly.

The fictional Gilford falls at the water jump during the Prix du Marat on the Auteuil track, and Butler dies in the crash. The actual Prix Murat was run much earlier in the season at Auteuil—March 12, 1922. Hemingway rearranged the racing season to use an actual steeplechase he had witnessed. In fact, Hemingway, who witnessed several racing spills that season, did not see any jockeys actually killed, nor did he need to. There were several stories in the Paris papers about fatal and near-fatal racing accidents that season, but if a man had seen one serious spill, he could easily imagine the death of the jockey. In fact, the same day as the real Ksar-Kircubbin race, a French jockey died in a spill at Marseilles. Two years later Hemingway said, "The only writing that was any good was what you made up, what you imagined. . . . Like when [you] wrote 'My Old Man' [you'd] never seen a jockey killed and the next week Georges Parfrement was killed at that very jump and that was the way it looked" (Baker 1969, 100–01).

It is worth noting that even in this seemingly honest statement, Hemingway was incapable of telling the exact truth if it did not fit his purpose. He wrote "My Old Man" in the late fall of 1922. Georges Parfrement, the most famous French jockey of the era, died the following April of 1923, not two weeks later as Hemingway said. Hemingway's Butler died at the Auteuil track; Parfrement died at the Enghien track. Moreover, Hemingway was in Cortina, Italy, when Parfrement's horse "came down at a stone wall" and fell on the jockey, killing him (*London Times,* 18 April 1923). Hemingway never saw Parfrement's fatal accident. Memory, as Hemingway warned us in *Death in the Afternoon,* is never true. Memory transformed by imagination becomes one man's fiction and another's history: both relatively true, both absolutely false. The past may be redeemable, but it is unknowable. With Hemingway there is no such thing as nonfiction; there are simply degrees of fiction: Some events are more fictional than others. "My Old Man" is a patchwork quilt of diversely acquired, accurate information—none of the parts fictional, only the total result.

What is most significant in the patchwork construction of "My Old Man"— Hemingway's first story begun after leaving Chicago—is his ability to blend limited firsthand observations with secondary information. He did not learn this technique from Anderson, Pound, or Stein, and he would use it for the remainder of his career. After he wrote *The Sun Also Rises,* most of his readers and more than one biographer assumed that all of his fiction was thinly veiled biography, which it almost never was. In *A Farewell to Arms* and *For Whom the Bell Tolls*—some of his most popular fiction—he relied heavily on secondary sources to construct his novels. As "My Old Man" clearly demonstrates, Hemingway mastered the technique early in Paris without benefit of tutors. We have no other evidence of what else he was learning in 1922, but this trick alone was extremely important in his development. Everything he wrote in Paris between December 1921 and December 1922 was lost except for this racetrack story. With no other evidence of Hemingway's crucial first year in Paris available to him, the literary biographer can ill afford to dismiss this story as Andersonian, to denigrate the only evidence he has for Hemingway's remarkable transformation.

As Hemingway told Scott Fitzgerald in 1925, "My Old Man" is "a good story, always seemed to me, though not the thing I'm shooting for. It belongs to another categorie along with the bull fight story and the 50 Grand [sic]. The kind that are easy for me to write" (Hemingway 1981, 180). All three stories— "My Old Man," "The Undefeated," and "Fifty Grand"—take their conflicts from the sporting life; all three stories center on over-the-hill athletes who lose: authority figures past their prime. These stories were easy to write only because they never happened. In each story Hemingway was able to describe a believable milieu by watching the sport, not by participating. Direct experience, he had discovered, was not necessarily the most reliable source of information for a writer: the actor could not observe himself in action, did not have time to analyze his reactions. Very early he learned that trick in the newspaper game and it carried over into his writing. "My Old Man"—the first story Hemingway began and finished in Paris—shows us a young writer already using the skills and techniques of a seasoned professional. It shows us a young writer who needed very little direction to become Ernest Hemingway.

Note

1. Hemingway spells Ksar with a "z."

References

Baedeker, Karl. *Paris and Its Environs.* Leipzig: Baedeker, 1924.
Baker, Carlos. *Ernest Hemingway: A Life Story.* New York: Scribner, 1969.
Chicago Tribune, Paris edition. 3 April, 22 May, and 27 July 1922.
Hemingway, Ernest. *Death in the Afternoon.* New York: Scribner, 1932.
———. *Selected Letters 1917–1961,* ed. Carlos Baker. New York: Scribner, 1981.
———. *The Short Stories of Ernest Hemingway.* New York: Scribner, 1953.
London Times, 17 August and 22 September 1922; 18 April 1923.

10

"Mons (Three)": An Unpublished *In Our Time* Chapter

Paul Smith

Of all the chapters of Ernest Hemingway's *In Our Time*—from the first six published in the *Little Review* in 1923 to the 12 added with *in our time* in the next year—only two (III and IV) are devoted to a single historical event, the defeat of the British Expeditionary Force at Mons, Belgium, on August 23, 1914. Hemingway recognized the two chapters' singular continuity from the start, for the second is the only one to bear a title in the 1923 series, "Mons (Two)." [1] But Hemingway followed that battle further, for there is an unpublished and unrecorded chapter recounting the beginning of the British retreat from Mons, a chapter to which I will give the nonce title, "Mons (Three)."

Hemingway's original source for the story of Mons was his close friend from the fall of 1918, Captain Eric Edward Dorman-Smith of the Fifth Northumberland Fusiliers. The two met in Milan in early November, shared anecdotes of the war; and one suspects that the veracity of Dorman-Smith's recollections of Mons and elsewhere may have elicited some of Hemingway's fictive accounts of leading the Arditi on Monte Grappa (Baker 1969, 53–56).[2] It was a favorable exchange for Hemingway. He would have heard of the Fusiliers' defense of the Mariette Bridge over the Mons-Condé Canal (Chapter IV). And if Dorman-Smith could not have told him of fighting "in a garden at Mons" (Chapter III), since "the city was not in the Fifth's sector" (Hagemann 1980, 255), no matter, for Hemingway's sharp ear for dialect caught the clipped accent and diction of the British officer.

The Battle of Mons was crucial in the early days of the war. The German "Schlieffen" strategy, to wheel through the Allies' flanks, surround them, and drive quickly on to Paris, nearly succeeded: the Belgian Army abandoned Liège and Namur; the French were defeated at Charleroi; and when the 90,000 British, in their first engagement with the Germans, were overwhelmed at Mons, the entire Allied line retreated to the Marne River. (Hemingway, a rising soph-omore at Oak Park High School, could have followed the battle in the pages of the Chicago *Tribune*.)

Although it can be argued that the action of Chapter III "in a garden at Mons" on the British side of the canal would have occurred *after* the defense of the bridge in Chapter IV, this inversion of the two events, both likely on the twenty-third of August, seems slight in the larger anachronistic ordering of the *Little Review* sequence of chapters (1915, 1923, 1922, 1914, 1922). Hem-ingway's implicit structure has less to do with the details of chronology than with the dramatic pattern in the narration of these chapters, III and IV from *In Our Time* and the unpublished "Mons (Three)":

Chapter III

We were in a garden at Mons. Young Buckley came in with his patrol from across the river. The first German I saw climbed up over the garden wall. We waited till he got one leg over and then potted him. He had so much equipment on and looked awfully surprised and fell down into the garden. Then three more came over further down the wall. We shot them. They all came just like that.

Chapter IV

It was a frightfully hot day. We'd jammed an absolutely perfect barricade across the bridge. It was simply priceless. A big old wrought-iron grating from in front of a house. Too heavy to lift and you could shoot through it and they would have to climb over it. It was absolutely topping. They tried to get over it, and we potted them from forty yards. They rushed it, and the officers came out alone and worked on it. It was an absolutely perfect obstacle. Their officers were very fine. We were frightfully put out when we heard the flank had gone, and we had to fall back. (Hemingway 1966, 104, 113)

("Mons (Three)")

We formed them in fours along the road. They were Gordons and very few of them were wounded. When we had lined up the last four the rest of them were gone along the road. "It's no good Charles," Buckley said. His face was red and he sounded sick. It wasn't at all like Sandhurst. We started along after them. The last of them were just going over the hill. They were keeping all together and they all had their rifles.[3]

The intensity, even the pitch of the speaker's voice rises from Chapter III to Chapter IV and falls again in "Mons (Three)"; the first and third of these chapters bracket the heightened language of the second with a lowered, almost contemplative, tone and with references to "Young Buckley," returning with his patrol from the enemy side of the canal to the garden in Mons and, here in the unpublished chapter, forming the troops of the Gordon Highlanders for the retreat. This chapter also returns us to Chapter III to reconsider an implication of the phrase "Young Buckley." The narrator there is clearly his senior in age and rank, but any other difference between the two goes unremarked. If, however, we assume a single speaker for all three chapters—a reasonable but not essential assumption—then the difference between the characters of Buckley and Charles in the last may argue for a more subdued, thoughtful, even quavering, voice than the exhilarated one some find in the last lines of Chapter III: "We shot them. They all came just like that." Something close to that quieter voice, suggesting an emerging awareness of the horror of the slaughter, would be consonant with the more explicit irony of "It wasn't at all like Sandhurst" in "Mons (Three)."

That silent remark is meant not only to dissociate the narrator Charles from Buckley but also to mark a momentary disavowal of the exuberant colloquialisms taken to be typical of the British officer. If the voices of understatement— in "Mons (Three)"—and overstatement—in Chapter IV—are expressions of one narrator, then the drama of the three chapters takes place within his character, and its conflict and resolution are signified by opposed manners of speech and their implicit moral positions.[4]

The first act of that dialectic drama (Chapter III) opposes the euphemistic "We waited . . . and then *potted*" the German soldier and he "looked *awfully* surprised" with the real and terrible act, "We *shot* them," and the officer's own awful surprise when "[t]hey *all* came just like that."

The second act of that drama (Chapter IV) seems to overwhelm the real action with the narrator's exaggerated pride in an "absolutely perfect, . . . simply priceless, . . . [and] absolutely topping" barricade; and in potting the enemy at close to point-blank range.[5] He remarks that the German officers "came out alone and worked on [the barricade, and] were very fine," recalling that aristocratic code of officers and gentlemen that transcended mere matters of nation or cause. But the chapter begins with the innocent remark that it "was a frightfully hot day," and it ends with the resounding pun, we "were frightfully put out when we heard the flank had gone."

The final act in "Mons (Three)" takes up the action from the previous chapter's last phrase, "we had to fall back." Here the British officer's voice is now assigned to "Young Buckley," while the more accurate perception of the retreat from Mons and the performance of the Gordon Highlanders is witnessed and silently affirmed by the chastened narrator. As the two officers form the battalion in a column of fours for the retreat, the first ranks march off before the last is formed and the column given the order to march. Young Buckley is infuriated by this breach of discipline, as discipline is defined in the textbooks of the British military schools like Sandhurst. But the narrator sees that the Gordons have behaved commendably for troops outnumbered and in retreat; "very few of them were wounded"; they had not thrown down their rifles and run, as had too many others; they kept "all together." Yet they are not waiting, as Buckley would have them do, to make this a textbook retreat. With what they have been through and the way they went through it, they deserve some respite from the rules, if only to start the long march to the Marne.[6]

With this last act of the Battle of Mons, it is as if the ambiguity in the

language that inspires men to battle as it obscures war's reality is finally re-
solved. Some, like Buckley, may still be "frightfully put out," at the infrac-
tions of an official code; but the narrator sees through that language to the fact
that they were, terrifyingly, "put out" of their lines at Mons and nearly out of
their lives. He sees that there is no such thing as an absolutely perfect barricade; that those fine enemy officers he so sportingly potted were, in fact, shot;
and at last that the language of absolutes—perfect, priceless, topping—is as
obscene as the language of abstractions—sacred, glorious, and sacrifice—would
become for Frederic Henry.

All this begs a nagging question: why did Hemingway exclude this unpublished chapter from those submitted to the *Little Review* in March of 1923 and
from those sent to William Bird for the forthcoming *in our time* in the fall of
that year (Baker 1969, 108, 113)? That he simply overlooked it seems unlikely:
In 1923 he worried over the thinness of both *Three Stories and Ten Poems* and
in our time and tried to pad them with blank pages.

The manuscripts offer little help with this question but do suggest two dates
of composition for "Mons (Three)": probably February 1923 in Cortina
d'Ampezzo and possibly August in Paris. One of the manuscripts in the mis-
cellaneous folder, Item 94A, is titled "ERNEST HEMINGWAY/IN OUR TIME"
and includes the six chapters submitted to the *Little Review* for its spring issue.
Each of the chapters is untitled, with the exception of the fifth, "Mons (Two),"
and each is concluded with three asterisks, as is the manuscript of "Mons
(Three)." Its probable date of composition, then, is the early winter of 1923.

One could be more certain of that date but for the fact that "Mons (Three)"
is typed on the reverse of a page that bears a draft of Chapter XII of *In Our
Time,* similarly untitled and concluded with asterisks. Since this chapter cele-
brates Nicanor Villalta's brilliant performance in Pamplona in July (Baker 1969,
112), one could claim a later date for "Mons (Three)." To do so, however, is
to discount the fact that more than once Hemingway picked up an earlier draft
of one work and parsimoniously composed another on its verso.

Whether it was composed in February in preparation for the *Little Review* or
in August for *in our time,* its exclusion from one or both collections may have
rested on a consideration of its function and effect within the first set of six or
the second set of 18 chapters.

The sequence of the first three *Little Review* chapters establishes three of its
motifs and locales: World War I, Champagne, 1915; Bullfighting, Spain, 1923;
and The Greco-Turkish conflict, Eastern Thrace, 1922. Following the two Mons
chapters and in a likely position for "Mons (Three)," Hemingway placed the
account of the execution of the six cabinet ministers in Greece in 1922. He
could have made that decision to exclude another Mons chapter to preserve a
more even emphasis, for with it four of the six would have centered his perspective on two years of World War I, three of them on one battle.

The same first six chapters introduce the *in our time* sequence, but by the late summer Hemingway had in hand two chapters from his own experience (Chapters VI and VII) and a revision of what was to become "A Very Short Story." He returned to Paris from Spain in August and wrote to Ezra Pound of his progress on *in our time:*

I will do the hanging [XVII]. Have done the death of Maera [XIV] altogether different and have fixed the others. . . .

When they are read altogether they all hook up. . . . The war starts clear and noble just like it did, Mons etc., gets close and blurred and finishes with the feller who goes home and gets clap. (Hemingway 1981, 91)

It would be difficult in a letter to Pound three years after the "Mauberley" poems to speak without irony of the war as starting "clear and noble." But if the terms indicate Hemingway's wish to maintain in the Mons chapters a sense of an untroubled conviction in a cause and an assured victory, then "Mons (Three)" would have been inappropriate for the early war chapters.

Finally, there is an interesting, if offhanded, chiasmus in that letter: "The war starts clear and noble . . . [then] gets close and blurred." If Hemingway intended *clear* to mean the sort of conviction and commitment I have suggested, then *blurred* would logically imply a loss of that conviction—as it does when Nick makes his "separate peace" (Chapter VI). Young Buckley's "clear" perception of the war is in fact clouded with textbook preconceptions, just as Nick's vision of the distorted scene of rubble and death and dirt is finally clear and precise—he "looked straight ahead brilliantly." And if those two terms exchange their meanings, then so do *noble* and *close*. The only noble war is one witnessed from the distance of a military college. Close to one's experience there is nothing about it that is noble or perfect or priceless or sacred or glorious. Paralyzed with a bullet and with that knowledge, Nick did all he could do—sweat and look.

If the decision to set aside this third chapter on the retreat from Mons offered a reason for the writing of the two chapters on the battle at Fossalta di Piave, then we are the richer for it. But there was some loss. "Mons (Three)" is a remarkably fine prose sketch, as good as or better than its two companion chapters. The Italian chapters need not and, in a way, could not replace it.

Finally, there is a fair chance that "Mons (Three)" may be unique among Hemingway's manuscripts. With Hemingway's celebrated "theory of omission" as a warrant, we have become too accustomed to assuming that all of his omissions were justified and even inevitable. "Mons (Three)," however, is inexplicably and unfortunately one of the "things left out" that never should have been.

Notes

1. The first six chapters appeared in the *Little Review* IX, no. 3 (Spring 1923), 3–5, Exiles' Number; 12 were added to *in our time* (Paris: Three Mountains Press, 1924);

and the accumulated 18 were rearranged and renumbered in *In Our Time* (New York: Boni and Liveright, 1925). Since that numbering is followed in the most available edition, *The Short Stories of Ernest Hemingway* (New York: Scribner, 1966), I will use it here. To clarify the discrepancies in numbering and placement among the three editions of the first six chapters, they are listed here with identifying phrases:

Little Review (1923)	*in our time* (1924)		*In Our Time* (1925)
"Everybody was drunk"	1		I
"The first matador"	2		(IX)
"Minarets stuck up"	3		II
"We were in a garden"	4		III
Mons (Two)	5	"It was a fright- fully hot"	IV
"They shot the six"	6		V

2. There is a telling line in "Soldier's Home": "His lies . . . consisted in attributing to himself things other men had seen, done, or heard of, and stating as facts certain apocryphal incidents familiar to all soldiers" (Hemingway 1966, 146).

3. Item 94A, The Hemingway Collection, The John F. Kennedy Library; copyrighted © 1990 by The Ernest Hemingway Foundation. Reprinted with its permission. The only revision on this Hemingway typescript is pencilled quotation marks around "It's no good Charles."

4. Other instances in Hemingway are familiar; for example, this conversation between Catherine Barkley and Frederic Henry in *A Farewell to Arms* when he affects a British diction:

"He . . . was killed in the Somme."
"It was a *ghastly* show."
"Were you there?"
"No." (Hemingway 1929, 18; emphasis added)

In the manuscript of the novel Hemingway first wrote "It was a terrible show."

5. There is a sinister, if only partial palindrome between *pot*ting and *top*ping which draws on the ironic pun of the soldiers "potted" in the garden.

6. If, as I suspect, "over the hill" was current in 1914–23 for absent without leave, there is another irony in this chapter.

References

Baker, Carlos. *Ernest Hemingway: A Life Story*. New York: Scribner, 1969.

Hagemann, E.R. " 'Only Let the Story End as Soon as Possible': Time-and-History in Ernest Hemingway's *In Our Time*," *Modern Fiction Studies* 26 (Summer 1980), 255–62.

Hemingway, Ernest. *A Farewell to Arms*. New York: Scribner, 1929.

———. *Ernest Hemingway: Selected Letters, 1917–1961*. Ed. Carlos Baker. New York: Scribner, 1981.

———. *The Short Stories of Ernest Hemingway*. New York: Scribner, 1966.

11

The Poetry of the Twentieth Chapter of *Death in the Afternoon:* Relationships between the Deleted and Published Halves

Donald Junkins

On John Dos Passos' advice, Ernest Hemingway deleted the first half of the twentieth and final chapter of *Death in the Afternoon* (DIA) after it was set in galleys.[1] At the time, Hemingway had doubts about it, but his critical hunches, exposed and confirmed by Dos Passos, led him to make this change even though some of his most graphic writing is in the deleted text.[2] What is most revealing, once again, in studying the Hemingway manuscripts, is Hemingway's creative process. More talk about Hemingway's iceberg theory risks a certain obviousness, but here we have two icebergs, one that he left out of *Death in the Afternoon* until the twentieth chapter, and one that he finally left out of that chapter. And although the author's ideas about what has or has not gotten into a text are not always normative, it is noteworthy that Hemingway said later that what *Death in the Afternoon* is about is in the twentieth chapter,[3] thus focusing his "Bibliographical Note" that it is a book about a specific and integral part of Spanish culture.[4] Perhaps more significantly, though, *Death in the Afternoon* also dramatizes Hemingway's writing process, his ways to a subject, the understructures of that subject and its themes, and how significant metaphors work toward significant presences in a controlled text. Hemingway's topic sentences in the published version allow the emergence of these significant presences.

It should have the smell of burnt powder

and the smoke and the flash and the noise
of the traca going off through the green leaves

of the trees and it should have the taste of horchata,
ice-cold horchata, and the new-washed streets in the sun,
and the melons and beads of cool
on the outside of the pitchers of beer; the storks
on the houses in Barco de Avila and wheeling
in the sky and the red-mud color of the ring;
and at night dancing to the pipes and the drum
with lights through the green leaves and the portrait
of Garibaldi framed in leaves. It should,
if it were enough of a book, have the forced smile
of Lagartito; it was once a real smile,
and the unsuccessful matadors swimming with the cheap
whores out on the Manzanares along the Pardo road; beggars

can't be choosers, Luis said; playing ball
on the grass by the stream where the fairy marquis
came out in his car with the boxer; where we made
the paellas, and walked home in the dark with the cars
coming fast along the road; and with electric lights
through the green leaves and the dew
settling the dust, in the cool at night; cider
in Bombilla and the road to Pontevedra from Santiago
de Campostella with the high turn in the pines
and blackberries beside the road; Algabeno the worst
faker of them all; and Maera up in the room at Quintana's
changing outfits with the priest the one year everyone
drank so much and no one was nasty. There really was such
a year, but this is not enough
of a book. (*DIA* 271)

Why Dos Passos suggested the cut and why Hemingway recognized the schema behind the suggestion relate to the unity of the manuscript of *Death in the Afternoon*. Everything that Hemingway knew about life and death went, in some way, into the writing of that book, and in the same way that the lyrical poetry of the twentieth chapter both personalizes and universalizes the tragedy of the bull within a specifically Hispanic culture, thus extending the human context of both bulls and matadors dying, the significant content of the deleted half of the chapter (significant as process, as preparatory understructure, and even as pure Hemingway pride-and-prejudice) would have subtracted from the published text.

The poetry, thus, of the published twentieth chapter is epiphanic.[5] Its imagistic richness, its rhythmic and melodic depths, and its passionately measured overtones combine to effect an ending to *Death in the Afternoon* that sheds light not only on *toreo* as a way of life, but also on death as a means toward enriching life. The aesthetics of the tragedy of the bull becomes the moral-aesthetic context for a way of living. The process of death is the process of

life. The complex, mysterious, sacramental, mystically pagan and religious nature of *toreo,* explicable in the interior text, is generative in the twentieth chapter. *Toreo* undergirds this chapter as it has infused the preceding 19 chapters.
Both are vital to the other, yet we do not realize the twentieth chapter until we
discover it, until it reveals itself to Hemingway as a conclusion that both focuses and expands the book. This is the true iceberg theory: Reciprocal metaphors of experience find counterparts in either stated or unstated contexts. Clearly
the passion which illuminates the twentieth chapter vitalized the preceding 19
chapters. Equally as clearly, its illuminations cannot be experienced except as
conclusion (which must be extension and clarification and embodiment).

Not only is the chapter a condensed narrative poem, in fabric and pace, but
once again, many of its sentences can be lined as individual poems.[6]

It should make clear the change in the country

as you come down out of the mountains and into Valencia
in the dusk on the train holding a rooster for a woman
who was bringing it to her sister; and it should show
the wooden ring at Alciras where they dragged the dead horses
out in the field and you had to pick your way
over them; and the noise in the streets in Madrid
after midnight, and the fair that goes on all night long,
in June, and walking home on Sundays
from the ring; or with Raphael in the cab. Que tal?
Malo, hombre, malo; with that lift of the shoulders,
or with Roberto, Don Roberto, Don Ernesto,
so polite always, so gentle, and such a good
friend. Also the house where Rafael lived
before being a republican became respectable
with the mounted head of the bull
Gitanillo had killed and the great
oil jar . . . (*DIA* 270–71)

Make all that come true again;

throw grasshoppers to the trout in the Tambre
on the bridge in the evening; have the serious brown face
of Felix Merino at the old Aguilar; have the brave, awkward,
wall-eyed Pedro Montes dressing away from home
because he had promised his mother he had stopped fighting,
after Mariano, his brother, was killed at Tetuan;
and Litri, like a little rabbit, his eyes
winking nervously as the bull came;
he was very bow-legged and brave and those three
are all killed and never any mention made about the beer
place on the cool side of the street underneath the Palace
where he sat with his father and how it is a citroen

show room now; nor about them carrying Pedro Carreño,
dead, through the streets with torches
and finally into the church and put him naked
on the altar. (*DIA* 272)

In the light of these centralizing images, we can see how the relationship of
the omitted last half-chapter to the retained version focuses the metaphoric
bondings of Hemingway's creative process. What he does in the deleted 2450
words is discuss thematically and formally the geography, ideas, and intentions
of the chapter, not unlike his originally planned beginning of *The Sun Also
Rises* where he discussed Brett's overall relationship to the story, trying to
create a larger perspective, then realizing, aided by Fitzgerald, that he could
more effectively present rather than explain the beginning.[7]

In a Fitzgerald letter to Hemingway criticizing what Fitzgerald called the
"elephantine facetiousness" of the first 7500 words of the originally uncut
version of *The Sun Also Rises,* Fitzgerald writes: "Appropos [sic] of your
foreward [sic] about the Latin Quarter—suppose you had begun your stories
with phrases like: 'Spain is a peculiar place—ect [sic]' or 'Michigan is interesting to two classes—the fisherman + the drummer.' "[8]

Remarkably, the first paragraph of the uncut version of the twentieth chapter
of *Death in the Afternoon,* where Hemingway leads with the identical formulaic
bad start that Fitzgerald needled him with as a hypothetical for-instance, begins:

It is a strange country, Spain, and few people have ever gone to it to find it as they
expected. Peninsulas often have much of the quality of islands without the feeling of
confinement that an island gives. They are islands with a road out and of the three
peninsulas that I have lived in, Michigan, Italy, and Spain; four really, for Michigan is
two peninsulas, the upper and the lower: upper Michigan was a true peninsula, but all
Michigan was a province; Italy was a true peninsula; and Spain is no peninsula but a
continent.[9]

Thus the deleted half-chapter discusses the three peninsulas (Michigan, Italy,
Spain) that held significance for Hemingway, and describes his passion for
each. Hemingway laments the changes in the Michigan landscape he once knew:
the slashed forests, abandoned farms, and fished-out and polluted streams ("you
will never know what it was like if you did not see it"). He says that his one-
time thought that the solution to his loss of Michigan could be his finding of
Italy was wrong, that he doesn't "believe any more that if you want to care
for anything, the best thing to care for is country."

He went to Spain from Italy via Paris "trying to learn to write well and well
cured of all abstract words" such as "liberty." He went to Spain and found
other things he "believed, in being practical and an opportunity to observe
others and in addition liked the bullfights and the country and some of the
people."

He defends himself against American critics who accuse him of not writing about America: "not to declaim the marvels of their newly acquired and discovered country is not always in us merely a lack of perception." He says that "no matter where we go, nor in what countries we live, we do not get away from those things we know, sometimes without wishing to know."

What follows is a lyrical essay on American corn, a metaphoric near-poem which highlights the cut-out material. It begins, "Nor is it necessary for us to declaim that we are Americans when we write since no one can fail to see it, nor could we lose it by changing our citizenship, nor escape it by changing our residence. The simplest thing to test with is a cornfield." Lining the passage that follows as a poem clarifies the essential difference between it and the poetry of the published chapter.

> Corn in America Is Maize
>
> Memories of the thin fields of New England; corn
> planted in a clearing in Pennsylvania; crows
> keeping just out of shotgun range
> while corn is being planted on a ploughed hillside
> in Michigan; memories of fine stands of corn
> on new land that has been taken from the forest; corn
> being hoed in the hot weather (the weeds
> cut at the roots by the hoe, its blade
> worn and shiny, and the earth being hoed
> to a fine dust around the corn
> roots): the great tall cornfields of Illinois
> and Iowa; cutting and shucking corn in the fall; ripe
>
> ears of corn thrown into a wagon; shocked corn
> in a field at night with the moon on it; hunting
> through a cornfield in the winter; not to mention
> corncob pipes, an uncle who lost a finger
> in a corn-sheller; the corncob as a joke, cobs
> around a grist mill; corn in a silo; corn
> whiskey in a charred oak keg (strapped to a horse;
> a keg on each side and the charcoal to be strained out
> before drinking); hundreds and hundreds of other things
> about the one word cornfield which you could fill a book
> with, that are in the subconscious and racial memory
> of the people who settled America. (*DIA* g. 78, JFK Library)

The corn soliloquy, as graphic as it is, is essentially a laundry list of corn images that do not generate a sense of mystery. And what follows the soliloquy is a defensive discussion about subject matter: that it is not important to defend yourself as a writer trying to prove that you know about things you know but have never written about. Hemingway says that although it is presumptuous for him to write about Spain, that he has no right to the things in Spain that the

Spanish people have fought for and paid for, he is still free as an American writer, having paid for things as an American that are American, to write English. This, then, leads him to the opening line of the published version of the twentieth chapter: "If I could have made this enough of a book it would have everything in it." [10]

Two points are pertinent to the deleted pages: (1) the material, in spite of being often graphic and poignant and interesting, talks about rather than demonstrates its ideas; and (2) the overall tone not only focuses the defensive stance of the excised material, but it undercuts the poignancy and drama of the published version. It lacks the poetic devices of juxtaposition and timing, and it lacks the melodic invention that characterizes the essential poetry of the published book. Hemingway seemed to be groping for poignancy through a kind of spreading intensity. The effect is a sense of arbitrariness.

This is to praise Hemingway, not to denounce him. After all, he deleted the material, and the whole point of writing is to open up oneself enough in the creative process to discover the finished work of art. First drafts provide openings, and in this one Hemingway wrote himself into the concluding epiphany. No literary origins determine literary or other kinds of validities, and we are only fortunate to see Hemingway's working drafts.

The idea of beginning the concluding chapter with a simple statement about making it enough of a book, then immediately introducing the image of the Prado museum, works because it evokes all of Spain and all of the world. Once Hemingway used the image of the Prado, he didn't need Italy and Michigan, nor his explicit statements linking moral and aesthetic principles. Under the umbrella of the cluster image of the museum, he directly presents Spain, simply, clearly, passionately.

It might seem, then, an obviousness to say that the deleted half of Chapter 20 was not worth publishing, but on the contrary, it was a question of context, of appropriate effect, not facility. When Hemingway wrote to Dos Passos that Dos Passos had better be right about his suggestions, the voices of Hemingway's intuitions were telling him that the writing was good writing, but not appropriate in a context that not only dwarfed it, but was blurred by it.

Those readers who study the original galleys in the Kennedy Library will undoubtedly conclude that much of the writing in the first 2450 words is very good indeed. Some may argue that the pages should have been included, that Hemingway should not have listened to Dos Passos. I think that they are wrong. Hemingway warmed up, in those deleted pages, to his true style in context, and wrote himself into the essential poetry of the twentieth chapter.

> We'll all be gone before it's changed too much
>
> and if no deluge comes when we are gone
> it still will rain in summer in the north and hawks
> will nest in the Cathedral at Santiago
> and in La Granja, where we practiced with the cape

on the long gravelled paths between the shadows, it makes
no difference if the fountains play
or not. We never will ride back from Toledo
in the dark, washing the dust out with Fundador,
nor will there be that week of what happened in the night
in that July in Madrid. We've seen it all
go, and we'll watch it go again. The great thing
is to last and get your work done and see

and hear and learn and understand; and write
when there is something that you know; and not before;
and not too damned much after. Let those who want to
save the world if you can get to see it clear
and as a whole. Then any part you make
will represent the whole if it's made
truly. The thing to do is work
and learn to make it. No. It is not enough
of a book, but still there were a few things
to be said. There were a few practical things
to be said. (*DIA* 278)

Notes

1. Hemingway cut approximately 2450 words, leaving approximately 3000 words in the published version. See galleys 78, 79, plus six lines of 80: "S404 Hemingway's Death," in the Hemingway collection at the John F. Kennedy Library, Boston.

2. Carlos Baker, ed., *Ernest Hemingway, Selected Letters 1917–1961,* (New York: Scribner, 1981), p. 360: To John Dos Passos, Havana, 30 May 1932. "Have gone over book 7 times and cut out all you objected to (seemed like the best to me God damn you if it really was) cut 4½ galleys of philosophy and telling the boys—cut all of last chapter except the part about Spain—the part saying how it wasn't enough of a book or it would have had these things. That is OK."

3. To Arnold Gingrich: Piggot, Arkansas, 4 December 1932: "Am glad you liked the last chapter in the last book [*Death in the Afternoon*]—it is what the book is about but nobody seems to notice that. They think it is just a catalogue of things that were omitted. How would they like them to be put in? Framed in pictures or with a map?" (Baker, ed., *Letters* 378).

4. Hemingway calls it "an introduction to the modern Spanish bullfight and attempts to explain that spectacle both emotionally and practically. It was written because there was no book which did this in Spanish or in English" (*Death in the Afternoon* [New York: Scribner, 1932], p. 517).

5. For discussions of Hemingway's prose as poetry, see my articles: "Hemingway's Contribution to American Poetry," *The Hemingway Review* 4 (1984): 18–23, and "Hemingway's Bullfighter Poems," *The Hemingway Review* 6 (1987): 38–45.

6. For discussions of relining Hemingway's prose as poetry, see the articles cited in note 5.

7. See Frederic Joseph Svoboda, *Hemingway and* The Sun Also Rises: *The Crafting of a Style* (Lawrence: U Kansas P, 1983). Svoboda says: "The tone of the material that

he eventually deleted is reminiscent of Hemingway's first-draft working out of ideas, motivations, and character-traits; it is essentially expository rather than dramatic'' (98, 100). About revisions Hemingway made prior to the galley cuttings, Svoboda says: "These discussions of method and direction in the first draft also seemed to serve as Hemingway's notes to himself, clarifying in an expository manner ideas that he later treated more organically within the scenes of the novel" (33). Both revisions consist of major cuttings from galley proofs, with the final text beginning with the next sentence after the cut material; and both were suggested by fellow writers. (For a discussion of Philip Young's and Charles Mann's discovery of Fitzgerald's actual role in the galley cuttings of *The Sun Also Rises,* see Svoboda, p. 98.)

8. As quoted in Bertram D. Sarason, *Hemingway and* The Sun *Set* (Washington, DC: NCR/Microcard Editions, 1972), p. 259.

9. Galley 78, S404 "Hemingway's Death" 11½-14-Scotch. Chapter 20, JFK Library. Of Italy, in the third paragraph of the same galley, Hemingway writes: "They say that everyone loves Italy once and that it is well to go through with it young and when you see the people who live at Fiesole, at Capri, at Taormina, at Rome and even at Rapallo, exception made for Mr. Pound as a friend, it makes you understand this and it is easy to see the unwisdom of loving such places too long. It was the north of Italy that I cared about. I never cared truly about any part of the peninsula south of Milan just as I have never loved France, nor any part of France except Paris and Provence when the wind was not blowing. But Provence really is a lapping over of Italy into France. But from Milan to Brescia, to Verona, to Vicenza, not from Vicenza to Padova, I hated Padova; but from Padova to Mestre, up to Treviso, all around the Venetian plain and then up to Barca di Cadore, all of the Dolomites, but especially the country between Toblach and Cortina, I cared about. . . . I loved Northern Italy like a fool, truly, the way I had loved northern Michigan" (Galley 78. S404 "Hemingway's Death" 11½-14-Scotch. Chapter 20).

10. Lined as a poem, the opening section reads as follows:

> If I could have made this enough of a book.
>
> it would have had everything in it. The Prado,
> looking like some big American college building,
> with sprinklers watering the grass early in the bright Madrid
> summer morning; the bare white mud hills
> looking across toward Carabanchel; days on the train in August
> with the blinds pulled down on the side against the sun
> and the wind blowing them; chaff blown
> against the car in the wind from the hard earthen
> threshing floors; the odor of grain and the stone
> windmills. It would have had the change
> when you leave the green country behind at Alsasua;
> it would have had Burgos far across the plain
> and eating the cheese later
>
> up in the room; it would have had the boy taking
> the wicker-bound jugs of wine on the train as samples;
> his first trip to Madrid and opening them
> in enthusiasm and they all got drunk including the pair
> of Guardia Civil and I lost the tickets
> and we were taken through the wicket by the two
> Guardia Civil (who took us out as though prisoners

because there were no tickets and they saluted
as they put us in the cab); Hadley, with the bull's ear
wrapped in a handkerchief, the ear was very stiff
and dry and the hair all wore off it
and the man who cut the ear is bald now too and slicks
long strips of hair over the top of his head and he was beau
then. He was, all right. (*DIA* 270)

12

Dealing with Robert Cohn

Barry Gross

I had recently published an article in *Commentary* on literary anti-Semitism in the 1920s in which I had used Hemingway's portrait of Robert Cohn in *The Sun Also Rises* to contrast the absence of anti-Semitism in Sinclair Lewis' novels of the same period. The text seemed clear and the matter central. And it was not a matter of the stray anti-Semitic line or two—or 12—I'd come across in T.S. Eliot and Ezra Pound, William Carlos Williams, and e.e. cummings, or the sleazy but at least secondary Broadway Jews in John Dos Passos' *Manhattan Transfer* and F. Scott Fitzgerald's *The Great Gatsby,* or even important characters like Bloeckman in Fitzgerald's *The Beautiful and Damned* and Marsellus in Willa Cather's *The Professor's House,* Jews whose Jewishness arises from the ambivalent and ambiguous feelings of their creators and elicits ambivalent and ambiguous responses from the other characters. Robert Cohn is a very important character—the most important character some Hemingway experts have argued—in what many consider the great American writer's best novel, and all the major characters in the novel come to hate Cohn and to equate what is hateful about him with his being Jewish.

How natural it seems, even for me, to call Jake Barnes Jake, Mike Campbell Mike, Bill Gorton Bill, Lady Brett Ashley Brett, and how unnatural, even for me, to call Robert Cohn Robert! As unnatural as calling Jay Gatsby Jay, but for wholly different reasons: Nick calls Gatsby Gatsby out of respect, awe even—and he *is* distant and unknowable, but Jake, and everyone else, calls Cohn Cohn *to* distance him, *to* differentiate him, as in "I . . . prayed for everybody I thought of, Brett and Mike and Bill and Robert Cohn and myself" or "There they were—Brett and Mike and Robert Cohn." He was never just Robert or Bob or Bobby, never called by just his *Christian* name.

It was also clear to me that the anti-Semitism expressed in *The Sun Also*

Rises was Hemingway's as well as his characters' and that it was not to be shrugged off, as Carlos Baker had done. Hemingway's "occasional use of terms like *frog, wop, jig,* and *kike* is regrettable," Baker wrote in 1981, "though we ought to remind ourselves that—like Frost, Pound, and Eliot, to name a few—he was born into a time when such epithets were regrettably commonplace in most levels of American society" (Hemingway 1981, xvii). But why oughtn't we to expect our writers—our *great* writers—to rise above the regrettably commonplace of their society, especially writers who made careers out of being critics of—out of being thoroughly contemptuous of—all that *they* considered regrettably commonplace in American society? As we ought to expect our critics and scholars—like Baker—to be able, 35 years after the war, after the "liberation" of the camps, to distinguish between the use of terms like *frog* and *wop,* on one hand, and *kike,* on the other. (I won't get into *jig*: If I were Black, I think I'd take as much offense at *jig* as, as a Jew, I take at *kike.*)

Baker knows there's a difference: He feels no need to apologize for Hemingway's Francophobia or Italophobia or Afrophobia, but he does feel the need to apologize for his Semitophobia. "Hemingway's anti-Semitism was no more than skin deep," Baker claimed. "It was mainly a verbal habit rather than a persistent theme like that of Pound" (Hemingway 1981, xvii). (Where would apologists be without Pound, compared to whose obsessive and lifelong Jew baiting and Jew hating all other literary anti-Semitism must seem positively benign?)

Jeffrey Meyers opines that "Hemingway's fashionably hostile feelings about Jews probably began when he entered artistic circles in Paris and met wealthy Jews who lived . . . on unearned income and seemed to him to exploit, rather than contribute to, the world of art and literature" (1985, 72). That might account for his complaining to Maxwell Perkins about a Samuel Roth who had pirated *Ulysses* and was similarly pirating Hemingway's work—"[It] does not make me love the Jews any better" (Hemingway 1981, 225)—but not for his apologizing to Sherwood Anderson for seeming to be "lining up on the side of the smart jews [sic] like Ben Hecht" (Hemingway 1981, 206).

Hemingway's "fashionably hostile feelings about Jews"—I wish Meyers hadn't said "fashionably": that makes anti-Semitism seem as trivial and harmless as deciding what kind of drink to order or gun to shoot—probably began much earlier. Meyers asserts that Hemingway's "anti-Semitism [must have] developed after he had left Oak Park, for no Jews lived in that town" (1985, 72), but since when do Jews have to be actually present for anti-Semites to hate Jews? At any rate, Hemingway's boyhood friend Bill Smith—and one of the two acknowledged models for Bill Gorton, who rivals Mike Campbell as chief Jew baiter in *The Sun Also Rises*—places it much earlier: He told an interviewer that both he and "Hemingway . . . disliked some of the very well-heeled Jewish people who summered in Charlevoix, Michigan" (St. John 1969, 19).

The other acknowledged model for Bill Gorton, Donald Ogden Stewart, told the interviewer that he "was basically anti-Semitic in those days [in Paris], as probably also was Hemingway" (St. John 1971, 24). Yet Meyers thinks that Hemingway's "hostility, though sometimes quite vociferous, was actually quite mild, for he spent a good deal of time with Jewish friends [and] established professional relations with them" (1985, 72). That "for" clause is as questionable as Meyers' for-no-Jews-lived-in-Oak-Park one—employing Jews, spending time with Jews, even having Jewish friends is, contrary to what one should or might even want to expect, no proof against anti-Semitism. (Even Pound had a Jewish friend.) To prove his assertion Meyers lists 22 Jews Hemingway spent time with—"girls, writers, agents, publishers, painters, bullfighters, bibliographers, lawyers, fishermen, photographers, doctors, soldiers, art historians, journalists and critics"—by name: "Irene Goldstein, Gertrude Stein, Alfred Flechtheim, Harold Loeb, Jules Pascin, Nathan Asch, Dorothy Parker, Leon Fleischman, Donald Frede, Sidney Franklin, Louis Cohn, Maurice Speiser, Michael Lerner, Robert Capa, Milton Wolff, Werner Heilbrun, General Morris Cohen, Bernard Berenson, Harvey Breit, Lee Samuels, Leonard Lyons, and Clara Spiegel" (1985, 586).

His lawyer Maurice Speiser? Hemingway was "needling [him] with unseemly epithets" in 1939 (Baker 1969, 338). Writer Dorothy Parker? Hemingway wrote "a nasty poem" about her in which he made reference to "the Jewish cheeks of [her] plump ass" (Meyers 188–89). Art historian Bernard Berenson? Hemingway scorned him as a "kike patron of the arts" (Meyers 429). Agent Leon Fleischman, Liveright's literary scout who had come to Paris with a contract for Harold Loeb's novel *Doodab?* According to Baker,

Harold would not rest until Ernest had met Leon. Kitty [Cannell] was . . . doubtful, having noticed Hemingway's occasional anti-Semitic outbursts. But Harold's will prevailed and a meeting was arranged. . . . As usual, Ernest was carelessly dressed. He froze visibly when the genial Fleischman received them in a velvet smoking jacket. . . . Leon said pleasantly that he would be glad to read Ernest's stories. If he liked them, he would send them along to Liveright with a recommendation. Something in his tone hinted that this would be a great favor. At least, Hemingway took it so, and his demon pride rose darkly. But he said nothing until the evening ended and they went down the stairs. Then he exploded profanely, calling Fleischman a low-down kike and a string of other epithets. (1969, 133)

This outburst by Hemingway against a genial Jew in a velvet smoking jacket who offers to do him a favor suggests something much more regrettable than regrettable verbal habit: Such anti-Semitic outbursts have to come from somewhere, and somewhere deep beneath the skin. Kitty Cannell's version—"Hemingway exploded into profanity: 'Double god-damned kikes!' "—is even more disturbing, confirming another persistent verbal habit, Hemingway's tendency to pluralize, to generalize: *kikes,* not *kike,* as in "smart jews [sic] like Ben Hecht" and "[Samuel Roth] does not make me love the Jews any better" (1968, 7).

As for Harold Loeb, he heard Hemingway "mutter, 'That damned kike' "
(1967, 11). Did Loeb hear what he wanted to hear—or, rather, not hear what
he didn't want to hear—a mutter instead of an explosion, *that* kike rather than
all kikes, and, hence, not him? Cannell warned Loeb that he would one day
be the butt of Hemingway's anti-Semitic hostility, but Loeb assured her that
was not possible: "If Hemingway thought of me as a Jew he wouldn't have
spoken that way in front of me" (Cannell 7).

That *does* stand to reason, but anti-Semitic outbursts and reason do not go
hand in hand. Hemingway not only thought of Loeb as a Jew: He told Cannell,
"I'm putting everyone in [*The Sun Also Rises*] and that kike Loeb is the vil-
lain" (Meyers 158). According to Cannell, "Cohn *was* Harold Loeb and everything Hemingway disliked in Jews—which was everything" (1968, 9).

When *The Sun Also Rises* was published, Cannell was "so angry she took
to her bed for three days" (Baker 179). Hemingway had put her in it as Frances
Clyne, and he had attributed to her things he disliked in Jews: He had based
part of the portrayal on a "Jewish secretary who had accompanied Harold Loeb
and Alfred Kreymborg from America to found 'Broom' " (Cannell 9). (Arthur
Waldhorn calls attention to Frances Clyne's "Jewish-sounding [but not Jewish-
spelled] name") (1972, 239). But Cannell's deepest indignation, says Carlos
Baker, "was less for herself than for the virtual crucifixion of Harold Loeb"
(1969, 179). Loeb, who had been so sure that Hemingway did not think of him
as a Jew, "felt as if he had developed an ulcer. What had he done to evoke
such malice? Had he not defended Ernest against the charge of anti-Semitism?"
(Baker 179).

In 1926 Hemingway shrugged off the charge: "Why not make a Jew a bounder
in literature as well as in life? Do jews [sic] always have to be so splendid in
writing?" (Hemingway 1981, 240). But as late as 1932 he was still thinking
of Loeb as a Jew—and worse: warning a friend against hiring a guide named
A. J. Klein, he observed, "One thing about Klein is that name—Does Clark
say he's one of those Kleins—Germans are swell—kikes not so good—We don't
want him to turn out to be Harold Loeb" (Hemingway 1981, 353). (Is Frances
Clyne one of *those* Kleins, as Harold Loeb is surely one of those *kikes?*)

Did he *ever* change? In 1939 he blamed what he considered an "appalling,
stupid, childish, ignorant, sentimental, silly" adaptation of *The Fifth Column*
on "The Jews" (Baker 338). In 1951, however, when Edmund Wilson asked
Hemingway's permission to include his 1926 letter to Sherwood Anderson in
The Shores of Light, the letter in which Hemingway had referred to "the smart
jews [sic]," Hemingway asked Wilson to change "Jews" to "New York people": "I was speaking of Paul Rosenfeld and Waldo Frank," he told Wilson,
"but I did not mean to give any derogatory or anti-Semitic meaning as it would
read today" (Hemingway 1981, 732).

I don't doubt that in 1926 he *did* intend a derogatory and an anti-Semitic
meaning. But 25 years later, and after Auschwitz, he did at least realize *how*
it would read "today," which is more than can be said for other of Heming-

way's contemporaries, not only the always embarrassing but ever-available Ezra
Pound but the apparently sane e.e. cummings who as late as 1951 was publishing poetry like this:

> a kike is the most dangerous
> machine as yet invented
> by even yankee ingenu
> ity (out of a jew a few
> dead dollars and some twisted laws)

What *I* heard in Hemingway's 1951 denial to Wilson was a confession—
"Guilty as charged!" He could change what he wrote in a letter because of
how "it would read today"—and in so doing change what he meant or, rather,
what anyone could make of what he meant—but what he had written in *The
Sun Also Rises,* those slurs which give the novel its anti-Semitic meaning,
could not be changed.

Yet after the war it was. In 1949 someone at Bantam expunged from a
paperback edition of *The Sun Also Rises* most of the anti-Semitic slurs: the one
kike, all six *Jewish,* and six of the 11 *Jew* and *Jews.*

1. *Scribner:* Robert Cohn was a member, through his father, of one of the richest
   Jewish families in New York, and through his mother of one of the oldest.
   Bantam: Robert Cohn was a member, through his father, of one of the richest
   families in New York, and through his mother of one of the oldest.
2. *Scribner:* He had a hard, Jewish, stubborn streak.
   Bantam: He had a hard, stubborn streak.
3. *Scribner:* "Haven't you got some more Jewish friends you could bring along?"
   Bantam: "Haven't you got some more friends you could bring along?"
4. *Scribner:* "Brett's gone off with men but they weren't ever Jews."
   Bantam: "Brett's gone off with men but they weren't ever steers."
5. *Scribner:* "He's got this Jewish superiority so strong that he thinks the only emotion he'll get out of the fight will be being bored."
   Bantam: "He's got this superiority so strong that he thinks the only emotion he'll
   get out of the fight will be being bored."
6. *Scribner:* "Let him not get superior and Jewish."
   Bantam: "Let him not get superior."
7. *Scribner:* "That kike!"
   Bantam: "That Cohn!"
8. *Scribner:* "Take that sad Jewish face away."
   Bantam: "Take that sad face away."
9. *Scribner:* "What do you think it's meant to have that damned Jew about?"
   Bantam: "What do you think it's meant to have that damned Cohn about?"
10. *Scribner:* "I said if she would go about with Jews and bull-fighters and such peo-
    ple, she must expect trouble."

Bantam: "I said if she would go about with Cohn and bull-fighters and such people, she must expect trouble."

11. *Scribner:* "I gave her a fearful hiding about Jews and bull-fighters and all those sort of people."
    Bantam: "I gave her a fearful hiding about Cohn and bull-fighters and all those sort of people."

12. *Scribner:* "Brett's got a bull-fighter . . . but her Jew has gone away."
    Bantam: "Brett's got a bull-fighter . . . but Cohn has gone away."

13. *Scribner:* "She had a Jew named Cohn, but he turned out badly."
    Bantam: "She had a guy named Cohn, but he turned out badly."

    Soon after the Bantam paperback appeared, a German publisher who had published a German translation of the 1926 Scribner edition of *The Sun Also Rises* was officially accused of anti-Semitism by a court of de-Nazification: a comparison of his translation with the Bantam paperback, the front and back covers of which said it was "complete and unabridged" and the last page of which stated, "This Bantam book contains the complete text of the original edition—Not one word has been changed or omitted," revealed to anyone who could read that the German had transformed a racially innocent novel into a blatantly anti-Semitic diatribe, sufficiently blatant and sufficiently anti-Semitic to warrant, in postwar Germany, criminal prosecution (Randall 1962).

    "What has Saul Bellow—or Bernard Malamud or Philip Roth—to do with Hemingway, . . . the defender of anti-intellectualism and polite anti-Semitism?" Leslie Fiedler once asked. "They cannot be considered descendants, or even collateral connections of Hemingway, but are rather anti-Hemingways, avengers of the despised Robert Cohn, Jewish butt of *The Sun Also Rises*" (1970, 64). Placing myself in their company I thought to bury Papa (not, of course, *my* papa: my *yiddische* papa never drank or hunted, fished or fought). My models were Michael Gold who, in *Jews Without Money,* recalled "spend[ing] long daylight hours wondering why the Christians hated us so, and form[ing] noble plans of how [he] would lead valiant Jewish armies when [he] grew up, in defense of the Jews," and Alexander Portnoy who, "on the staff of the House subcommittee investigating the television quiz scandals," gets to prosecute Charles Van Doren, "the ur-WASP"—"Yes," he says, "I was one happy yiddel down there in Washington, a little Stern gang of my own, busily exploding Charlie's honor and integrity."

    But the more I reread *The Sun Also Rises*—the harder I reread it—the harder I found it to be certain—and it seemed very important to me to be certain—that it was the open-and-shut case of anti-Semitism I thought it was and—yes, I admit it!—wanted it to be. (Are there no open-and-shut cases about *anything* anymore, or is it one of the conditions—cop-outs?—of middle age that, as one squints through those particular bifocals, nothing *looks* open-and-shut?)

    I'd come up against lines and moments that, despite my assumptions and intentions, made me pause and gave me pause, especially the famous definition of moral and immoral behavior, the most oft-quoted lines from *The Sun Also Rises*, from all of Hemingway probably: "That was morality; things that made you disgusted afterward. No, that must be immorality." I hadn't realized before that what made Jake disgusted afterward—what made him feel immoral—was his enjoyment at the way Cohn was being mistreated. The full quote is: "I liked to see him hurt Cohn. I wished he would not do it, though, because afterward it made me disgusted at myself. That was morality; things that made you disgusted afterward. No, that must be immorality."

Jake, characteristically, immediately undercuts the importance of what he's said (it's not cool to be hot, to be passionate about things, to take things too seriously): "What a lot of bilge I could think up at night. What rot, I could hear Brett say. What rot!" But it's not bilge and it's not rot—Hemingway doesn't think so, Jake doesn't think so, and Brett doesn't think so: At the end of the novel Brett comes up with an almost identical definition of morality—"I feel rather damned good . . . deciding not to be a bitch." Nor, to my atheist ears, does Brett's similarly characteristic disclaimer—"It's sort of what we have instead of God"—detract from the definition's power and significance.

If the way the Jew is treated—mistreated—in *The Sun Also Rises*—and the enjoyment derived from his mistreatment—is the litmus test for immoral behavior, then the whole matter of anti-Semitism in *The Sun Also Rises* must be very complex indeed, far too complex for me to rush to judgment about it. I would have to fish that particular swamp longer and harder.

I a fisher of swamps, I who have never even *held* a fishing rod? I who was so very sure that I had nothing to do with Hemingway, was neither descendant nor collateral connection? I who was so very sure that I neither shared nor even really understood his metaphors, those objective correlatives for norms of national behavior which I denied were mine? Never could be mine. Never wanted to be mine.

But why had I been so sure? Why did I derive a secret pride from what I thought of as my unconnectedness to him and to the American culture I thought he stood for? Was it to forestall "being treated as a Jew," being "made [to] feel . . . different from anybody else," as Robert Cohn was at Princeton? Was it to forestall being called a kike, being told to take my damned Jewish face away, as Robert Cohn was some sixty summers ago? But that was another swamp I would have to fish another day.

References

Baker, Carlos. *Ernest Hemingway: A Life Story*. New York: Scribner, 1969.
Cannell, Kathleen. "Scenes with a Hero." *Connecticut Review* 2, no. 1 (1968): 5–9.
Fiedler, Leslie. *Waiting for the End*. New York: Stein and Day, 1970.
Gross, Barry. " 'Yours Sincerely, Sinclair Levy.' " *Commentary* 80, no. 6 (1985): 56–59.

Hemingway, Ernest. *Selected Letters 1917–1961*. Ed. Carlos Baker. New York: Scribner, 1981.

———. *The Sun Also Rises*. New York: Scribner, 1926.

Loeb, Harold. "Hemingway's Bitterness." *Connecticut Review* 1, no. 1 (1967): 7–24.

Meyers, Jeffrey. *Hemingway: A Biography*. New York: Harper & Row, 1985.

Randall, David A. " 'Dukedom Large Enough': Hemingway, Churchill, and the Printed Word." *The Papers of the Bibliographical Society of America* 56 (1962): 346–53.

St. John, Donald. "Interview with Hemingway's 'Bill Gorton.' Part II" *Connecticut Review* 3, no. 1 (1969): 5–23.

———. "Mr. and Mrs. Donald Ogden Stewart Abroad." *Connecticut Review* 4, no. 2 (1971): 23–36.

Waldhorn, Arthur. *A Reader's Guide to Ernest Hemingway*. New York: Farrar, Straus and Giroux, 1972.

IV

Hemingway in Italy

13

The Ritualization of Death and Rebirth: The Reconstruction of Frederic Henry

Robert E. Gajdusek

The ninth chapter of Ernest Hemingway's *A Farewell to Arms* is an important stage in the development of that richly structured work. In it, Hemingway establishes the symbolic and intellectual coordinates of his novel: he ventures into death to covertly explore in ritual and myth the significance of rebirth; he studies both the process and the sexual, religious, and mythic necessities for effective psychic rebirth.

That it is in the ninth chapter is itself an important fact, for numerology is as structural a device in this early work as it was to be in *To Have and Have Not, Across the River and into the Trees,* and *The Old Man and the Sea.* In this novel Catherine will announce the fact of her nine-month pregnancy at nine o'clock, in September, the ninth month. Such use of nine as a generative symbol, suggesting the beginning of a new cycle, appears frequently in the novels. In *The Sun Also Rises,* for example, Jake, beginning a new cycle in his experience, arrives in Bayonne at nine; after the metaphoric death of the male principle at the end of Book II, the third and last book begins as he awakens at nine. In this work, Catherine's nickname, Cat, allies her with the mythical cat whose life proverbially ends on its ninth cycle, Catherine's own fate. But in the cat/nine metaphor, Hemingway has joined the opposites of birth and death. That which gives birth at the end of the ninth cycle is joined to that which ends at this same moment: The moment of death has been made into a simultaneous moment of birth. Birth is forced back on death as it was in the first chapter when the soldiers who go toward their deaths are seen as women heavy with child, and as it will be in the last chapter when Catherine dies in childbirth. When Hemingway put his nick-named Cat together with Catherine, the saint who underwent her martyrdom on the wheel, he has joined cat and saint in one person and lined-out much of the intellectual action of the novel.

Later, in *For Whom the Bell Tolls*, his Maria in her nickname Rabbit will bind together the eternal reproductive natural cycles to the virgin of immaculate conception. Hemingway's ubiquitous cats—whether the 57 that Norberto Fuentes recorded that Hemingway kept at the Finca Vigía outside Havana (1984, 79), or the one who represents fertility amidst sterility in "Cat in the Rain," or Boise, the one who tries to reconcile Thomas Hudson to life after the death of his trinity of sons in *Islands in the Stream*—continually express the healing synthesis of opposites.[1] In *this* chapter, where Frederic experiences death-in-life, where he undergoes death and cyclical resurrection, opposites are joined, even as they are when love is thrust into the midst of war. These oppositions, studied in dialectical opposition as well as in synthesis, prepare the reader for the antagonisms and loves of lovers and the battles and capitulations of warriors. *A Farewell to Arms* exists to force love and war together. This is partly because Hemingway was both warrior and lover. His ironic recognition, however, is that each may become its opposite: Love, that tends to bond lovers together creatively, and war that tends to oppose warriors destructively—love and war are the archetypal sources of birth and death—may invert, so that love may beget death (as it does for Catherine and Frederic) and war create birth (as it seems to in the imagery of the "pregnant" soldiers and in Frederic's multiple violent rebirths that the novel studies).

Frederic's wounding suffered in his night journey to the other side, and his return from that wounding bearing the special knowledge of that other kingdom, is fashioned of the classical coordinates of all such mythic journeys: The ninth chapter is, as completely as is "Indian Camp," a traumatic exposure of the culture hero to the mysteries, and his subsequent return with that wisdom. But Hemingway has carefully prepared for this crossover and its religious and mythic and psychic meaning on the pages of the immediately preceding eighth chapter when, in describing Frederic Henry's reconnoitering visit to what will be the scene of his life/death encounter, he has him recognize in the external world the necessary syntheses and reconciliations that he must, in the ninth chapter, at risk of death, psychically experience. In the preceding chapter, in elaborate landscape description that is filled with religious overtones, he has Frederic Henry ascend into the hills while the dust is rising under the wheels—that image in itself a sharp, controlled metaphor (taken from *The Sun Also Rises* and the first chapter of *this* novel) speaking of death and resurrection caught in cyclical recurrence.

His physical journey is one that climbs high to hills to confront distant peaks in the snow and then descends low to valleys to study the waters, farms, and fruit and produce there: high sterility and low fecundity. He takes his four cars up into the hills, always conscious of the three he can see and not see. It is equally a journey where he must weave back and forth between the two sides of the river, between the heights and the lowlands, actively stitching them together in his movements as he observes imaginatively from his vantage above the turning wheels. He thinks, as he drives, of the two facing but separated armies, and he considers the water in flow as well as its pebbly bed. In sun and then in shadow, he looks forward and back, to the north and to the south, and above and below. He is alert to the lines *and* curves of the river and, in the valley, to the *straight* line of the railroad bridge as well as the *arched* stone bridges. He considers the *lines* of trees that lead his sight to the flowing river, and later lets the trees lead his sight to the *line* of the river. The road goes back and forth—there are straight ways and rounded turns—and, climbing and descending, he considers the high white loveliness of the mountains and, below, the low green darkness. On the journey, he is responsive to road line, river line, tree line, crest line, snowline, and battlelines between armies, as well as to both sides of the river, of the road, of the bridges, and those taken by armies in the larger picture of war. But that whole chapter had been based on the necessity to separate or divide Catherine and Frederic Henry in their love—the two lovers who have attempted in their love to become one indivisible whole—as he, as soldier, held by war, goes toward the front to consider the divided landscape.

As Frederic goes towards this front to consider such *divisions* in landscape, Catherine, staying behind, gives him a Saint Anthony in a capsule to wear. An interval separates his spilling the saint into his hand and then spilling him back into the capsule: In it, he watches his driver take a similar Saint Anthony from under his tunic with his right hand while his left holds the wheel. To emphasize the split/synthesis of spirit and flesh (hand on the saint or hand on the wheel), Hemingway writes, "His right hand left the wheel." [2] In *To Have and Have Not,* he will similarly play with words: "He turned to the right as he left the dock" (Hemingway 1934, 146). Play of this sort is a sure index to the density of the intellectual structure being built. But this play, with the encapsulated saint, is the paradigm of the spirit's separation from and return to the flesh Hemingway studies in the ninth chapter when Frederic feels his soul slide out of his body and then slide (spill?) back again. All the landscape dynamics of the eighth chapter are preliminary to the event they are meant to focus upon: the death and resurrection, life/death experience of the wounded hero, that he undergoes in the next chapter.

In the ninth chapter, Hemingway develops a consistent imagery of birth that runs concomitantly with the facts and imagery of death. Carefully, he sets the stage for a caesarian birth, no less difficult than the one in "Indian Camp" if more covert. His first sentence reads: "The road was crowded and there were screens of corn-stalk and straw matting on both sides and matting over the top so that it was like the entrance at a circus or a native village." Few have noted how inappropriate an imagery of circuses and aboriginal simplicity is to the frontlines of battle. It is, however, necessary to Hemingway, who is establishing at the very beginning of his ninth chapter an imagery of cycles of nativity and of return to primitive sources. "Native" speaks of natal. The corn-stalk screens additionally speak of Demeter/Ceres and Persephone, of birth and death and cyclical renewal, of seasonal fruition and the birth of crops, as well as of the death and reaping of the harvest. Hemingway lets us see that this entrance to the place of wounding/death experience is patently a return to the womb itself. As they drive slowly down the straw matting–covered tunnel to emerge in a bare cleared space sunken below the level of the riverbank, they confront holes in the earth that are filled with infantry. These men in the holes will variously emerge to live and die, and some will die *in* them—a foreshadowing of Catherine's child's death in the womb later in the novel—and others will need assistance to be lifted from them and brought to life. The uterine journey inward down the life/death covered tunnel (made of materials that speak both of death and of life and the cycles of life and death) is one that has literary precursors, of which Hemingway could scarcely have been unaware. It is perhaps only as we reread Melville's "Tartarus of Maids" that we discover that we are *not* being taken on a tour of a paper mill but rather on an expedition through the biology, the reproductive organs, of a woman—and *these,* indeed, *are* the Tartarus of maids. In Hemingway's biological journey, the holes in the earth where the doctors function are described as the ovens of this setting which was a brickyard. The sense of the oven as a hot source out of which emerge fully formed and created "bricks" is part of the total structure, and Hemingway twice emphasizes a distinction between the straw matting of the tunnel and the life-endorsed "obstetric" ovens from which may emerge living men restored to life. In the main "oven," Frederic notes the instruments shining in the light and the basins. This is the oven to which he must be brought after he is wounded and before he is finally delivered to the world. But before rebirth, he must first undergo wounding and death. In the wounding, he knows he is "dead," and then he feels himself "slide back." The shock of this moment is carefully described as a "blastfurnace door . . . swung open." Hemingway so describes it to suggest the trauma of a man being destroyed *or* that of an infant being expelled from the womb, and he describes it in terms that carefully and distinctly relate it to the "oven" from which he will later emerge, fully restored to life. When Frederic goes on to exclaim that it is a mistake "to think you just died," the bewildering "just" is a real clue to one major insight of the novel: birth as death, death as birth. This journey into death and back again into life is the replication in miniature of the mythic heroic journey to the other side that the true hero must make—the rebirth-return as important as the death journey in the archetype of heroic adventure.[3]

Much of the birth imagery of the chapter is associated with the feminine reproductive system of the mother, which is associated with death, darkness and disorder, but *this* imagery is annealed to a sustained parallel imagery of the father/obstetrician role in that "delivery," which is associated with light, control, and spiritual resurrection/redemption. The two threads of imagery together produce an imagery of a doubly endorsed rebirth/restoration, one part of which is physical, the other spiritual: however, it is the spiritual resurrection which seems to save Frederic from encirclement in the womb, the fate his son suffers.

The birth/rebirth imagery takes the reader on an internal journey to the womb itself where primitive feeding occurs. It is a world of oppositions, where there are interchanges but no resolution, recognition of opposition but no definition, where passion and reason are mixed. Life in that dugout hole is a sitting on the earth or a crouching in darkness. This point is made as a small lighter is lit and passed around by these men whose backs are most frequently described in the telling Hemingway phrase of "against the wall," but the first words said by one of the soldiers are "Why didn't we see?" Frederic, saying, "I'll go and *see* now," prepares to go back to the lighted world of the doctors he has left, and when he goes out, it is to "look" and to "see." The point is made that his men can either stay where they are *or* "look around," but sight is not a function of the cave.[4]

It is in this almost sightless sunken hole that the men are nurtured and prepared for either life or death. There Passini dies, and from there three others emerge naturally under their own power. Frederic has to be forceably lifted and brought out and so brought to the doctors in the light who subsequently "cut" him free and act to set him forward on his journey into the world. Hemingway uses the word "severing" to describe the doctor's action; then he writes, "The flesh was cut," and this child/man of questionable paternity is then carried toward the waiting world, undergoing a baptism of blood as he goes.

Hemingway carefully lets us see the intricate relationship between father and son in this victory over death and process. It is described as a spiritual victory of paternal expertise and definition over darkness and chaos in a maternal realm where dirt rains down and where multiple inversions and dissolutions are recommended. The major who is responsible for the food Frederic receives and the medical attention he is given, and who has great expectations for Frederic, is one of a group of three doctors Frederic Henry knows. To emphasize his alliance with the paternal doctor ideal, later established in Valentini, the major is given the same rank and upturned mustaches as Valentini and bears wound stripes to tell of his own successful encounters with death. It is with this trinity of doctors that Frederic first shares spirits in this lighted place amidst surrounding darkness. When he later returns to this same lighted arena to get food for his men, he finds the major sitting on a box, and it is then he sees, as the major again offers him spirits, the instruments "shining in the light" and the basin and stoppered bottles.[5] For his men, Frederic is given pasta asciutta and cheese, pointedly retrieved from a dark hole in the back and out of sight, which he receives in a basin. This separation of the cheese/pasta from the alcohol/light is a careful separation exercised in that lighted oven/hole in the earth and speaks of the demarcations and sunderings overseen by the father figures. Later, after Frederic's wounding, after he has officiated via that basin with cheese and wine at a black mass communion offered by him as perverted priest to his men, the religious significance that Hemingway has been developing about the trinity of doctors with their implements, vaguely suggesting a mass to sustain the spirit as well as an operation to save/restore the body, is established.

After Frederic is wounded, he is unable to move, and so he must be lifted out: "Some one took hold of me under the arms and somebody else lifted my legs." Before he is lifted, he notes that a trinity has survived: that the explosion that almost meant his death has effectively removed from him the contaminating fourth, Passini: "That left three." Being carried to the oven where three doctors await, he is twice dropped. The imagery of his wounding is that of death/resurrection, and that of his lifting is the classical imagery of Christ's Descent from the Cross. The subsequent falls on the journey to the oven suggest the stages of the cross on Calvary. That this imagery seems reversed should not trouble a critic who has studied similarly frequent ironic inversions of religious ritual in *The Sun Also Rises, Green Hills of Africa,* and "A Clean, Well-Lighted Place." Such inversion is central to Hemingway's statement: Frederic is, after all, coming back to life through a sort of rebirth and not being brought to heaven through death.[6]

The spiritual/obstetric part of the process of spiritual/physical rebirth takes place at the main oven, formerly dominated by the three spirit-giving doctors. Here the question of paternity is the first question raised. First Frederic is called the legitimate son of President Wilson, and then he is described as "The only son of the American Ambassador." At this frontline aid station, he now confronts a *new* trinity of totally admirable paternal role models. Later, the reader will see Frederic in Milan confronting three inadequate nurses (mother figures), then three rear-echelon impotent ineffective false doctors (surrogate fathers)— all before Valentini arrives to look after him. Now, at the ovens, the first male of three who take charge of Frederic is the tall British driver who has arrived there with three ambulances. He is active, effective, concerned, and spirited. He steps carefully among the wounded, speaks perfect Italian, bypasses procedure and protocol by seizing control of events, and establishes Frederic's fictional paternity to give him special status and attention, as he also anticipates Frederic's subsequent needs. Next, the little Italian major oversees the operating room, readily speaks French, and shows resilience as he accommodates to the driver's rearranged priorities, and active control as he continues to operate on others while accepting Frederic. A third officer takes Frederic on his operating table. As he dictates and talks while investigating, probing, injecting and cutting Frederic, he demonstrates the easy reconciliation of humanity and expertise, efficiency and humor, objective curiosity and concern, speed and accuracy, that mark the humanity of the Hemingway hero: his hands move "fast," his bandages come "taut and sure." He offers brandy (spirits) to Frederic, has a cross put on both Frederic's legs, and to him Frederic offers his three exclamations, "Christ, yes!" and, twice, "Good Christ!"

It is part of Hemingway's sustained iconography that as Frederic emerges from under the care/concern of these three "fathers," he comes out to have the sergeant-adjutant kneel down "beside me where I lay." The chapter ends as he is baptized by the stream of blood that falls upon him from above, from the man who dies above him in the slings.

Throughout the novel the struggle between worldliness and the priest, as to who is to be mocked or to have authority at the mess, establishes the alternatives of mess and mass, an ambiguity that suggests the alternative meanings of these feasts, life as biological process or life as spiritual sacramentalized event. What Frederic first brings to his men to share in communion together are *Macedonias*—but he brings them to men who prophesy the road will be a *"mess"* and who prefer to eat, and it is to honor their request that Frederic gets *"mess"* tins and food. They have effectively converted the mass to mess.[7] However, as Frederic prepares the food for his men in the dugout, he carefully separates the dust and dirt from the cheese while Gavuzzi at his side hands him the basin. He then elevates the cheese and macaroni. Hemingway writes:

> I . . . lifted. A *mass* loosened.
> "Lift it high, Tenente."
> I lifted it to arm's length and the strands cleared. I lowered it into the mouth, sucked and snapped in the ends. [my emphasis].

He describes the taking of the food: "They were all eating, holding their chins close over the basin, tipping their heads back." This profane communion mass, where Frederic officiates as the profane priest, seems to be a challenging fusion of mass and mess that is answered immediately by three celestial comments from the skies. The communion is of cheese and wine, and although Frederic and his men eat four times, he drinks wine three. As he takes this profane communion the second time, "Something landed" and "shook the earth." Returning to their eating, a second explosion "shakes the earth," but then precisely as Frederic eats the cheese and drinks the wine once more, the "blast-furnace door" swings open and the third explosion strikes, the one that is his "death"/wounding. There are actually four pagan communions answered by three blows from heaven. The last of these almost fatally wounds Frederic and does so wound Passini, of the four men the unbeliever-anarchist who would break down the definitions that Frederic tries to erect; the man who, refusing to attack across into, or intellectually venture into, the side of his enemy, would wish to bring Frederic over to *his* "side," to "convert" him. Dying, Passini, true to character to the end, cries out to both "purest lovely Mary" and to "Mama mama mia," avatars of both spiritual and biological birth. Passini refuses to accept the patriarchal terms of battle, duty, orders, uncomprehended if received logics, or to go out and go over and across the frontline to meet perhaps death on the other side because of them, and he is identified with those who endorse anarchy, sexual prowess, with being "Always with the girls," and with the loss of property rights and with the overthrow/dispossession of the father—the fathers of those shot for cowardice lose their civil rights "and cannot even vote." He is the one who says "I do not believe," and then, "I don't believe" and exclaims that "even the peasants know better than to believe in a war." The argument between Frederic and the unbelieving Passini is basically between dualism and synthesis. Battlelines or the dissolution of battlelines is the question—and Passini, whose argument endorses the both/and ambiguities of the mothering cave, dies in that womb enclosure crying out in his last words "mama mia," while Frederic is separated from and borne away from it *to* the fathers and *by* them cut loose and carried clear. His cry has been neither to "mama" nor "Mary," but rather "Oh God . . . get me out of here." It is the doctors in the light who "cut" him free and act to set him forward on his journey into the world.[8]

The religious imagery has a double function, to sacramentalize Frederic Henry's relations with the world—and this explains the perverse inverted mass at which he officiates as priest, as well as the redemptive spiritual iconography associated with the three-in-one father image—and to establish his unique role as the sacrificed and resurrected god/child returned to the world. That Frederic is last seen in the chapter being raised to the "top" by wheels is part of a pattern that clearly exists throughout Hemingway's work, and it exists to name Hemingway's very particular religious belief: his Christ/Saviour imagery—lavishly overlaid on Santiago, Cantwell, Robert Jordan, Harry Morgan, and Steve Ketchel, among others of his protagonists—always shows these redeemed redeemers as resurrected to an eternal return. They come to terms with and religiously redemptively *necessarily* accept the cycles of life, the wheels upon which they discover the still point. They pointedly do *not* disappear into isolating and abstract heavens. The novel ends as Frederic, having seen Catherine in death as a fixed "statue," at last walks away "in the rain" Catherine has feared. The rain is the icon of those cycles which include death (and also the birth because of which she dies) and so deny the changeless state she had desired and apparently attained. Colonel Cantwell, possessor of the unchanging portrait of Renata, carefully dies on wheels in the back seat of his automobile; Robert Jordan, who has found his eternal Now in orgasmic love, whose ecstasy moves the earth, who has discovered a lifetime in 72 hours, in his last gestures acknowledges and accepts the fallen pine needles beneath him that speak of the cycles of the *un*changing evergreen; Harry Morgan, after sacrificially hanging on "the wheel," accepts the "roll" of the eternal cyclic moon-driven sea that he has been throughout his life resisting; and Santiago lies with his Christlike wounded hands outspread on the bed of sleep from which he will arise in the morning. As emphatically as D.H. Lawrence, who in *The Man Who Died* mated his Christ with a Priestess of Isis that she might become pregnant by Him, Hemingway rewrites received orthodox belief to refuse his nature gods an escape into the skies: bound to the wheel, like the sun that must forever "also rise," they endorse spirit bound to life, where eternity can be found in time, and "always" perpetually rediscovered.

It is important to note the many details of "Indian Camp" that resurface in this chapter. To see this is to know the boy/man here but another portrait of the youth there—for both undergo a crossover night journey to a wounding in a primitive dark place where a caesarean birth, accomplished finally only by

virtue of the sight, light, tools, and technique of a father figure, with his basin
beside him, brings out of darkness to light a child whose paternity is covertly
questioned, and where the host that is elevated—in "Indian Camp" the newborn child itself; in *A Farewell,* the cheese in the mothering hole that sets in
motion the rebirth—is related to the release of the child from womb darkness
to life. In "Indian Camp," it is Nick himself who is the surrogate newborn (or
reborn) given to life at the end of the story. There, he goes forward into a new
day with a sense of immortality, partly achieved through his father's command
and partly the result of the reconciliations he himself has made between two
discrete realms—while he endorses the cyclical rings that spread about him and
envelop him. Frederic Henry makes comparable affirmations, having visited
both sides of existence, and debated and observed their differences. In "Indian
Camp," a second father figure dies in a bunk above. We might ask just whose
is the blood that falls at the end of this chapter upon Frederic from the unseen
anonymous man who dies above him in the slings. I would like to know if that
detail was added to the novel or written after Hemingway's own father's suicide.

Notes

1. The imagery of Chapter XXXVII will express Frederic's rowing across Lago
Maggiore to Switzerland as a crucifixion/death/rebirth, and when the journey has at last
been successfully made to Brissago, Frederic exclaims, "I couldn't be any happier,"
and immediately "A fat gray cat with tail that lifted like a plume crossed the floor to
our table and curved against my leg to purr each time she rubbed. I reached down and
stroked her" (p. 279). This cat who both crosses and curves, reconciles death and life
and welcomes Frederic and *Cat*herine to their momentary idyll in Switzerland.

2. Throughout this chapter I quote briefly from Chapter IX. I do not, however, include page references to a specific edition for these, since the text I quote from is at
once so readily and variously available and so very circumscribed.

3. There is a series of watery deaths and rebirths structured for Frederic throughout
the novel, and after each he is seemingly offered the alternative of one or the other of
two surrogate "fathers." After his wounding, he is offered the services of either Rinaldi, who calls him "Baby," or the priest, who is truly a padre. After his emergence
from the Tagliamento after his escape from execution, the imagery of his emergence
from the river as he crawls ashore is that of a newborn child, and he is soon under the
aegus of either the barman or Count Greffi. After his night crossing of Lago Maggiore,
where he is given to the reader in the imagery of Christ crucified, he emerges from the
lake and steps ashore to come under the alternative care/concern of the two quarreling
customs officials, who insist on opposing alternatives for the direction his life will take.

4. It is interesting that the "lighter," which is described as shaped like "a Fiat
radiator," does not give light, although it is associated with radiation, only fire for the
linear cigarettes. The men in the holes hand "around" the lighter and twist their cigarettes to keep the tobacco from spilling. Such circulating of the light and cycling of the
line should not be missed.

5. The square, sun-struck top of Kilimanjaro is but one of many descriptions in

Hemingway that identify the box (square), light, and spirits found *here* as related to the Father principle.

6. Students of film may remember Elia Kazan's brilliant reversal of the order of execution, death, the Pietà, and Stations of the Cross imagery in his *On the Waterfront,* created by a similar need to reverse redemptive imagery and ritual.

7. It is Frederic's men who prophesy "They'll shell the ____ out of us" and that the "road will be a mess." Hemingway through such remarks focuses on the virtue/heroism of holding in/holding fast as opposed to the moral and physical self-soilure of spilling or not being able to hold fast. He lets the reader see that these men, whose coordinates are mouth and anus, have yielded the spirit for the flesh: "soul" and "mass" are the antitheses of "shit" and "mess."

8. This opposition between Passini and Frederic, suggesting their alternative devotions, involves significant inversion: physical Passini uses words (abstractions) to destroy faith and spirit; mental Frederic uses food to restore faith.

<h2>References</h2>

Fuentes, Norberto. *Hemingway in Cuba.* Trans. Consuelo E. Corwin. Secaucus, NJ: Lyle Stuart Inc., 1984.

Hemingway, Ernest. *A Farewell to Arms.* 1929. New York: Scribner, 1969.

———. "Indian Camp." *In Our Time.* 1925. New York: Scribner, 1958.

———. *To Have and Have Not.* 1934. New York: Scribner, 1965.

Lawrence, D[avid] H[erbert]. *The Man Who Died.* 1929. First published as *The Escaped Cock; St. Mawr and the Man Who Died.* New York: Vintage, 1953.

Melville, Herman. "The Paradise of Bachelors and the Tartarus of Maids." *Stories, Poems, and Letters by the Author of Moby Dick: Herman Melville.* Ed. R.W.B. Lewis. New York: Dell, 1962.

14

Hemingway's Study of Impending Death: *Across the River and into the Trees*

Charles M. Oliver

The common critical judgment on *Across the River and into the Trees* (*ART* 1950) is that it is not a very good book. And most of the criticism has taken a biographical stance, insisting with varying degrees of disappointment—including anger and contempt—that Hemingway merely wished the fulfillment of his love story and that, therefore, he wrote with diminished talent. Colonel Cantwell has been referred to as a "joke," a "caricature," a "comic figure," a "poor soul who, with romantic self-delusions . . . takes himself far too seriously" (Vanderbilt 1965, 285). The book has been called "self-serving" (Kobler 1985, 145); the tone has been called "mawkish" and the dialogue "contrived" (Whitlow 1984, 40).

Perhaps the two most important deviations from this standard criticism are *The Divine Comedy* interpretations, one or two of which are extremely important works of literary criticism, and the deviation that argues the novel as tragedy—both may be the best starting points for future work on this novel.[1] The purpose of this chapter, however, is to make two interpretive points, one which has been suggested before but not with the emphasis it deserves and the other which has not been made previously.

First, Colonel Cantwell has had four heart attacks when the novel opens "two hours before daylight" on Sunday morning, Cantwell recalling the fourth (which had occurred the day before) in flashback two-thirds of the way through the novel; and then he has the attacks which kill him on Sunday evening after the return to time-present near the end of the book. Chapter I and the last six chapters are in time-present (Chapter I takes place on Sunday morning, the last six chapters on Sunday evening), while Chapters II through XXXIX take place in Cantwell's remembering as he thinks about the recent events leading to and including his Venice weekend and up to the final goodbye to Renata on Saturday afternoon. Neither Renata nor Venice appear before the reader in time-present, but only as they are recalled by Cantwell in flashback. In fact, the physical setting of the novel is not Venice at all, but the duck blinds in the marshes at the mouth of the Tagliamento River, the "long low stone house by the side of the canal," where Cantwell and Alvarito meet at the end of the day, and the road back toward Venice as far as Alvarito's villa. But the more important setting is not physical, but spiritual—or at least mental—in the mind of Colonel Cantwell as he is able to transcend the physical catastrophe taking place in his body.[2]

Second, Barone Alvarito *does* appear in time-present, suggesting a more important role for him than has previously been acknowledged and, therefore, the motif of the relationship between Renata and Alvarito and the understanding that develops about that relationship among the three main characters.

If one accepts these two interpretive points, the novel then becomes the story of a man struggling heroically to control the terms of his own impending death. The duck-hunting trip is the frame-vehicle through which Hemingway creates a character whose recent life moves before his memory as he awaits, with sure knowledge, the next heart attack and death. Cantwell is not at all a caricature or authorial wish-fulfillment, but a fully drawn persona 50 years old, selecting very carefully both the things he does on his last weekend and the things he remembers about it during the Sunday duck-hunt. Both the actions and the memory of them are carefully controlled so that he can feel within, at least, that he faces up to death with dignity. Wirt Williams says that by transcending the catastrophe of death, Cantwell "defines and elevates himself to [a] truly tragic stature" (Williams 1981, 170).

The first mention of Cantwell's impending death comes as a transitional device which stimulates his remembering and sends the novel into its flashback sequence. Chapter I ends with Cantwell trying to hold back his anger at the boatman because the Colonel remembers that *this* hunt could be his last:

I do not understand him [the boatman] but I must not let him ruin it. I must keep it entire and not let him do it. Every time you shoot now can be the last shoot and no stupid son of a bitch should be allowed to ruin it. Keep your temper, boy, he told himself. (*ART* 7)

Cantwell is angry because the boatman is interfering with that "control" the colonel wants to maintain during his last few hours. The remembering begins and ends with a repetition of the "boy" reference. Chapter II begins, "But he was not a boy" (*ART* 8) and near the beginning of Chapter XL, Cantwell is brought fully back to the reality of time-present by the sight of ducks coming in:

Boy, hell, he thought. You beat-up old bastard. But look at them [the ducks] come now. (*ART* 279)

"Boy, hell" connects to the reference at the beginning of Chapter II and so emphasizes both Cantwell's concentration on the intervening events of his remembering and the frame for the novel's time structure.

Perhaps even more important to indicating this "frame" structure are the verb tenses. Cantwell's time-present memories are, appropriately, told by the narrator in past-tense verbs; the narrator is telling the story of a man's attempt to control the terms of his own death. But at the beginning of Chapters II and III there are past-perfect verbs that shift the story into its flashback sequence: "he *had taken* enough mannitol hexanitrate," "The surgeon *had been* quite skeptical" (*ART* 8), "he *had driven* down from Trieste" (*ART* 12), etc. Hemingway does not continue the past-perfect narrative because once he has established the idea that events are taking place only in Cantwell's memory, it isn't necessary to continue what would eventually become an obtrusive verb tense structure. It is argued that the narrative point-of-view is confused, but the very subtlety of this tense shift makes it unlikely that Hemingway made a mistake. That is, his mistakes were mistakes of facts and not of emotional responses to actions. Further, the narrative point-of-view is not at all confused if one sees Cantwell as the narrator and hero of his own narration—like Walt Whitman in *Song of Myself,* but told in the third person.

Cantwell's memories are quite naturally focused on the more pleasant things which have happened to him, particularly his love for Renata, his military career, and his awareness of Alvarito's importance. But underlying all these thoughts is the one thought which dominates without being obtrusive either to himself or to the reader—the thought of impending death. In fact, the point here is precisely that the dominant element is so unobtrusive that readers simply miss the novel's larger meaning.

The idea that he must keep his temper reminds him of his Thursday visit to the doctor's office where the Colonel had been given a "clean" bill of health by a skeptical army surgeon. Cantwell had taken mannitol hexanitrate to speed up his blood flow in order to pass the doctor's test, but the doctor was not fooled:

don't you ever run into anything, or let any sparks strike you, when you're really souped up on nitroglycerin. They ought to make you drag a chain like a high-octane truck. . . .
    "Your cardiograph was wonderful, Colonel. It could have been that of a man of twenty-five. It might have been that of a boy of nineteen." (*ART* 9)

The doctor knows that Cantwell had forced the cardiograph to look good so he would be allowed the trip to Venice. Cantwell knew he did not have long to live (he had already had three heart attacks), and he wanted the trip as a kind of final farewell to the things he had most enjoyed in life. And it is important to see that in spite of all that has been said about the role of Renata, Cantwell chooses to spend the last day of his life not with her but with Alvarito and the other duck hunters. Further, the reader doesn't even meet Renata, even in

Cantwell's memory of the weekend events, until Chapter IX (*ART* 80) when he recalls their Friday evening meeting at Harry's Bar—one-quarter of the way through the novel.

The first real indication of Cantwell's impending death comes (in his remembering) as he arrived at Harry's Bar. He recalls saying, as he looked at the church of Santa Maria del Giglio,

Damn, I wish I might walk around this town all my life. All my life, he thought. What a gag that is. A gag to gag on. A throttle to throttle you with. Come on, boy, he said to himself. No horse named Morbid ever won a race.

Besides, he thought, . . . I don't feel so badly. There is only the buzzing. . . .

Then, as he climbed, he felt the twinges. . . . There's a lot of oxygen in this air, he thought, as he faced into the wind and breathed deeply.

Then he was pulling open the door of Harry's bar and was inside and he had made it again, and was at home. (*ART* 77–79)

The first *direct* statement of Cantwell's impending death is handled matter-of-factly by Renata as she and Cantwell discussed it over drinks at Harry's. Cantwell had told her she looked sad:

"I am not, really [she said]. I am as happy as I ever am. Truly. Please believe me, Richard. But how would you like to be a girl nineteen years old in love with a man over fifty years old that you knew was going to die?" (*ART* 91)

Later, he compared his own heart attacks with his old army friend, the *Gran Maestro*. Cantwell had asked him about his health and learned of his friend's "small cardiac condition." The *Gran Maestro* had indicated two attacks:

"I'm ahead of you," the Colonel said. "But let's not be macabre. Ask Donna Renata if she wishes more of this excellent wine."

"You did not tell me there were more," the girl said. "You owe it to me to tell me."

"There has been nothing since we were together last." (*ART* 138)

Renata knows Cantwell is going to die, and she had worried that he had not told her about every attack. On the other hand, he is more objective about it, certainly more controlled about his impending death than she, at least in his biased remembering of the scene. And before Renata had gone home that night (Friday), Cantwell had asked her if she would call him in the morning:

"Yes. But why do you always wake so early?"

"It is a business habit."

"Oh, I wish you were not in that business, and that you were not going to die."

"So do I," said the Colonel. "But I'm getting out of the business." (*ART* 160)

His business is the army, but he's not talking about retiring; he's talking about death.

Still thinking about Saturday's events, he remembers his fourth heart attack, after he had called Renata in the morning:

> Coming out of the telephone booth he suddenly did not feel good and then he felt as though the devil had him in an iron cage, built like an iron lung or an iron maiden, and he walked, gray-faced, to the concierge's desk and said, in Italian, "Domenico, Ico, could you get me a glass of water, please?"
>
> . . . and he took four tablets of the type that you take two, and he continued resting as lightly as a hawk rests. (*ART* 196)

This is apparently the most powerful attack yet. He remembers he had rested "lightly and without illusion" and that he had given an envelope to the concierge, to be "called for either by myself, in person, or in writing, or by the person you have just put that call through to." He had been careful to see that in the event of his death, Renata would be given the envelope.

When Renata had asked him where he would like to be buried, he made a "quick decision," saying, "Up in the hills. . . . On any part of the high ground where we beat them" (*ART* 228). And, when Renata told him she would like to go along when he dies, he had scolded her:

> "That is the one thing we do alone. Like going to the bathroom."
>
> "Please do not be rough."
>
> "I meant that I would love to have you with me. But it is very egotistical and an ugly process." (*ART* 228)

Both Renata and Cantwell had shown awareness of his impending death in nearly everything he remembers they had said to one another. Time is pushing Cantwell as much as it does Robert Jordan in *For Whom the Bell Tolls*. Jordan, however, knows only that he *may* soon be killed, whereas Cantwell knows he *will* soon die.

All of this, then, is Hemingway's attempt to recreate for the reader the true felt emotion of Cantwell's final hours. At the highest level, it is a psychological study of the hero dying. Cantwell is like any other hero beyond his heroism and no longer a hero except to his close friends who are still glad of his presence, yet the hero who sells his soul by the minute to those events which not even his clear memory can imitate or recover. The lost heroism is in the surface meaning of the story, within the memory of the protagonist. But the emotions which Cantwell feels and attempts to control as he lives his last few hours are in the seven-eighths of the iceberg. Ironically, and for the only time in Hemingway, the knowledge that does not have to be stated is closer to the reader than the knowledge that is. The emotions which result from Cantwell's attempt to control the circumstances of his own death are the very emotions the reader hopes will result whatever the circumstances of *his* own death.

Beneath the death theme, which is closely tied to the whole structural framework (that is, Cantwell's remembering of these things), moves another, key element. There are four passages which suggest the developing relationship between Renata and Alvarito and which tie directly to the theme of Cantwell's attempting to control the terms of his impending death.

Renata and Alvarito were childhood friends:

> "We knew each other as children, . . . But he was about three years older. He was born very old." (*ART* 130)

Alvarito and Cantwell are also "good friends," and it was Alvarito who had invited Cantwell on the duck hunt. The Italian is in another boat as the novel opens and is waiting by the fire in the stone house when Cantwell lands his boat at the end of the book. Alvarito's presence before the reader in the book's only time-present scenes lends emphasis to his role as the third in the triangle of mutual love and respect about which Cantwell thinks and about which he talks indirectly with Alvarito late Sunday.

While Renata and Cantwell were having dinner together at Harry's Bar, the Barone walked up to their table. It is the reader's introduction to Alvarito, and he is described by the omniscient narrator of Cantwell's memory:

> He was almost tall, beautifully built in his town clothes, and he was the shyest man the Colonel had ever known. He was not shy from ignorance, nor from being ill at ease, nor from any defect. He was basically shy, as certain animals are, such as the Bongo that you will never see in the jungle, and that must be hunted with dogs.
>
> "My Colonel," he said. He smiled as only the truly shy can smile.
>
> It was not the easy grin of the confident, nor the quick slashing smile of the extremely durable and the wicked. It had no relation with the poised, intently used smile of the courtesan or the politician. It was the strange, rare smile which rises from the deep, dark pit, deeper than a well, deep as a deep mine, that is within them. (*ART* 129)

This careful description of Alvarito's shyness is significant for a writer who depended on similar details to create the emotional dimension so essential to an understanding of his fiction. Alvarito understands the three-way relationship which has developed and is aware that he and Renata will soon be alone to develop their relationship fully. And the hint of jealousy which comes through in the language of Cantwell's remembering allows the reader to know that Cantwell, too, understands this relationship. But, of course, it is natural that the subject would *not* be mentioned openly: as natural as the young lovers in "Hills Like White Elephants" *not* mentioning the abortion; as natural as Frederic Henry and Catherine Barkley concentrating on the details of the jewelry-store window in order *not* to think about Frederic's departure on the midnight train; as natural as Jake Barnes concentrating on the details of his Paris taxi ride in order *not* to think about his sexual problems; as natural as Nick Adams in "Big Two-Hearted River" *not* thinking about whatever it is that disturbs him. It is knowledge which does not have to be stated.

After having said that they had known each other as children, Renata had not spoken again (while Cantwell and the *Gran Maestro* discussed good wines) until she was asked what she wanted for dessert. Then she is remembered by Cantwell as having been

quiet and a little withdrawn, since she had seen Alvarito. Something was going on in her mind, and it was an excellent mind. But, momentarily, she was not with them. (*ART* 131)

When Cantwell had asked her what was wrong, she had been distant. And when he asked her if he had to take it "like a corn cob," she had said, "No . . . not understanding the colloquialism," as Cantwell realizes, "but understanding exactly what was meant, since it was she who had been doing the thinking" (*ART* 132). She is thinking about both Cantwell's impending death and her relationship to both men—even, perhaps, the potential development of her relationship with Alvarito.[3]

In the next significant reference to Alvarito there is further suggestion of Cantwell's coming to awareness of the developing understanding. He remembers that Renata had asked,

"Don't you think I should go to the shoot?"
"No. I am quite sure. Alvarito would have asked you if he wanted you."
"He might not have asked me because he wanted me."
"That's true," the Colonel said. (*ART* 199)

Then again, but back in time-present at the end of the novel, the shyness is what is noted first:

Alvarito, the Barone, was standing by the open fire in the middle of the room. He smiled his shy smile and said in his low pitched voice, "I'm sorry you did not have better shooting." (*ART* 300)

Alvarito's shyness enhances one's understanding that there can be no open discussion about the three-way relationship. Then, after small talk about their duck-shooting luck, there is this significant exchange between the two men:

"I always love the shoot," the Colonel said. "And I love Venice."
The Barone Alvarito looked away and spread his hands toward the fire. "Yes," he said. "We all love Venice. Perhaps you do the best of all."
The Colonel made no small talk on this but said, "I love Venice as you know."

"Yes. I know," the Barone said. He looked at nothing. Then he said, "We must wake your driver." (*ART* 301)

The Barone's shyness gives him away here, for it is not Venice but Renata they are speaking of; it is reflected in Alvarito's looking away when Venice is mentioned. And what they are *not* saying is "no small talk." There is understanding here between the two men; each is aware of the other's love for Renata, and there is respect. It is an emotion for both which is impossible for them to state, but which the reader feels more strongly than if it had been stated. A little later, the Colonel drops Alvarito off at his villa and they say goodbye:

"You're sure you won't come in?"
"No. I must get back to Trieste. Will you give my love to Renata?"
"I will. Is that her portrait that you have wrapped in the back of the car?"
"It is."
"I'll tell her that you shot very well and that the portrait was in good condition."
"Also my love."
"Also your love."
"*Ciao,* Alvarito, and thank you very much." (*ART* 303)

There is tacit understanding here which has worked in Cantwell's thinking until he has become aware of the triangular relationship but not sure enough of it to express it openly, and even only by indirection in his remembering.

Finally, riding toward Trieste in the car late Sunday and thinking about a last note to Renata but rejecting it because they had "said everything," Cantwell thinks yet again about the "understanding" that has developed among the three characters.

You have said good-bye to your girl and she has said good-bye to you.
That is certainly simple.
You shot well and Alvarito understands. That is that. (306)

Cantwell is now fully aware of what has developed. The control over the terms of impending death is everything.

At one point Cantwell tells Renata that he is "preparing the best way to be over-run" (*ART* 104). It is an army metaphor not relevant to their conversation—he denies ever being lonely and she wants to give him the gift of emeralds. She misses his point, and it is easy for the reader to as well, but in that sentence lies the very theme argued here. He cannot avoid being "over-run"—no one can—but he can prepare "the best way."

Human beings tend to hide truth from themselves at all costs—especially the truth about their own impending deaths. So the rendering of Colonel Cantwell, a 50-year old man struggling through the pain of a series of recent heart attacks, to maintain some dignity, some control over the circumstances of his own death, is one of the most powerful and moving character portrayals in all of Hemingway.

Notes

1. See Wirt Williams, *The Tragic Art of Ernest Hemingway,* for the best general discussion of the theme of tragedy in Hemingway; for the discussion of *ART,* see Chapter VIII (155–71). Williams says that "Cantwell is in part the designer and contriver of his own life, and therefore, like Dante, of his own hell—just as he is, in part, Christ crucified" (Williams 1981, 167). See also Gerry Brenner, *Concealments in Hemingway's Works,* for the best discussion of the Dante parallels, including quotes from *The Paradiso.* Brenner says, for example, that "particularly apt to the memory-ridden Cantwell would be the river Lethe. Its waters of forgetfulness wash away memory and so lead to the 'everlasting forest,' the sacred wood of the earthly paradise" (Brenner 1983, 154). There are other positive reactions to the novel, of course: Philip Young, *Ernest Hemingway: A Reconsideration,* suggests that "perhaps someday it can be shown how the calculus, which is often described as a symbolic means of 'grasping the fleeting instant,' throws a more attractive light on the novel than has yet been observed" (Young 1966, 275); and Carlos Baker, *Hemingway: The Writer as Artist,* was the first, I believe, to call *ART* a fable, "a lesser kind of *Winter's Tale* or *Tempest.* It's tone is elegiac. It moves like a love-lyric" (Baker 1972, 287).

2. For a discussion of the frame structure of the novel, see Peter Lisca, "The Structure of Hemingway's *Across the River and into the Trees,*" especially page 243. This is one of the few articles available on the structure of any of Hemingway's major works, and Lisca suggests a number of other ideas that need to be thoroughly considered before scholars give up on *ART.*

3. For example, Delbert Wylder (1969, 188), among others, argues that Renata is pregnant. This reading would certainly enhance one's understanding of the triangular relationship. Alvarito would marry Renata and be the father to Cantwell's child. Wylder centers his argument around Renata's statement to Cantwell, "I have a disappointment for you" (*ART* 110) and makes an interesting case for pregnancy. But the statement may also mean merely that it is the wrong time of the month for sexual intercourse. However one reads this passage, there are two important arguments against pregnancy: first, they treat the idea too casually for such a crucial difference in their lives (it is not mentioned again, not even in Cantwell's memory); and second, a statement Renata makes earlier in the same scene confirms the importance of such a difference:

Everything is known in Venice anyway. But it is also known who my family are and that I am a good girl. Also they know it is you and it is I. We have some credit to exhaust. (*ART* 109)

There would be no credit left in Venice for a 19-year old countess pregnant out of wedlock. On the other hand, Hemingway was a master at handling intensely subtle situations.

References

Baker, Carlos. *Hemingway: The Writer as Artist.* Princeton, NJ: Princeton UP, 1972.
Brenner, Gerry. *Concealments in Hemingway's Works.* Columbus: Ohio State UP, 1983.

Hemingway, Ernest. *Across the River and into the Trees*. New York: Scribner, 1950.

Kobler, J. F. *Ernest Hemingway: Journalist and Artist*. Ann Arbor, MI: U of Michigan Research P, 1985.

Lisca, Peter. "The Structure of Hemingway's *Across the River and into the Trees*." *Modern Fiction Studies* 12(1966):232–50.

Vanderbilt, Kermit. "The Last Words of Ernest Hemingway." *The Nation* (October 25, 1965):284–85.

Whitlow, Roger. *Cassandra's Daughters: The Women in Hemingway*. Westport, CT: Greenwood P, 1984.

Williams, Wirt. *The Tragic Art of Ernest Hemingway*. Baton Rouge: Louisiana State UP, 1981.

Wylder, Delbert. *Hemingway's Heroes*. Albuquerque: U of New Mexico P, 1969.

Young, Philip. *Ernest Hemingway: A Reconsideration*. University Park: Pennsylvania State UP, 1966.

15

To Die Is Not Enough: Hemingway's Venetian Novel

John Paul Russo

Morire non basta.

D'Annunzio

Across the River and into the Trees (*ART* 1950) has long been undervalued by Hemingway's readers and critics who have failed to understand it as a signifi- cant, late representative in the tradition of the European Venetian novel. An extremely potent and complex symbol, Venice has thrived on the historical and literary imagination. It has been "painted and described many thousands of times," Henry James remarks, "and of all the cities of the world is the easiest to visit without going there" (1909, 3). One result of its overwhelming cultural importance and visual splendor is that few writers or (post-eighteenth century) painters—Byron, Turner, Ruskin, D'Annunzio, Mann, Pound, possibly Barrès— have succeeded in controlling the representations of Venice. Whether Heming- way should be added to the list depends on an assessment of his ability to shape the abundant Venetian materials at his disposal. One should resist the temptation to understand *Across the River* as an equivocal reprise of his leading themes (the soldier hero, code behavior, stoicism, vanity, the mysterious wound, love and death, the mystic land). In such terms the novel will likely disappoint, as it has almost universally disappointed readers. Rather, Venice is the key to this novel. The myths of Venice should be seen to overlay the thematic com- plexity of the novel, to give it organizational strength and subtlety, and to help explain odd structural features, integrally linked symbols, and tangled linguistic undergrowth.

Historically considered, the two chief myths of Venice may be conveniently labelled "classical" and "romantic." The former is now by far the more ob- scure. Hemingway valued them equally and they are often seamlessly intercon-

nected in the novel. Renaissance humanists linked Venice to an ideal of republican *virtù* and liberty. This essentially classical myth, a "civic cult of mystic
patriotism," goes back to the medieval period and the translation of Saint Mark's
body from Alexandria to Venice (ca. 827), and ultimately to the origins of the
city in the seventh century (Muir 1984, 24). Venice owed its life to the resourcefulness, economic aggressiveness, civic and moral discipline, courage,
and endurance of a people who withstood barbarian invasions from the north
and marine invasions from the south and east.[1] For a thousand years La Ser-
enissima was inviolable save by the tidal waters of the lagoon bathing her 117
islands. Modern readers will be more familiar with the city's romantic myth
and its associations with play, carnival, aesthetic refinement, orientalism and
luxury, illusion and reality, perverse sexuality, dissolution, and, in Mann's
phrase, the "voluptuousness of doom."[2] Georg Simmel referred to Venice as
the "ambiguous" city and Mann agreed: This was the "humblest adjective that
can be applied," "this musical magic of ambiguity still lives."[3] Hemingway's
allusions to ancient mythology often cross both his "classical" or "romantic"
mythic patterns, which is the case with the opening chapter. This "story about
death" (Lewis 1965, 183) begins with allusions to the watery outskirts of Hades.

The swamp is the real origin of Venice—the novel begins there and ends
there, and nowhere do we long forget the presence of water. The swamp is a
traditional Western symbol for chaos and undifferentiation, the unhealthy mixture of land and water, luxuriant uncontrollable life and decomposing matter,
pollution, disease, and death. In the Book of Job, Behemoth (the hippopota-
mus) and Leviathan (the crocodile) are swamp monsters, and in Isaiah, Rahab
is a marine dragon or chaos monster. In Revelation, the vision of new heaven
and new earth begins: "there was no more sea" (Rev 21:1; Auden 1950, 7–
8). Flaubert and Pound, two writers whom Hemingway revered, associate the
swamp with the feminized Orient, luxury, decadence, and the unconscious.
These writers present the "familiar paradox of Oriental fecundity and sterility,
enormous abundance and enormous barrenness," argues Robert Casillo (1984);
in Pound specifically it symbolizes the "parthogenetic feminine, which ignores
the priority of the phallus and threatens to overwhelm the masculine order or
agriculture with its undifferentiated and proliferant confusion" (Casillo 1984,
281, 285). With its organizing mark of the phallus, the sign of plough and
stylus, the male principle preserves hierarchy against the chaotic and violent
energies of the swamp-feminine. In Pound, Venetian history is one of the scenes
in which these warring principles engage. Likewise in Hemingway, the swamp
is a culturally overdetermined symbol: the lagoons and canals of Venice are a
displacement for the power of the feminine and the lure of death.

The title *Across the River and into the Trees* is taken from General Stonewall
Jackson's dying words and announces the theme of the watery passage to death.
Richard Cantwell is an American colonel stationed in Trieste in the years immediately following the Second World War. *Cant*ankerous, given to exposing
cant, no politician, he has recently been demoted in rank from general and,

with a serious heart condition, is thinking of retiring to Venice. There he has
a few soldier friends from the First World War and has recently become infat-
uated with a young Venetian contessa named Renata. The novel tells the story
of a two-day visit to Venice that ends in his death. But we only begin to learn
these details in Chapter 2. Chapter 1 opens mysteriously at a duck shoot set in
the littoral swamps and lagoons near Venice, at low tide, in the pre-dawn hours,
on a cold, windless winter night. Gradually the light comes up to a "gray dim
sky" (*ART* 5); the sun has not yet risen by the end of Chapter 1. People are
unidentified except for "boatman" and "shooter." Like the infernal Charon,
the boatman is surly ("What the hell is eating him?" *ART* 4), powerful ("tall,
heavily built" *ART* 4), violent ("shoved the boat savagely," "smashing with
his oar at the ice," *ART* 4) and inhuman ("big brute" *ART* 4). Charon would
be angry that his passenger is not yet *dead*. The shooter (Cantwell) has over-
taxed himself in rowing out, complains to himself of discomfort, and asks for
water. The boatman replies "No water" (no life) and warns with a cruel sadism that the lagoon waters are "unhealthy" (*ART* 4) too. The shooter manages
to kill two birds, as it were, sacrifices for the god of death; but the boatman
continues to be unhelpful. "To hell with him," thinks the shooter, who knows
that "[e]very time you shoot now can be the last shoot and no stupid son of a
bitch should be allowed to ruin it" (*ART* 7). The shadowy light, the marshy
terrain, the two generalized characters, the curses ("hell"), all place us within
the outer precincts of the city of Death.

Hemingway labored over the progression and disjunction of the opening and
closing chapters, which provoke an unsettling, uncanny response. Chronologi-
cally, the novel begins with Chapter 2, Cantwell's medical check-up in Trieste,
"the day before yesterday" (*ART* 12). Chapters 3–15 comprise "Yesterday"
(*ART* 12): the day-long journey from Trieste to Venice, the late afternoon and
night in Venice at the Gritti, including the nocturnal gondola ride. Chapters
16–39 narrate events of "today" (*ART* 123): morning and midday passes in
Venice; Cantwell leaves Venice in the afternoon (*ART* Chapter 39) and repairs
to a country villa in preparation for the duck shoot the next morning. Projected
as an eternal tomorrow, outside of the present according to the strict chronology of the novel, the swamp scenes and duck shoot comprise Chapter 1 *and*
Chapters 40–44; Cantwell dies in the afternoon (*ART* Chapter 45), a "prema-
ture" death before nightfall. Hemingway picks up the narrative in Chapter 40
precisely where he left off in Chapter 1: the shooter (Cantwell) alone in the
sunken hogshead, the wind just coming up, the sun *about to rise,* the boatman's surliness still unexplained, and the shooter's "anger" (*ART* 281) inten-
sifying to a point where he must take heart pills. Indeed, when from his ad-
vanced location the "sullen boatman" starts killing the birds that would have
come to "the shooter," the shooter "fired at him twice" (*ART* 281)—warning
shots, but the implication is obvious: psychologically speaking, he wants to
"kill" the boatman and defeat the power of death. We learn after the duck
shoot that the boatman's "hatred" (*ART* 302) of the shooter is due to the fact

that Moroccans had raped his wife and daughter during the Allied invasion; in the boatman's mind an American Colonel also in the war shares in the act. (If there were two separate duck shoots instead of one, the Colonel would have had ample opportunity to discover the source of the boatman's hatred in between—he talks with his host Barone Alvarito [*ART* 129–30] and the subject is not raised—and probably would have asked for another boatman.) Cantwell dies shortly afterward on the road back to Trieste (*ART* Chapter 45). The swamp thus "encloses" the novel with its central events in Venice, surrounding the city of Death and permeating its atmosphere by the ever-present waters of the canals. But beside this framing effect, the swamp is also "outside time." From the swamp life emerges; to it life returns; and like the unconscious, for which it becomes an apt symbol, it knows no time.

The long drive from Trieste to Venice gives Cantwell an opportunity to reminisce about his early experiences in the surrounding location and in Venice, while establishing Venice itself as the distant goal, the feminine love object, and the attraction of death. His first "serious" wound was received defending the "queen of the seas" (*ART* 35); it gave him his first sense of death or rather the "loss of the immortality" (*ART* 33), and so Venice is implicated in his death from his youth. He fought to protect Venice without having seen "her" (*ART* 45) (a lack: her absence must be filled by the imagination), without even having "command of the language" (*ART* 45). He means the Italian language; but the context suggests a helpless child who does not have a "language" that can speak for the unconscious and declare its love for its mother, another lack that will be continually associated with his relation to Venice. For a brilliant commander like Cantwell not to have "command" of something is a breach in his armor—Hemingway's fondness for turning colloquial or idiomatic expressions inside out is succinctly illustrated.

If Cantwell suffered his first wound defending without seeing Venice, a second "small wound" required actually going to the city for treatment. So it will not have been that "small." Again, Venice is associated with wounding and a "small" wound might indicate a *symbolic* wound. On this first journey he said that he saw Venice as a "queen" and "rising from the sea" (*ART* 45), an allusion to the birth of the goddess Venus from the ocean foam, the sperm of the castrated Uranus; later, Renata will describe herself as "rising from the sea" (*ART* 97). This conjunction of city, woman, and goddess occurs in the most famous example of the topos in English, by another soldier-writer, Byron, in *Childe Harold's Pilgrimage* (IV.11): "She looks a sea Cybele, fresh from ocean,/Rising with her tiara of proud towers." In Byron's amalgamation of classical and romantic myth, "Venice" as both queen and fertility goddess wears her "towers," the male sexual symbol, her trophies, in castrated form: She is the beautiful Medusa, her beauty is the transformed opposite of her horror, the repressed castration anxiety. Venice is the "*sea* Cybele" because Cybele is normally associated with the land. In the older strata of Cretan and

Anatolian religion, Cybele is the Mother God who is accompanied by a "subordinate figure of the male attendant, half son, half lover," for example, Adonis and Attis (Harrison 1963, 48–49). The terrified Attis castrates himself after sleeping with her; Cybele's priests castrate themselves in ritual commemoration. Towers (male trophy symbols) also stand for the mural wall or battlements; they form the woman's headdress signifying the city as a protective enclosure; the "goddess crowned with an image of her city is the Mediterranean's oldest emblem of sovereignty" (Davenport 1989, 162). In short, Hemingway's "queen of the seas" is an overdetermined symbol which is well equipped to be associated with her "subordinate" "male attendant," with Cantwell and his brush with death, his first "serious" wound—and his even more serious "small wound."

Cantwell's next thought after the small wound is "Merde . . . we did very well that winter up at the juncture" (ART 45), a place of military engagement. Death is the undesirable, the enemy; "Death," he thinks later, "is a lot of shit" (ART 219). By swearing "Merde" (French, "excrement" but also a play on *madre* and murder) he shows a "command of the language" and symbolically desecrates the city that will, after a few near misses in his youth, inevitably be linked to his death. His thought—doing very well "at the juncture" (English ed.: "junction"—contains a buried reference to successful sexual penetration and also to a fateful crossroads. A similar layering of geographical, sexual, and fate metaphor is employed by Sophocles to depict Oedipus' killing his father Laius ("at the crossroads"—a juncture) and marrying his mother. Since the juncture concerns a military engagement with the Austrians, one concludes that in resisting and defeating "them," Cantwell reenacts an oedipal scenario, destroys the father, and claims the mother incestuously.

Throughout the novel Cantwell is obsessed by loss and death: his youth, his health, his generalship, his "three battalions," and "three women" (a doubling), and "where the hell does it end?" (ART 95). He consumes his waning psychic energies fighting thoughts of death, which he must continually repress as "morbid," a favorite word (ART 34, 47, 78, 168, 291). His efforts fail because at the same time he longs for death as the end of his suffering and loss.[4] "*Komm süsser Tod,* he thought" (ART 88): Bach's choral melody "Come, Sweet Death" on death and rebirth. Cantwell turns things into death, projecting a massive death instinct onto the birds that he shoots; onto the fish that he sees in the market; onto a cooked lobster, "a monument to his dead self" (ART 115); onto General Custer's body, "unspeakably mutilated"; onto the "metallic agony" (ART 46) of the *motoscafo* engine, bought in one of the "graveyards of automobiles" (ART 43); onto his wife "Deader than Phoebus the Phoenician" (ART 213) (unlike Eliot's "Phlebas the Phoenician,"[5] Phoebus Apollo returns every day from "death"; the feminine antagonist, compared to a male plague god, will rise to claim her victim); onto "mutilated" soldiers (a "German dog eat a good German soldier's ass" [ART 257]) and cripples—"he was a sucker for crips" (ART 71). He plans his burial, imagines the "mulch" (a swamp image) (*ART* 34–35) of his buried body, and thinks his brother's corpse may have "deliquesced" on a Pacific island in the war (another swamp image) (*ART* 257); he conceives both deaths in terms of the decomposition of organic life by water. In the city of trade and death, death is his "strange trade" (*ART* 40); "killing armed men" is "my trade" (*ART* 63), his "sad trade" (*ART* 94), his "*sale métier*" (114), a "sad science" (133), the "*triste métier*" (253).[6] In battle, by his own count, he has a record of "one hundred and twenty-two sures" (*ART* 123), a real killer. And now he has recurrent anginal pains and takes two heart pills at 6–7 hour intervals in the novel (*ART* 12, 33, 92, 166, 266, 281, 294): it gives him pleasure to "take them dry" (*ART* 33)—*no water*.[7] With unconscious irony, revealing her sadistic streak, Renata calls him Richard the "lion-hearted," which he characteristically "corrects" by way of an aggressive reference (defecation) to the "crap-hearted" (*ART* 229). When, on what will be his final journey to Venice, Cantwell suddenly realizes that he will arrive in half an hour, he takes two heart pills (*ART* 33), a doubling and overcompensation, to lower his blood pressure and pep up his heart, as if protecting himself from the city, another killer.

It takes four chapters to arrive in Venice, reminiscent of the long delay of Aschenbach's arrival in Mann's *Death in Venice*. Surely the point is that one does not start but ends in Venice. Analyzing the struggle between the death instinct and the sexual or "self-preservative" instincts (or "life instinct," which includes the sexual instincts), Freud speaks of the "circuitous paths" and "ever more complicated *détours*" that the individual organism takes to its death. The self-preservative instincts enable it "to ward off any possible ways of returning to inorganic existence other than those which are immanent in the organism itself. . . . Thus these guardians of life, too, were originally the myrmidons of death" (Freud 1955, 18: 38–39). The journey across the Veneto, with its many stops and detours ("where I grew up very rapidly," *ART* 93) enables Hemingway to elaborate upon the stages of Cantwell's youth and age. Throughout the journey Cantwell tries to keep "strictly controlled" (*ART* 20), repressing his thoughts of death, and "unthinking his great need to be there" (*ART* 20). He realizes the mortal danger in his strenuous pastime (duck shooting) and his passion (Renata).

The butt of Cantwell's frequent neurotic outbursts is "the driver," a feckless American soldier named Jackson; the name parodies the great general's. Cantwell's regular driver is away and the substitution signals a new and unknown experience. Initially uneasy (to add to his uneasiness), Cantwell is comforted at finding Jackson a "good driver" (he is a garage mechanic—*his* trade *is* driving itself). Cantwell's "big Buick" (*ART* 20) is fit for this fatal journey, a "tumbril" (*ART* 228), "god-damned," "over-sized," and "luxurious" (*ART* 307), a hearse; he is "still paying for it" (*ART* 23), and it will never be paid for. This journey is paid with one's life.

The countryside passes dizzily by Cantwell; it may be the effect of the pills. Also, "I'm not sure I like speed" (*ART* 14), an instance of longing for stillness and repose. His thoughts travel back to the scenes and battles of his youth. Only three weeks earlier, he had revisited the ground nearby where he had suffered his severest wound in the First World War. Fixing the spot by triangulation, he desecrated it by defecating and then buried a knife and a "brown" (*ART* 18) (color of organic death) ten thousand lire note (a considerable sum just after the Second World War). Cantwell surrenders his weapon and offers a worthy tribute of money to the victor Pluto, the god of death whose name in Greek means "wealth." From the earth all wealth comes and to it all returns. But according to Norman O. Brown (1959), the feces are both a gift and a massive, violent act of aggression against the other. Cantwell's behavior typifies his desire to get rid of death, to project it onto the other. Cantwell "attacks" his enemy for having violated him. The money he gives to the earth is a kind of payment as substitute for himself. By making the exchange, he only buys time (and time is money): no one escapes the great economy of Death. Thus the act which attempts to cancel or negate violence only repeats it. Cantwell defecates as a sign of protest again in Venice, one of the many doublings in the novel, on the very morning after Cantwell has had to sleep alone, Renata having refused him (*ART* 167–68). As he "sat there" in the bathroom, he first thinks of Renata: her absence, his long wait for her telephone call, her depriving him of company and pleasure. The train of thoughts that follows is: the army (where there is as much privacy as in a "professional shit-house"), "shit-house" ambassadors, "wives." Linked together are violence, "merde," the system that has denied him his generalship, the feminine. And there are other links between the expulsion of human waste, anal sadism, and protest against Renata (or the feminine) along with the deep desire for privacy, which represents male independence. On first arriving at the Gritti he asks a porter to get Renata on the telephone while he (Cantwell) goes to urinate (*ART* 68). In his earlier reverie he had linked "merde" and "her" (Venice) (*ART* 45). Another time he jokes with Renata who cannot grasp the colloquial use of the word "go" in "going to the bathroom": "That," he says, "is the one thing we do alone" (*ART* 228).

Near the end of the journey to Venice, Cantwell asks Jackson to stop so that they can admire the view of the "square tower" of the Church of S. Maria Assunta on the island of Torcello. In the language of the American frontier, he gives Jackson a thumbnail sketch of the men who "pioneered" (*ART* 28) Venice. Visigoths, Lombards, and "other bandits" had driven local inhabitants from the mainland to Torcello. However, its lagoons silted up and mosquitoes brought malaria, so the "Torcello boys" eventually built Venice which was more "defensible." (Cantwell makes the transition smoother than it actually was. According to Giulio Lorenzetti, Torcello flourished well into the Middle Ages when it was overtaken by the "greater wealth and power of Venice" and suffered the "gradual silting up of its water" [1975, 834]: Venice is a predator.) A "Torcello boy" smuggled the body of Saint Mark out of Alexandria to Venice to give the Venetians their patron saint (*ART* 29). Numerous references to "boys" indicate a priority over the father: the "boys" were there at the origins and lay claim to autochthonous authenticity. In all, "the boys from Torcello . . . were very tough" (*ART* 28). Cantwell thinks of Venice as "my city" (*ART* 26); he is "part owner" because he had defended it in his youth, on account of which the Venetians "treat me well" (*ART* 26) and accept him as one of them, unlike the French who only resent him for having shamed them in the Second World War. Cantwell is also "tough," shares possessions, and claims priority by identification with the "tough" pioneers and defenders of Venice. The founding myth is reinforced when Cantwell says that Venice is a "tougher town than Cheyenne" (*ART* 35) (Jackson is from Wyoming); and although Venetians have refined manners and delicacy, Venice is as "tough as Cooke City, Montana" (*ART* 36) (Cantwell is from Montana).[8] Despite its reputation for aesthetic refinement, carnival, and pleasure, Venice preserves its founders' independence and resourcefulness and "makes a living on its own" (*ART* 35). Cantwell—and Hemingway—hated and feared the dependency syndrome, though both fell victim to it.

Cantwell thus identifies his own youth with that of Torcello and its military prowess. But there is already a displacement: Torcello is not Venice. Torcello's "square tower" is frequently linked to Cantwell: the phallus as impenetrable monolith. The square, sentinel-like bell tower of Torcello rises *next* to the church dedicated to the Virgin Mary; it is not connected to it. Cantwell prefers the "good taste" and "geometrically clear" (*ART* 28) simplicity of the old church on Torcello to Saint Mark's which is feminized as "pretty Byzantine" (*ART* 29). Moreover, he sees the square tower on Torcello against the bell tower on nearby Burano where men "make bambinis" (*ART* 29), but these phallic tower images hardly need the extra associations. One bartender likens Cantwell himself to a *"campanile,* or even the old church at Torcello" (*ART* 39). The headwaiter imagines staging an event with Cantwell for the fictitious military "Order of Brusadelli" (the in-group) "in some historic place such as San Marco or the old church at Torcello" (*ART* 61). Still another waiter refers to local gossip involving Cantwell: "Some people don't understand the Torcello part" (*ART* 75).[9] "Some people" include the reader because this is one of two references with no clear referent in the novel, thereby enhancing the mysterious relation to Torcello: Cantwell's phallocentrism and desire for origins. Finally, Cantwell wonders when they will tear down the "Cinema Palace" (a reductive reference to Saint Mark's) and build a "real cathedral." Only when they bring back Saint Mark's body a second time is Renata's reply. Venice is already a doubling or displacement: Saint Mark's body is moved from its "origin" to establish another "origin." If Mark is the origin, he is already *marked* (St. Mark), and in deconstructionist terms, his very name signifies an absence, lack, and trace. "That was a Torcello boy," says Cantwell. Renata answers: "You're a Torcello boy" (*ART* 161); the Venetian contessa affectionately confers honorary status on the "boy."

These references to Torcello underscore Cantwell's identification with sol-

dierly, pioneering Venice and its "classical" myth, and his love of an art of
power, directness, and simplicity. To summarize the opposition between Torcello and Venice, Venice signifies the feminine, the unattainable, the sense of
lack, the lure of death; Torcello with its square tower signifies completeness,
phallocentrism, the masculine virtue of being closed up in oneself, autonomy.
Death ties in with lack because it implies otherness and difference. The fact
remains that the individual is not complete and self-sustaining—and hence not
immortal. Torcello was silted up in its later history, its inhabitants driven out
by invaders and malaria, its churches abandoned. It was absorbed by Venice.
The fate of Torcello is the fate of all things.

If Cantwell protests on behalf of Torcello, he is nonetheless strongly attracted by the romantic myths of Venice. A major motif of this myth is play
and carnival. In *Across the River* "fun" is one of those quite ordinary words
(like "boy," "trade," "engine," "lovely," "jerk," "tough," "hell") on
which Hemingway works many changes. Often enough Cantwell must remind
himself that he has come to Venice to "have fun" (*ART* 27, 71, 101, 152,
281), because he fears that he is not and that time is running out. On the way
to the Gritti, he passes the palazzo of D'Annunzio (1863–1938) and Eleonora
Duse (1858–1924). "Christ they are dead," he thinks, hoping "they had fun
in that house" (*ART* 51). Gliding by the contessa Dandolo's palazzo, he notes
that the contessa, though "over eighty," acts "as gay as a girl," does not
"fear dying," and dyes her hair "red" (*ART* 47), an overt sexual reference;
Dandolo is an ancient Venetian name, proving the blood is still energetic.
Whenever people visit her, they are "cheerful" because "they are going to see
the Contessa Dandolo." Then, Cantwell never walked in Venice "that it wasn't
fun" (*ART* 45), even though climbing the bridges triggers anginal pains. "No
one is ever old in Venice" (*ART* 93), a typical example of Cantwell's self-
deception. Venice seems to transform reality and is contrasted, to its advan-
tage, to Milan. Only gondoliers and waiters seem to work. The Order of Brusadelli is a source of humor and magic "spell" for Cantwell who is its "Supreme Commander," with his former sergeant, now headwaiter only near the
Gritti, as *Gran Maestro*. Cantwell enjoys the in-jokes and for a time the "spell
works" (*ART* 62); the *Gran Maestro* notices that "this taking of towns had
pulled him out of his depth" (*ART* 62), that is, his brooding depression. But
appearances cannot be kept up for long, and the "spell was broken" (*ART* 64).
Revealed by Cantwell at the end of the novel, the "Supreme Secret" of the
Order combines "love," "fun," death by water, and oriental opulence: "Love
is love and fun is fun. But it is always so quiet when the gold fish die" (*ART*
271). Which, appropriately enough, is positively banal.

Regression and infantilism inform this absolute necessity for fun: Cantwell
and Renata "have fun" (*ART* 116, 127) with their food. Shopping together
will be "fun" (*ART* 141). Trying to change places in a gondola is "fun" (*ART*
152). Cantwell has had "as much fun shooting" at the duck shoot "as I ever

had'' (*ART* 281)—more self-deception, considering his condition; and so forth. Even though the weather is cold and windy, Cantwell likes the windows of his hotel room thrown wide open and guesses that a "hell of a tide" will flood Saint Mark's Square: "That's always fun" (*ART* 167). The pleasure derived from the destructive elements is another sign of projected aggression. Maybe if he tears down the great cathedral he can restore the origin, Torcello. In the "hell of a tide" on St. Mark's one notes the Romantic-Decadent motif (cf. Poe, Barrès, Debussy, De la Mare) of the "engulfed cathedral," an apocalyptic vision of stillness, sunken beauty, and death. Irked by the fact that Jackson worries too much, will not drink with him (*ART* 41), and does not know how to "have some fun" (*ART* 58), Cantwell *orders* him to "have yourself some fun," an order which Jackson rephrases absurdly in military terms (*ART* 58). The *Gran Maestro* assumes that Jackson is "One of those *sad* Americans" (*ART* 58), repressed and unimaginative, not one of us.

Heavy drinking on a delicate heart condition and strong medication can be extremely dangerous, "and he knew that it was bad for him" (*ART* 70). Cantwell's fun is self-destructive. He drinks his first "double" upon arriving at the garage (*ART* 39) in Venice and has eight more drinks of hard liquor *before dinner* (*ART* 55, 63, 69, 82, 92, 101, 116).[10] At dinner with Renata he shares a bottle of Valpolicella and a bottle of expensive champagne; another bottle of champagne is placed in the gondola; a bottle of Valpolicella is by his reading light in his hotel room (*ART* 164). He drinks it before going to sleep and, on rising, he finds a second bottle of Valpolicella (*ART* 172), and he begins to drink. His entire experience of Venice is thus suffused in a haze of alcohol, a "drug" that undermines the effect of the heart drugs. The drinking may also explain why he does not notice much in Venice, except in general terms. Further, the occasional stupidity of the dialogue may be the result of intoxication.

Hemingway avoids Venetian scene painting but creates an atmosphere consistent with theme and characterization. Only indirectly does he allude to the Venetian beauty, mystery, and decay that have long haunted writers and painters. In D'Annunzio's *Il fuoco,* translated as *The Flame of Life* and given by Hemingway "to several women he dated" just after the First World War (Reynolds 1986, 127), the "true spirit" of the "temptress" Venice is to be found "in the silence and, most frighteningly—be certain of it—in full summer, at noon," like the epiphany of "great Pan," the god of totality and dionysian destruction ("panic") (D'Annunzio 1982, 46, 117). In *La Mort de Venise* Barrès represents the city as the "despair for a beauty which journeys to its death," either the extreme of experience or innocence: "the song of an old corruptress or a sacrificed virgin" (Praz 1970, 337).[11] In *Death in Venice* Mann's Gustav von Aschenbach arrives in bad weather but stays into the high season (hot summer)—and the cholera epidemic which kills him. D'Annunzio's Stelio Effrena is young; Aschenbach is in his fifties but physically well. It seems appropriate, in light of Cantwell's precarious health and soldierly virtue, that the "true spirit" of Venice in *Across the River* reveal itself in winter, at night, in the "same strong, wild, cold, wind from the mountains" (*ART* 184); in evening walks between the Gritti and Harry's where climbing each little bridge gives him heart spasms; in a nocturnal gondola ride with Renata under a heavy army blanket, possibly a literary reminiscence of Jordan and Maria in *For Whom the Bell Tolls*.

Because of Hemingway's decision to cross over frequently into interior monologue, he is careful to keep his own perceptions close to Cantwell's, so that we see Venice largely through Cantwell's eyes; and they are sensitive eyes. The Grand Canal looks "as grey as though Degas had painted it on one of his greyest days" (*ART* 71). Nothing seems "dull" along the canals, and it "doesn't all have to be palaces and churches" (*ART* 44). On his way to Harry's he passes Santa Maria del Giglio, compares its "compact," "air-borne" (*ART* 77) structure to a P47, and anticipates reading up about it (perhaps the heavy drinking may explain how this heavy, baroque church could fly). What pleasure he will have in learning that, endowed by the Barbaro, a famous Venetian military family, the church is one of the few in Christendom decorated with carvings of military fortifications on its façade: a soldier's church. He loves taking walks through the "strange, tricky town" (*ART* 45), which is like "working cross-word puzzles" (*ART* 45), full of bridges, junctures, crossroads, a symbol for the linguistic puzzles of a text. For Venice is "a game you play" (*ART* 185), "fun" to be sure, but also a treacherous labyrinth, an unknown and mysterious terrain where one gets lost playing *"solitaire ambulante"* (*ART* 185) in the labyrinthine city of death. Taking a gondola across the Grand Canal, he sees the "black-clad people" climbing out of a "black-painted vehicle" (*ART* 185), as if disembarking on the Isle of the Dead (another Romantic-Decadent motif—see, e.g., Tennyson's "The Voyage of Maeldune," Boecklin, Rachmaninoff); they would "not give you a penny" for your thoughts. Earlier he tried to pay off death by giving a lot of money. The weather is not only *"brutto,"* but *"Bruttissimo"* (*ART* 183); his coat is "wind-proof" but not "water-proof" (*ART* 194), making him vulnerable to the quintessential Venetian element.

Cantwell's main reason for going to Venice, its central attraction, is the Contessa Renata. We first know her as the contessa (*ART* 68), only after 20 pages as Renata (*ART* 88), and Hemingway never gives her last name. Perhaps this could serve as a key to her generalized, ambiguous character: She is deliberately presented in vague terms (which has been mistaken for a failure of characterization [12]) and seems rather a screen upon which one may, as does Cantwell, project fantasies or, like the critics, offer widely varying interpretations. She is the impossible Romantic love: a young and beautiful woman who is 32 years younger than Cantwell, a foreigner, a wealthy aristocrat. *Renata* means reborn in Italian; she is both the vehicle and goal of Cantwell's longing: to be "reborn," to achieve the "great miracle" (*ART* 288) of love, to regain something of the spirit of lost youth, won by almost clairvoyant memory in many passages, and to ease the passage to death. To be reborn is another powerful indication of the search for origins, a repetition of the novel's ultimate action, a finding of death, Thanatos marked by Eros.

Hemingway takes great pains to identify Renata with Venice: She is not only a Venetian but actually born in the city (whereas he is a "Torcello boy"). When Cantwell, evoking the soldierly myth, asks how many people in her family fought for the city, she replies proudly, "Everybody," "Always . . . and several of them were Doges" (*ART* 219). Although Hemingway says "they were not Othello and Desdemona" (*ART* 230), like the Venetian Desdemona, Renata begs her "Othello" to tell his war stories; but like the innocent Miranda, she twice falls asleep while he is telling them (they are a trifle boring; she is a trifle drunk). She describes her own portrait as if it were a person "rising from the sea without the head wet" (*ART* 74), possible only for a goddess, in other words, Venus "rising from the sea" (*ART* 45) with whom Venice had been earlier identified.

Venice is a city of oriental splendor, precious gems, and fabled riches. As Cantwell's gift for her, Renata picks out the "small Negro" (another reference to a diminutive Othello and perhaps to a blackamoor servant, which one occasionally sees beside Venetian ladies in paintings). The Negro wears a turban of chip diamonds (*ART* 105): the decorated phallus as trophy. She gives him both her portrait and two large square emeralds, green being the symbolic color of Venice, jewels symbolizing oriental luxury, and squareness signifying the geometric, the nonnatural, and the uncanny, but also a paired opposite of the "square" tower of Torcello (the only other time that "square" or "squared" appears in the novel). The two square emeralds are her symbol, just as the square tower on Torcello is Cantwell's. Renata asks him to feel in his pocket for her two "stones" (*ART* 103) which will remind him of her. Cantwell realizes that these jewels are worth a quarter of a million dollars and, embarrassed, returns them. He prefers the nonluxurious, the simplicity of Torcello.

Besides her associations with innocent heroines and heroic Venice, however, Renata also embodies the sinister qualities of the Romantic Fatal Woman typified by Keats's *Belle Dame Sans Merci:*

> I saw pale kings, and princes too,
>   Pale warriors, death pale were they all;
> They cried—"La belle dame sans merci
>   Hath thee in thrall!"

According to Mario Praz, innocence itself may be a quality of the Fatal Woman because innocence may cast a spell even more alluring (because less initially threatening) than experience (see, e.g., Monk Lewis's Matilda). Typical attributes of the Fatal Woman include a pale complexion; diabolical beauty; a Medusa smile; algolagnia (or sexual sadism and masochism); a close relation between the erotic, the aesthetic, and the exotic (for the "love of the exotic is usually an imaginative projection of a sexual desire"); frigidity; perversion; slaughter-lust; vampirism and satanism; Sphinx-like or cat-like "knowledge"; a devotion to the cult of the moon; and the cruel desire to be idolized like a Venus figure or the Eternal Feminine (Praz 1970, 207). "The typical Fatal Woman is always pale," writes Praz, pallor being spectral or death-like (1970, 231). Renata has "pale, almost olive-colored skin," a "profile" that could "break your, or anyone else's heart" (Cantwell has heart trouble), and hair of an "alive texture" (*ART* 80), the feral talisman. The "unnatural" aspect of their intimacy is not just represented by the great difference in age (which bothers her [*ART* 272]), but by a mock-violation of the incest taboo. Cantwell frequently calls her "Daughter" and she participates in the fantasy. But when he objects to "incest" (*ART* 98), she attempts to excuse it: "I don't think that would be so terrible in a city as old as this and that has seen what this city has seen" (*ART* 98). Either Venice has seen so much sin that one more makes little difference; or, Venice is so "old" that it is virtually presocial, that is, natural, and therefore sexually permissive and promiscuous. Praz comments, "Crime is natural, and therefore innocent" (1970, 276). The incest theme is closely related to the quest for rebirth and the origin: incest-longing, as in Byron, Chateaubriand, and Poe, implies a desire to give birth to oneself, not to acknowledge difference.

Renata gives hints of depressive affect and needs to be whipped up by stories of violence. She repeatedly asks to hear war stories, teasing him not to be too "rough," but never giving up on the slaughter-lust (*ART* 123, 125, 126, 133, 138, 139) until Cantwell finally objects, "Let's skip war," on page 217 *(ART)*. "No. I need it for my education," Renata replies. Then follow chapters 29 to 35, concerned with Cantwell's Second World War exploits. "Tell me some more please," she says when she wakes up, "and be just as bitter as you want" (*ART* 240). Renata can be as "rough" (*ART* 212) as Cantwell, and he thinks of enrolling her in the Order of Brusadelli; it happens late in the novel after she has truly proven herself a killer (*ART* 270). Her utterance of a crucial "disappointment" (*ART* 110) (refusal of sex?—this is the second reference lacking a clear referent[13]) sounds to Cantwell like "the worst" from a batallion commander. She can be severe and demanding: "you never give me presents" (*ART* 102). As a figure of demand she shakes his monolithic impenetrability. He protests that on a colonel's pay (which must have been further reduced by his alimony payments) he can only afford drinks, meals, and "small things from the PX" (*ART* 102), which will not long satisfy a Venetian contessa. Stopping at a jewelry shop, she remedies the lack and selects a gift for herself—he has to borrow money from the wealthy owner of the Gritti to buy it. The ebony figurine of the "small Negro" has *no legs* (*ART* 259), a mark of her castrating power. Later, in silent protest, he claims that he never "gave" it to her because *she* had picked it out (*ART* 290). He calls her "gentle cat" (*ART* 155), the animal known for its stealth, silence, and predatory indifference. Feline narcissism may explain her bland affect. A cat is also a sphinx, possessor of forbidden knowledge. Renata asks Cantwell, "how would you like to be a girl of nineteen years old in love with a man over fifty years old that you know was going to die?" (*ART* 91) Is this the fatal knowledge? Rightly shocked, Cantwell has to admit, "you put it a little bluntly" (*ART* 92). But she repeats the sentiment with astonishing frankness at dinner: "Oh, I wish . . . that you were not going to die" (*ART* 160); and the next day, "that is the good thing about you going to die that you can't leave me" (*ART* 211). A death goddess, she will forever possess him. Can this be "fun"?

One can only interpret Renata's protestations as veiled acts of sadism. In the same vein she enjoys holding his "hurt hand" (a common dream symbol for the penis). She dotes on his wound; "all last week, every night," she dreamt that his wounded hand was "the hand of our Lord" (*ART* 84), which reverses the roles of divinity and supplicant. She is now the worshipper, he the worshipped. Such "jumping" of poles or opposition, in psychoanalytic terms, masks desire and intensifies conflict. Inflicting pain, Renata enjoys pain herself: She makes him kiss her so that "the buttons of your uniform hurt me" (*ART* 110).

The power of the Fatal Woman to punish and wound is connected to Renata's vampirism. He carries her square emeralds, which (she says) "come" from "dead people" (*ART* 103), the war trophies of Renata's family. She draws his blood like a vampire, for they kiss so hard that he feels the "sweet salt" (*ART* 111) of his blood in his lips, exactly the wound that La Foscarina inflicts upon Stelio Effrena in *Il fuoco* (D'Annunzio 1982, 164). Cantwell's most serious "blood" wound is his heart condition which rapidly deteriorates on this visit to Venice. At one point he "reminds" Renata's portrait to "keep your Goddamn chin up so you can break my heart easier" (*ART* 173).

As implausible as it may first appear, Renata belongs with Semiramis, Marguerite de Bourgogne, and Théophile Gautier's Cléopâtre (in *Une nuit de Cléopâtre*) who had "massacred in the morning the lovers who had passed the night with her" (Praz 1970, 214). In one of the novel's most important scenes, the nocturnal gondola ride, Renata is in control from the start, makes arrangements with the gondolier (a figure of the Other), chooses the route, and sets the ground rules for sexual behavior. Cantwell notes the "dark-ed [*sic*] symmetry" of the gondola and the fact that Renata, with her hair blown back in the wind, looks like the "figure-head of a ship" (*ART* 149), a phallus. Sorceress, vehicle, and goal, Renata is identified with the gondola and reminds Cantwell of the "same magic, as always, of the light hull." (Brett Ashley has the curves of a racing yacht.) So, too, the gondolier lays "her partly on her side" to have "more control" (*ART* 151). Under the blanket Cantwell feels Renata's body with what she calls his "hurt hand" (not the penis, but its castrated symbol) and helps her experience three orgasms to Cantwell's none. The first orgasm happens and "the bird" flies out the "closed window" (*ART* 154)—a miracle. Then, "please wait until after we have gone under the second bridge," at a juncture, a clear sexual reference (*ART* 154); and, third, "do you think we could once more if it would not hurt you?'' (*ART* 157). It "hurts" him because of his heart condition, ''hurt hand,'' and the denial of sexual gratification.

But Renata has satisfied her selfish desire: She has experienced three orgasms, avoided sexual penetration, and refused orgasm to her partner. Her behavior the next morning confirms her sexual terror. Cantwell and Renata meet in St. Mark's Square which, as if in response to his wish, has been flooded overnight. He likes it; she does not: "It is only really fun toward the last when the children play" (*ART* 200).[14] Renata projects her fear of penetration onto the female Venice who has been violated by the destructive sexual overflow of the male sea god (Neptune, *il mare;* the classical sea, as opposed to the romantic one, is masculine). At the same time her refusal of sex provokes Cantwell's most violent fantasies: the next morning he "jokes" about military secrets such as "energy crackers" that prevent erections, "like the atomic bomb, only played backwards" (*ART* 197). He wants to destroy Venice, "give all Venice botulism from 56,000 feet" because "they give you anthrax" (a disease of *sheep*).

Renata's body becomes a representation of the islands and canals of Venice, a trope that Hemingway may well have borrowed from D'Annunzio's *Il fuoco* where Venice is the "magnificent and tempting city in whose canals, as in the veins of a voluptuous woman, a fire was beginning to burn" (1982, 62). In the nocturnal gondola ride Cantwell's wounded hand "coasted" (*ART* 152) along her body as he "searched for the island," that is, the vagina, "for good and for bad," bad because no sooner taken than it is "lost"; there is no penetration. She asks that he also "hold the high ground," referring to her breasts. In the symbolic geography of the swamps and lagoons, this is another island, the *riva alto* (Rialto) or high bank on which Venice was founded. Cantwell feels he is "assisting, or had made an act of presence, at the only mystery that he believed in except the occasional bravery of man" (*ART* 153). In this profanation of religious language, he is like a priest "assisting" at the revelation of a "mystery" in which he "believed," that is, the body of the woman floating in the gondola in her primeval realm of the swamp. The champagne, which they drink in the gondola, is the sacramental wine. Likewise in *Il fuoco* Stelio Effrena rhapsodizes over the sexual penetration of the male sky god Autumn into the canals of the goddess Venice, "the hour of the highest Feast," not the revelation of the Host as in Wagner's *Parsifal*, but sexual consummation, "as if the wild bridegroom were waving his purple banner as he drew near in his fiery chariot" (1982, 84):

The mutual passion of Venice and Autumn, which exalts each to the highest level of their sensuous beauty, has its origin in a deep affinity: because the soul of Venice, the soul which the old artists created for the beautiful City, is autumnal. (D'Annunzio 1982, 87)

Searching for, "finding" and then "losing," an "island" (*ART* 153) or the "unknown country" (*ART* 155) upon which to land and relieve oneself of the burden of a "nomadic" life (*ART* 142) and loneliness is an enduring theme in Hemingway's fiction. To name just two examples, the title of *For Whom the Bell Tolls* recalls the famous phrase in Donne's Sermon, "no man is an island"; and there is the posthumous *Islands in the Stream*. In Venice, the hundred-odd islands, linked by canals and bridges, retain their independent existence but form a larger, organic whole. In one respect, early, pioneering Venice and whatever is preserved of that spirit in the modern period may represent Hemingway's ideal of social solidarity. Yet the overwhelming impression is of Cantwell's loneliness and failure to communicate—a failure continually expressed by the virtually seamless narrative shifts into isolated, interior monologue. In the market, facing the "attack" of shoppers, Cantwell forms an *"îlot de résistance"* (*ART* 190) against them. In one of the final scenes Cantwell stands in a sunken oak hogshead waiting for the ducks to fly over, a solitary man-made island in a "frozen lagoon" and "far" from the "sedge-lined shore" (*ART* 280). As in Keats's "La Belle Dame Sans Merci," for this "pale warrior," the "sedge has wither'd from the lake." Marina Gradoli rightly speaks of the novel in terms of "a gradual detachment of the Hemingway hero from his own country" (1985, 148).

If Venice transforms life into art, and Renata is a true daughter of the city, then her portrait, which she presents to Cantwell, is the most powerful representation in the novel of that transformation. Everything associated with the portrait is tainted by her ability to render weak and helpless. It was painted by a *"pédéraste"* who has "false teeth" (loss of aggressive power) because he was attacked by other pederasts under a "full moon" (*ART* 96), almost certainly for being ashamed of his pederasty (later he makes a show of dating women). In Flaubert's *Salammbô* and Swinburne's *Atalanta in Calydon,* "a man dies under the eye of a frigid woman, devoted to the cult of the Moon, herself an idol" (Praz 1970, 253). Renata is a devotee of the moon, the symbol of the "huntress-maiden" Artemis in her brightness and the death goddess Hecate in her "dark spectral side" (Harrison 1963, 88). When Cantwell says that she can have any planet she wants, she chooses: "I'll be the moon" (*ART* 99). For one course at dinner Renata chooses lobster, a precious luxury food from what Cantwell describes as *"our* rich coast" (*ART* 117) symbolizing both possession and victimization. He explains that "lobster fills with the moon," meaning that it feeds better when there is light at night, that it supplies its lack. When the moon is dark, "he" is "not worth eating" (*ART* 117); the male lobster is being fed and consumed in the presence of the moon, which is female, at the height of her power. Cantwell identifies with the cooked lobster and is generally fascinated by the obscure universe—witness his fascination with the fish and crustacea in the market (*ART* 192). "When you want to be the moon and various stars and live with your man and have five sons," Renata says, "looking at yourself in the mirror and doing the artifices of a woman is not very exciting" (*ART* 118), a disavowal of narcissism that rings false: to be the moon requires sacrifice, and Renata chooses something that she really likes doing. Like an oriental goddess, she suffers no rival women around her and no daughters; but she will have an undifferentiated horde of men ("five sons"). Half-seriously, Cantwell thinks that she now wishes to marry him and have children: "Then let us be married at once." " 'No,' she said" (*ART* 118).

In Renata's analysis, her portrait is "very romantic." The hair is "twice as long" as normal, and hence more potent, and she looks as though she were "rising from the sea." But the painting falsifies reality, because "you rise from the sea with the hair very flat and coming to points at the end." This is "almost the look of a very nearly dead rat" (*ART* 97). "Very ugly," as she admits, the portrait and her description evoke the face of the Medusa encircled by snakes ("coming to points"), symbols of the castrated penis. As Freud notes in "Medusa's Head," the multiplicity compensates for the fear of losing the one penis in one's possession (Freud 1955, 17:28). Feelings of horror and repulsion are transferred onto the male rat, which is dead, associated with the swamp, predatory vermin, disease, and undifferentiated nature. Renata has "killed" another potential aggressor (a "rat pack," symbol of male sexual predatoriness). Mesmerized by both the real and the portrayed Renata, Cantwell utters, "I think of you when you come from the sea too" (*ART* 97); he thinks of her both as in the portrait *and* as the Medusa-like woman described by Renata. This Medusa does not rise like a queen from the sea but like a rat from the swamp: the other Venice rising from the littoral marshlands.

Renata will not spend the night with Cantwell at the Gritti. In her stead—and it is a wholly depressing spectacle—he has her portrait brought to his room and propped on chairs near his bed so he can look at and talk to it. His first thought is what "went wrong tonight . . . Me, I guess" (*ART* 165). Yet, the fault must be shared with Renata, who abandons him to this frightening substitute, her iconic double, while she sleeps alone. The picture is silent, unresponsive, "indefensible" yet menacing, not unlike the real Renata, as life and art fuse together. "You are two years younger than the girl you portray," Cantwell addresses the portrait, "and she is younger and older than hell; which is quite an old place" (*ART* 176). The remark underlines the trait of the vampire "successively incarnate in all ages and all lands, " according to Praz, "an archetype which united in itself all forms of seduction, all vices, and all delights" (1970, 219–20). Earlier her kiss drew blood; he will soon call "her" daughter in three languages (*ART* 266), an eternal presence, a *Magna Mater*. The *locus classicus* of the Romantic-Decadent *topos* of timeless vampire beauty is Pater's great passage on the Mona Lisa which Yeats considered the first modern poem[15]: "She is older than the rocks among which she sits; like the vampire, she has been dead many times, and learned the secrets of the grave; and has been a diver in deep seas, and keeps their fallen day about her; and trafficked for strange webs with Eastern merchants" (1929, 103). Cantwell's "younger and older than hell" might possibly connect Renata's portrait with Pater's Mona Lisa; her Venetian ancestors trafficked with Eastern merchants; and "hell" reinforces the association of her fatal and satanic beauty, which is not reduced, but rather accentuated by his attempt to joke about it ("quite an old place"). His most frequently used curse, "hell," is often on his lips (*ART* 4, 6, 52, 63, 92, 118, 165, 166, 172, 173, . . . 245, 253, 279, 281, 282, 289) and therefore on his mind. " 'The hell with you,' the portrait said, without speaking. 'You low class soldier' " (*ART* 174). He projects this harsh thrust of aristocratic disdain onto the picture which turns it back on himself, punishing him for his social inferiority and psychological insecurity. "The hell with you"— he is in hell, among the swamps.

The Gioconda smile, the Medusa smile in romantic tradition, is so hackneyed a motif that one might expect Hemingway, at this late date, *not* to exploit it or to do so only indirectly. While one looks in vain for any smile from the portrait (or from Renata), the smile is subtly displaced from Renata onto her double the Barone Alvarito, Cantwell's sexual rival. Alvarito is a Venetian aristocrat like Renata; "about three years older" (*ART* 130) than Renata; "almost tall" and "beautifully built" (*ART* 129) just as Renata has a "tall striding beauty" (*ART* 80). He is a hunter (*ART* 129); she the moon, the huntress. She says that "we knew each other as children" (*ART* 130) (regressive merging) and that he was "born very old" (*ART* 130) (like the vampire portrait). Some hidden communication takes place between them since she "had been quiet and a little withdrawn, since she had seen Alvarito" (*ART* 131). Later she teases Cantwell about the real reason why Alvarito did not invite her to the duck shoot: "He might not have asked me because he wanted me" (*ART* 199). Death has been claiming the older men around them: Renata's and Alvarito's fathers have died recently. Their mothers share a peculiar trait. Still in mourning, Renata's mother "sees almost no one" (*ART* 93) and "can't live" in Venice "too long at any time because there are no trees" (*ART* 205); she "lives" in the country. Alvarito's mother is "tired of there not being trees in Venice" (*ART* 48). Living in the country, both women are associated with the chthonic powers and rites of the dead; both are Demeter figures who in a primitive matrilinear era claim priority over the dead fathers. Alvarito is Cantwell's host at the duckshoot, surely knows of his heart condition, and is therefore implicated in his death; he purveys a killing form of fun as surely as Renata.

Now Hemingway devotes an entire paragraph to Alvarito's smile:

It was not the easy grin of the confident, nor the quick slashing smile of the extremely durable and the wicked. It had no relation with the poised, intently used smile of the courtesan or the politician. It was the strange, rare smile which rises from the deep, dark pit, deeper than a well, deep as a dark mine, that is within them. (*ART* 129)

Alvarito's "strange" smile is removed from all social purposes and is even at odds with them. It expresses the remote, the unbidden, the irrational, "the uncanny," which is the return of the repressed. "[D]ark" and "deep" as within the (mother) earth, "deeper" (from a pit, to a well, to a mine), its origin

represents the womb of prenatal bliss. But equally the smile conveys unconscious pleasure in accordance with Freud's constancy principle by which pleasure results from the lowering of tension, from the loss of self and return to
inorganic nature, the ultimate goal of the death instinct (1955, 18:9, 36–39).
Birth and death join hands in celebration of the mystery of life.

Alone at night Cantwell feels the "stones" (the square emeralds) which are
"hard and warm against his flat, hard, old, and warm chest." He notes "how
the wind was blowing," looks at the portrait, drinks another glass of Valpolicella, and reads "Red" Smith in the *Herald Tribune* (*ART* 166). The train of
associations leads from the emeralds, felt "against" his chest and parasitically
drawing their warmth from his warmth, to the death wind from the north, the
drug of wine, and diversion ("fun"—the sports page). Suddenly he realizes he
should take his medicine but "the hell with the pills" (*ART* 166). At this point
the desire for death seems momentarily stronger than the desire for life. But
the sexual instinct and life instinct, whose object is represented by the portrait,
wins out as he decides to take the pills. The next morning, he asks the portrait,
"why the hell can't you just get into bed with me" (*ART* 172). Then he concedes ultimate defeat: Renata would "out-maneuver" him every time (*ART*
173); Renata always gets the upper hand ("manus").

Both D'Annunzio's Venetian novel *Il fuoco* and his notebook-diary *Notturno*
(1921) provided motifs for *Across the River,* while D'Annunzio himself is an
important point of reference in the novel and, indeed, in Hemingway's career.
In *Il fuoco,* the poet and composer Stelio Effrena is the younger partner; the
Venetian actress La Foscarina is the aging one. (D'Annunzio was only five
years younger than La Duse.) They have long delayed consummating their
love, which occurs between scenes in the novel, and during which La Foscarina
inflicts the "wound" by biting Effrena's lower lip and drawing blood. Afterwards they decide to resume a more or less platonic relationship. She goes
back to her "nomadic" life, affirming her desire to bring art to the "barbari"
across the Atlantic; he, "the Life-Giver," assumes the role of Nietzschean
superman.[16] *Il fuoco* also has a victim of heart disease: Effrena helps Richard
Wagner from his gondola and up the *fondamenta* when he has heart spasms.
The novel closes with Wagner's death from a heart attack in the Palazzo Ven-
dramin and his funeral cortège in which Effrena serves as pallbearer. D'Annunzio addressed *Notturno,* a series of memories and reflections, to his daughter
Renata—the name may well have contributed to Hemingway's choice of Renata for his heroine. D'Annunzio's daughter helped him through his convalescence in Venice in 1916 when, having lost an eye in a plane crash, he was
forced to bandage the other eye and lie immobile for months. Hemingway's
Renata similarly comforts the ailing Cantwell and listens to his war stories.
Cantwell's Italian must have been fluent because *Notturno* has never been
translated and it is the only book by D'Annunzio that he mentions by name:

"the great, lovely writer of *Notturno*" (*ART* 52). Pound also admired *Notturno,* leaner and simpler (more like Torcello) than D'Annunzio's rich early style; he could have recommended it to Hemingway.

Cantwell's (and Hemingway's) relationship to D'Annunzio goes back to the First World War. Riding up the Grand Canal Cantwell points out famous palazzi to Jackson. Passing by the one in which Byron lived, Cantwell says that he was "well-loved in his town," despite his "errors." "You have to be a tough boy in this town to be loved" (*ART* 48). As we have seen, Cantwell takes pride in the fact that the Venetians "treat me well" in "my city" (*ART* 26) and he defines a "tough" man as one "who backs his play" (*ART* 49), surely a Cantwell. Byron created the Romantic archetype of the poet-warrior which culminates in D'Annunzio and, to a lesser extent, in Hemingway himself. D'Annunzio's "little villa" is the very next one that Cantwell points out to Jackson. "[L]ittle" is not merely descriptive but pejorative. The villa is also "ugly" (the only ugly thing Cantwell seems to notice in Venice), "close up against the water" (the destructive element—but what palazzo is not?) and "overrun with badly administered trees" (*ART* 49), not an image of nature in the wild but of bad art. In a parody of D'Annunzio, Hemingway launches into a few sentences of "bad" rhetoric tonally at odds with the novel's stylistic norm and immediately recognizable as a false note:

They loved him for his talent, and because he was bad, and he was brave. A Jewish boy with nothing, he stormed the country with his talent, and his rhetoric. He was a more miserable character than any that I know and as mean (*ART* 49).

D'Annunzio never wrote such bad rhetoric and was not Jewish, as Cantwell shortly concedes. Within its context the anti-Semitic remark, which is not Cantwell's only one, [17] sets D'Annunzio apart, making him a scapegoat for certain qualities that Hemingway secretly admired and wished to reject in himself. Meanness is also a quality of Cantwell's. Such "mimetic hostility," writes Robert Casillo, informs the relations between Jake and his double the "Jewish" Cohn: the "doubling results from Jake's projection of self-loathing onto Cohn" (Casillo 1986, 124–25). Like D'Annunzio, Hemingway is (by 1950) a famous writer, a paramilitary figure, and lover—married four times (to Cantwell's two, possibly three). D'Annunzio "lost an eye" in a crash "flying as an observer"; Hemingway was wounded handing out chocolates and cigarettes to Italians in the trenches. D'Annunzio "flew, but he was not a flier. He was in the Infantry but he was not an Infantryman and it was always the same appearances" (*ART* 50). Cantwell may be partially justified in his criticism, and yet Hemingway could be accused of "the same appearances" as D'Annunzio, and with much less to credit them. D'Annunzio was a genuine and much-decorated war hero, he did the military part better—he also did it first.[18] D'Annunzio and Cantwell are doubles, and by means of Cantwell's attitude towards D'Annunzio, Hemingway attempts to vent his hostility, project his envy and self-hate, and resolve his own attitudes towards his ideal of the poet-warrior and death.

Colonel Cantwell refers to D'Annunzio as "Lieutenant Colonel" (*ART* 51) and seems pleased to have risen higher in the ranks (but did Cantwell—or Hemingway—ever take over a large city and hold onto it with machine guns?). His profound distaste stems not so much from professional jealousy as from a rejection of D'Annunzio's war mentality and a rhetoric that has little to do with true patriotism (the original, soldierly myth of Venice) and a great deal to do with megalomania and Romantic narcissism. In a scene too reminiscent of the famous passage in *A Farewell To Arms,* Cantwell recalls standing with the troops in the rain and listening to a "discourse, speech, or harangue" (*ART* 51) by D'Annunzio. With his patched eye and his "white face . . . looking thirty hours dead," D'Annunzio is "shouting": "Morire non basta" (To die is not enough).[19] Cantwell, then a lieutenant, thinks reasonably to himself: "What the muck more do they want of us?" (*ART* 50). To answer the question from the standpoint of D'Annunzio, the romantic myth requires that one be "half in love with easeful death" (Keats): this experience must not be left to nature, *that* is "not enough." One must long for death, fill it with meaning, will one's death, dramatize one's death. This view is undercut by its own language: "death" is not "enough," not totality, does not fulfill life, is not, in Keats's words, "life's high meed." In a "classical" soldier's plain thinking death is the end of life.

In this scene many soldiers cannot hear D'Annunzio because there are no loudspeakers. When D'Annunzio asks for a moment of silence for "our glorious dead" (*ART* 50), the soldiers misconstrue the situation and take it as a cue to shout *"Evviva d'Annunzio"* (*ART* 50). While others die, may D'Annunzio live on! In classical epic tradition, the poet preserves the name and glory of the warrior by singing his exploits, the pagan version of immortality. In the romantic myth, D'Annunzio is the Superman triumphing over the "slaves" who exist merely to serve him. He combines both functions of poet and warrior.

Yet D'Annunzio undergoes further satiric reduction. The great writer shouting into the air without anyone hearing him is a little ridiculous. The men know what he says because they had heard him before, "after victories, and before defeats, and they knew what they should shout if there was any pause by an orator" (*ART* 50). So they are complicit in his will to power. But, "loving his platoon" (*ART* 51), Cantwell wishes to show solidarity; he too shouts *"Evviva d'Annunzio"* in order to "share their guilt" (*ART* 51). Hemingway may be attempting to atone for his hero-worship of D'Annunzio by means of satiric reduction and shared guilt.

Hemingway's ambivalence toward D'Annunzio extends across his career. In an unpublished story written in 1919, "The Passing of Pickles McCarty" or

"The Woppian Way," D'Annunzio is both a "great amourist" and one who has "set the decrees of nations aside by his filibuster," filibustering being a negative comment on D'Annunzian rhetoric. D'Annunzio is a "lover who had failed in only one pursuit, that of death in battle" (quoted in Reynolds 1986, 58). Still, the narrator, a journalist, and Nick Neroni decide to join D'Annunzio at Fiume. By the following year, in "The Mercenaries" Hemingway may have undercut D'Annunzio's stature as an "amourist" and even his physical courage. Il Lupo (the wolf), an Italian air ace and celebrity, may be a thinly veiled portrait of D'Annunzio. According to Michael Reynolds, in this story an American mercenary has an affair with Il Lupo's mistress, prompting a duel. Il Lupo's courage wavers and the American shoots the pistol out of his hand (Reynolds 1986, 125). By 1920–21, in "D'Annunzio" Hemingway completed the demythologization, turning directly to the war exploits:

> Half a million dead wops
> And he got a kick out of it
> The son of a bitch. (Hemingway 1979, 28)

The spare, caustic language and jargon is Hemingway's answer to D'Annunzian rhetoric. D'Annunzio enjoys a horrid version of the false sublime ("a kick") at the expense of the "wops." In a letter to Pound in 1924 Hemingway referred to D'Annunzio as the "Principe di Monte Nervosa" (prince of nervous mountain), a play (or a slip?) on the actual Monte Nevoso (snowy mountain) (Hemingway 1981, 114).

What is Hemingway's final estimate of D'Annunzio? In *Across the River,* Cantwell interrupts his thoughts on D'Annunzio to tell Jackson the name of the person who lived in the villa, "Gabriele d'Annunzio, who was a great writer," and to recommend "some fair English translations" (*ART* 51). Jackson asks for his name again—the name is already forgotten[20]: " 'D'Annunzio,' the Colonel said. 'Writer' " (*ART* 51). The tone is lapidary, public, final; but it hardly suffices and Cantwell silently resumes his mental traveling: "writer, poet, national hero, phraser of the dialectic of Fascism, macabre egoist, aviator, commander, or rider, in the first of the fast torpedo attack boats, Lieutenant Colonel of Infantry without knowing how to command a company, nor a platoon properly, the great, lovely writer of *Notturno* whom we respect, and jerk" (*ART* 52). A "jerk," as we learn, has "never worked at his trade *(oficio)* truly, and is presumptuous in some annoying way" (*ART* 97). Finally, Jackson never will read D'Annunzio (nor Hemingway?). He prefers "Comic books" and can find anything he wants "from superman on up to the improbable" (*ART* 301–02) in Trieste. The Italian Superman is brought down to the exchange level of the American comic book Superman.

After *Across the River,* the only significant reference to D'Annunzio in Hemingway appears in an interview with Eugenio Montale in Venice in 1954. Montale asked the ailing Hemingway about his opinion of D'Annunzio, "He leaped from his bed and tried to imitate him, shouting: 'To live is not enough!' Then he remembered, it seems to me with praise, *Notturno.*" [21] The very name of D'Annunzio energizes Hemingway, makes him jump out of his sickbed to "imitate" and parody his old hero, though there is also the balancing praise for the great writer. *To live* instead of *To die is not enough* is a slip, as in dreams which show "a preference for combining contraries into a unity or for representing them as one and the same thing" (Freud 1955, 4: 318). To live and to die do not, however, make up a unity. Rather, each concept separately implicates the sense of lack. Our life and death concepts leave us equally with an absence of fulfillment.

Death resolves the soldierly classical and the romantic myths. While Venice precipitates Cantwell's death, however, he does not die in Venice. Death is pollution, and the goddess must not be profaned by the sight of death. Death is natural, and Venice is aesthetic, inorganic ("no trees"), permitting no natural death. Cantwell plans a trip with Renata back to Wyoming; she imagines that "we could see the trees when we woke up" (*ART* 265); he expresses his love for trees by naming them, "Pine mostly, and cotton-wood along the creeks, and aspen" that "turn yellow in the fall" (*ART* 265). Cantwell says farewell to Renata near the garage under trees with "no leaves on them" (*ART* 276). On the detour on the road to Trieste Cantwell suffers a heart attack and quotes Stonewall Jackson's dying words, "let us cross over the river and rest under the shade of the trees" (*ART* 307). But Hemingway's title is stronger, primal: not under the trees, but "into the Trees," like Frost's "Into My Own," where the poet wants to disappear into "those dark trees," "Into their vastness." As in Frost, Hemingway's deepest affinity is not for the city but for the land. Cantwell does not die on the battlefield: He is too good a soldier and too lucky. Yet he dies a soldier's, not an artist's, not an aesthete's death: not in Venice, but near the battlefield where, long before, he lost his "immortality" (*ART* 33), where his death properly began, for, as Ruskin said, "the ceasing to breathe is only the *end* of death."

Cantwell's final order to Jackson is to return the portrait of Renata and the shotguns, symbols of love and war, to their owners (Renata and Alvarito) through the Hotel Gritti. Not the great general Jackson, but a modern flunkey and ignoramous Jackson has the "last words." "They'll return them all right," Jackson thinks, "through channels" (*ART* 308). This mimesis and parodic reduction of the Venetian canals is Hemingway's final comment on the fall from beauty in the modern, mechanized, administered society. A new pestilential form of "death by water" has spread through the world, where everything feeds through administrative "channels."

Time and Form in *Across the River and into the Trees*

Chronological Time		Narrative Time	Cantwell's Time
Italy, late fall, 1946 or 1947			
Chapter 1	Day 4	"tomorrow"; duckshoot in swamps near Venice, two hours before dawn	"boatman" and "shooter" in marshes
Chapter 2	Day 1	"day before yesterday"; a medical examination in Trieste	prognosis
Chapter 3-15	Day 2	"yesterday"; drive from Trieste to Venice; afternoon drinks at Gritti; evening with Renata; nocturnal gondola ride; returns to hotel; portrait	memories of early career in WWI: first visit to Venice
Chapters 16-39	Day 3	"today"; morning and lunch with Renata; leaves Venice for duckshoot	recounts later military career in WWII to Renata
Chapters 40-45	Day 4	"tomorrow"; dawn; the duckshoot; and death on road back to Trieste	realm of the dead

Notes

1. As Jacob Burckhardt wrote of Venice, no state "has ever exercised a greater moral influence over its subjects" (1960, 42).

2. Thomas Mann to Elisabeth Zimmer, 6 September 1915. *Letters 1971*, p. 76.

3. Thomas Mann to Erika and Klaus Mann, 25 May 1932. *Letters 1971*, p. 187.

4. In one of the most important essays in Hemingway studies in the past decade, "The Festival Gone Wrong: Vanity and Victimization in *The Sun Also Rises*," Robert Casillo has analyzed the interrelation between desire, mediation, code-followers, and death (Casillo 1986).

5. Eliot's Phlebas appears in *The Waste Land*, IV: "Death by Water." Cantwell, misquoting Eliot, unconsciously identifies himself with Eliot's "Phlebas the Phoenician, a fortnight dead."

6. According to J. J. Bachofen, by the law of tellurian generation (and thus of the swamp) life is an exchange for death: In the soldier's trade, he gets paid for killing.

7. Hemingway gives large prominence to Cantwell's heart trouble (and other physical ailments) and medication, devoting the second chapter to a medical examination. Cantwell suffers from high blood pressure and severe angina pectoris, and he has sustained about ten concussions in battle. Before his medical examination he takes an extra large dose of mannitol hexanitrate in order to "pass" and be given permission to go on the duck shoot near Venice. Mannitol hexanitrate is a longer acting member of the nitrite family (nitroglycerin is a related drug) and would have forestalled symptoms or signs on his cardiogram. In general nitrates act on blood vessels by "causing muscle fibers to relax," particularly arterioles, capillaries, and veins; "the lumen of the vessel is increased, the blood pressure is reduced, and the capillary flow is increased" (Krug 1960, 432). "The primary effect on the heart is acceleration" (Solis-Cohen 1928, 1330). Dilation of the retinal vessels may increase intraocular tension, and dilation of the meningeal vessels increase intracranial pressure and may cause severe headaches. But Cantwell's overdose backfires. Not fooled by it, the "skeptical" surgeon notes, after taking two readings, that the excessive medication is "definitely contra-indicated in increased intra-ocular and intra-cranial pressure" (*ART* 8). Cantwell cannot wait for the examination to end because he is suffering from nausea, a typical side-effect of large doses (Solis-Cohen 1928, 1329). Mannitol hexanitrate lasts for 6–7 hours, which are roughly the intervals between which Cantwell takes the drug. Hemingway may have chosen this particular nitrite because of one of its more unusual characteristics: It is "very explosive" (Solis-Cohen 1928, 1328). The surgeon jokingly tells Cantwell not to "let any sparks strike" him when he is "souped up" on his medicine (*ART* 9)—a parody of a soldier's death. The surgeon also flatters Cantwell that his "cardiograph" is "wonderful" and "could have been that of a man of twenty-five" or a "boy of nineteen" (*ART* 9). While a "normal" cardiogram of a healthy nineteen-year-old might be slightly different from the "normal" cardiogram of a healthy fifty-one-year-old, there would not be typical findings to warrant the surgeon's remark. More likely he is trying to cheer up the ailing colonel who is even more seriously ill than he thinks. The "boy of nineteen" would bring him back to his precise age during the Italian campaign in the First World War and leave him a few months older than Renata's present age. (I am indebted to Dr. Thomas J. Mattimore, Harlem Hospital and Columbia College of Physicians and Surgeons, for the research, information, and interpretation in this note.)

8. These comparisons point up a rather adolescent attitude on Cantwell's part.

9. Here is an instance of Hemingway's typical romanticizing of waiters and their special "knowledge" which at any rate remains superficial. Hemingway actually condescends to waiters even as he pretends to glorify them.

10. In this count, a double equals two drinks (three of Cantwell's nine orders are doubles). But it should be noted that Italian hard drinks are rarely at the strength of British or American drinks—even at Harry's.

11. According to Praz (1970, 429), Barrès was opposed to the reconstruction of the *campanile* of Saint Mark's after its collapse in 1902. The collapse, thought Barrès, was proof of his interpretation of Venice. But the *campanile* was reconstructed—and disproved his interpretation.

12. "Between a solid beginning and a solid end," writes E. M. Halliday, "we meander through a spongy middle of prolonged conversation wherein the hero expresses to his dream-girl *contessa* numerous prejudices, often malicious and often irrelevant to what meaning the book could have" (1952, 217). "Spongy" indeed, those marshlands of the scenes with Renata contain the clue to the entire work!

13. Robert Lewis (1965, 186) suggests that Renata may whisper of being pregnant, but surely they would have discussed a pregnancy—and his fatherhood—further. It seems highly unlikely that Renata has ever had intercourse with Cantwell. She later stops Cantwell from taking off his "tunic" (*ART* 211) in his hotel room, a clear sign of a refusal that he reluctantly must accept.

14. She may want children, but not by Cantwell. Or this is a dredged-up memory of her childhood, her love of "fun."

15. Yeats placed the passage, in free verse form, at the beginning of his *Oxford Book of Modern Verse* (1939). Hugh Kenner discusses Pater's influence on Hemingway in *A Homemade World:* "What has been less routinely noticed . . . is the wholly aesthetic basis of all his values: aesthetic, decadent, in the *fin de siècle* sense: the sense of the forlorn aesthetes, Dowson and Symons, Pater and Oscar Wilde (1979, 141–42). For Pater, the Mona Lisa, and Modernism, see Harold Bloom, introduction to *Selected Writings of Walter Pater* (New York: New American Library, 1974).

16. In *Il fuoco* the eponymous flame is a complex symbol for the all-consuming power of love; sexual union; the color of pomegranates which are sacred to the death-goddess Persephone, yet bursting with life-giving seed; the destructive and creative fire, as at the glass furnaces on Murano where the novel reaches its climax in La Foscarina's declaration; the burning of light upon or behind water which is captured by Venetian glass, for the fire is the masculine creative power and the water or glass the woman's refracting medium (e.g., the actress La Duse) through which it expresses itself. Hence the flame reflected on or behind water is a synecdochic condensation of Venice itself.

17. See the references to "Benny Meyers" (*ART* 184, 188) a "typical" Jewish name. "Meyers" is accused of staying home and making money selling bad products to the army.

18. Michael Reynolds (1986, 211), first concedes that D'Annunzio was a "difficult act to follow," then goes on to imply that Hemingway actually succeeded in following it: "Hemingway's own military adventures in World War Two were to bear a striking resemblance to those of the Italian writer." But Reynolds's list of these "striking resemblances" only serves to show how truly *un*like the experiences of the two men were: "D'Annunzio led single-boat raids on the Austrians; Hemingway outfitted his fishing boat to attack German submarines single-handedly. D'Annunzio flew bombing missions; Hemingway flew intercept missions with the R.A.F as a reporter. D'Annunzio gathered

his own army to liberate Fiume after the war; Hemingway gathered his band of irregulars after the Normandy invasion and was the first military group into Paris.'' One cannot find a "striking resemblance" between D'Annunzio's numerous raids in hostile territory and Hemingway's fishing boat exploits in Cuba. Nor can D'Annunzio's liberation of Fiume be seriously compared with Hemingway at Paris. Reynolds had previously called for a "moratorium on nostalgia," said he was "bored with psychoanalysis," and urged a resumption of "the practice of the trade for which we were trained" (1980, 28).

19. Hemingway had cited D'Annunzio in correct Italian ("Morire non basta") in a report to the *Toronto Daily Star* (5 October 1923), translating the remark "It is not enough to die," and intepreting it "You must survive to win" (Hemingway, *Dateline: Toronto: The Complete* Toronto *Star Dispatches, 1920–24,* ed. William White [New York: Scribner, 1985], p. 320). For a further discussion, see my "Hemingway and D'Annunzio," forthcoming in *Il Veltro.*

20. This is true: The Modern Library has long ceased to reprint *Il fuoco (The Flame of Life), The Triumph of Death,* and so on.

21. Eugenio Montale, Interview with Ernest Hemingway, *La Corriere della sera,* 26 March 1954: "Ha letto D'Annunzio? Fa un salto sul letto e cerca di imitarla gridando: 'Vivere non è basta!' Poi ricorda, mi pare con lode, il *Notturno.*"

References

Auden, W. H. *The Enchafèd Flood: or The Romantic Iconography of the Sea.* New York: Random House, 1950.

Bachofen, J. J. *Myth, Religion, and Mother Right.* Trans. Ralph Mannheim. Princeton UP, 1967.

Brown, Norman O. *Life Against Death: The Psychoanalytical Meaning of History.* 2nd ed. Middletown, CT: Wesleyan UP, 1959.

Burckhardt, Jacob. *The Civilization of the Renaissance in Italy.* New York: Phaidon, 1960.

Casillo, Robert. "The Desert and the Swamp: Englightenment, Orientalism, and the Jews in Ezra Pound." *Modern Language Quarterly* 45 (1984), 263–86.

———. "The Festival Gone Wrong: Vanity and Victimization in *The Sun Also Rises.*" *Essays in Literature* 13 (1986): 115–33.

D'Annunzio, Gabriele. *Il fuoco.* Milan: Mondadori, 1982.

Davenport, Guy. "Persephone's Ezra," in *New Approaches to Ezra Pound.* Ed. Eva Hesse. Berkeley and Los Angeles: U of California P, 1989. 145–73.

Freud, Sigmund. *Beyond the Pleasure Principle. The Standard Edition of the Complete Psychological Works.* Vol. 18. London: Hogarth Press and The Institute of Psycho-Analysis, 1955.

———. *The Interpretation of Dreams. Standard Edition.* Vols. 4–5.

———."Medusa's Head." *Standard Edition.* Vol. 17.

Gradoli, Marina, "Italy in E. Hemingway's Fiction." *Revista Studi Americani. Italy and Italians in America.* Ed. Alfredo Rizzardi. Acts of the Seventh National Conference, Associazione Italiana di Studi Nord-Americani. 4–5 (1985): 145–52.

Halliday, E. M. "Hemingway's Narrative Perspective" *Swanee Review* 60 (1952): 202–18.

Harrison, Jane. *Mythology*. New York: Harcourt, Brace, 1963.

Hemingway, Ernest. *Across the River and into the Trees*. New York: Scribner, 1950.

———. *88 Poems*. New York: Harcourt Brace Jovanovich, 1979.

———. *Selected Letters*. Ed. Carlos Baker. New York: Scribner, 1981.

James, Henry. *Italian Hours*. Boston: Houghton Mifflin, 1909.

Kenner, Hugh. *A Homemade World: The American Modernist Writers*. New York, Knopf, 1979.

Krug, Elsie E. *Pharmacology in Nursing*. 8th ed. St. Louis: C. V. Mosby, 1960.

Lewis, Robert W., Jr. *Hemingway on Love*. Austin: U of Texas P, 1965.

Lorenzetti, Giulio. *Venice and Its Lagoon*. Trans. John Guthrie. Trieste: Lint, 1975.

Mann, Thomas. *Letters of Thomas Mann*. Trans. Richard and Clara Winston. New York: Knopf, 1971.

Montale, Eugenio. Interview with Ernest Hemingway. *La Corriere della sera*, 26 March 1954.

Muir, Edward. *Civil Ritual in Renaissance Venice*. Princeton: Princeton UP, 1984.

Pater, Walter. *The Renaissance*. New York: Boni and Liveright, 1929.

Praz, Mario. *The Romantic Agony*. Trans. Angus Davidson. 2nd ed. London: Oxford UP, 1970.

Reynolds, Michael. *Hemingway's Reading: 1910–1940: An Inventory*. Princeton: Princeton UP, 1980.

———. *The Young Hemingway*. Oxford: Basil Blackwell, 1986.

Solis-Cohen, Solomon, and Githens Thomas Stotesbury. *Pharmacotherapeutics: Materia Medica and Drug Action*. New York: D. Appleton, 1928.

16

The Way It Never Was on the Piave

Frank Scafella

I had tried to write ["A Way You'll Never Be"] back in the twenties, but had failed several times. I had given up on it but one
day here (in Key West), fifteen years after those things happened to me in a trench dugout outside Fornaci, it suddenly
came out focused and complete. Here in Key West, of all
places. Old as I am, I continue to be amazed at the sudden
emergence of daffodils and stories.

Hemingway to Hotchner,
in *Papa Hemingway*[1]

In "A Way You'll Never Be" (1933), Nick Adams returns to the war front at
Fossalta on the Piave River, to the exact location of his wounding several
weeks (or months) earlier. He crosses a field of battle where the dead lie slumped
and bloated, makes his way through the town of Fossalta, and comes out onto
the west bank of the river where his parent battalion of Italian troops is dug in.
The Austrians hold the east bank of the river from which, periodically, they
shell the Italian positions on the west bank.

But the focus of the story is not on the war between the Italians and the
Austrians. It is on the effects of war in Nick Adams's psyche. There, inside
Nick, it is a standoff between *I* and *myself*. For in the moment of Nick's
wounding, as in the wounding of Frederic Henry in *A Farewell to Arms, I* felt
myself rush out of *myself*. *I* knew *I* was dead, says Lieutenant Henry, and that
it had all been a mistake to think you just died. "My soul went out of me,"
says Nick in a manuscript version of "Now I Lay Me," "and sailed a long
way out and I was dead until it came back" (Ms. 638). And from that moment
on, at night when Nick lay down to sleep, *himself* threatened once more to rush
out of *himself,* and *I* could stop it only by a very great mental effort.

So that is what's behind what's going on in "A Way You'll Never Be." Nick Adams returns to Fossalta di Piave, to the exact location of his wounding, consciously seeking a way to keep *myself* from rushing out of *myself* once more. For Nick has decided that by returning to the exact location of the loss of *myself*, *I* might discover why that event has made darkness and sleep such forbidding presences. And according to what Hemingway allegedly said to Hotchner, Nick Adams in fact solves the mystery of his vagrant soul there on Paravicini's cot in the command dugout on the west bank of the Piave. That is what Hemingway implies when he calls the story "focused" and "complete," and by way of the story and an early manuscript version of "A Way You'll Never Be," I wish to demonstrate that in this instance we can indeed take Hemingway at his word.

Let us enter the published story by way of its climax. In the battalion commander's dugout on the west bank of the Piave, Nick Adams lies down on Paravicini's bunk.

He shut his eyes, and in place of the man with the beard who looked at him over the sights of the rifle, quite calmly before squeezing off, the white flash and clublike impact, on his knees, hot-sweet choking, coughing it onto the rock while they went past him, he saw a long, yellow house with a low stable and the river much wider than it was and stiller. (*Short Stories [SS]* 1938, 414)

For the first time since his wounding, in this memory Nick sees the man who shot him, feels the impact of the bullet, tastes the blood of his wound, and coughs it (his soul) onto a rock *before* he sees the familiar but frightening objects of a recurrent nightmare, namely, a long, yellow house with a low stable and the river much wider than it was and stiller. Always during the weeks prior to this moment of lucid recall on Paravicini's cot, Nick "has" the yellow house in the recurrent nightmare but *not* the Austrian soldier, the club-like impact, the hot-sweet blood, and his soul on a rock. In other words, in the nightmare which comes on him unaware he has the psychic result (the long, yellow house) but not the sensory details of the event that underlies it. But lying there on Paravicini's bunk long after the actual event, on the very river bank where he was wounded, awake and in the daylight, in full consciousness of its coming, Nick "has" the yellow house once more—that house that meant more than anything to him, that was what he needed but it frightened him— but this time, for the first time, he has the house *in place of* the Austrian soldier, the clublike impact, the taste of his own blood, and the loss of his soul. He has the yellow house, that is, *in place of* having died. So the long, yellow house of his recurrent nightmare is, quite clearly, a projection from the unconscious psyche of Nick Adams *himself* more frightened than he had ever been, and Nick's consciously having the yellow house *in place of* the sensory details of his wounding and death is Nick's becoming conscious of himself frightened, cowardly, "yellow" in face of his own death. And to grasp his cowardice thus is to begin moving beyond it.

Nick had in fact gone back to the front at Fossalta with the conscious intention of locating the yellow house and of examining it to discover why it frightened him so. Long before his return to Fossalta he was fully aware of something extraordinary about the house, for night after night in his dream, in the world of *myself,* "outside of Fossalta there was a low house painted yellow with willows all around it and a low stable and there was a canal" (*SS* 1938, 408). But out of his dream, in the daylight and under ordinary circumstances— in the world of *I*—Nick remembers that he had actually been outside Fossalta "a thousand times" and had never seen that house. Yet there it was in his dream every night and "it frightened him."

So when Nick passes through the town of Fossalta on his way back to the river he looks for the low yellow house and finds, as he already knows, that "there was no house" like the one in his dream. "Nor was the river that way" either, wider than it was and stiller. If so, "Then where did he go each night and what was the peril," Nick asks himself, "and why would he wake, soaking wet, more frightened than he had ever been in a bombardment, because of a house and a long stable and a canal?" (*SS* 1938, 408, 409)

Notice how Nick puts it: He does not ask, why do I have this nightmare? but, *where do I go* each night? The dream is a terrain in which he moves, the yellow house an object that he needs there. Hence it is not, for Nick, a matter of dispelling fear by demonstrating that the house is merely oneiric. Nick's problem is to track to its origin in experience the nightmare journey of *himself* to the low yellow house by the river *in his dream.* And the origin of the house, as we have seen, is revealed to Nick as he lies on Paravicini's bunk and relives the event of his wounding. There it becomes clear that the low yellow house is Nick Adams *himself* in the form of a low, yellow house more frightened than he had ever been. The nightmare repeatedly forces this fact on Nick's conscious mind, demanding that *I* face *myself* frightened, cowardly, "yellow." But frightened of what?

The common answer is, frightened of death. And of all Hemingway's stories, "A Way You'll Never Be" is commonly regarded as *the* story which "masks" most perfectly (in Frederick Hoffman's words) the compulsive repetition of the traumatic shock of the unreasonable wound (*SS* 1938, 74). In other words, Nick Adams is understood as a mask worn by Ernest Hemingway in order that he might conceal, in the very act of revealing, that "core of shock" (Philip Young 1966, 52), shell shock, or fear of death which grips the psyche of Ernest Hemingway the man with a firmness which destines him to repeat compulsively the wounding which he can neither face directly nor ever understand. It follows that there is more "obvious hysteria" in "A Way You'll Never Be" than anywhere else in Hemingway's fiction (Rovit 1963, 80), so much hysteria, in fact, that "one never knows what is going on in this story" (Young 1966, 52). Hugh Kenner puts it this way: Hemingway's achievement "consisted in setting down, so sparely that we can see past them, the words for the actions that concealed the real action," namely, Hemingway's own experience of shell shock and terror of death (1975, 156). Thus the critical task has been to get at the "real-life experience" behind the mask of fiction. Kenneth G. Johnston summarizes this critical agenda most explicitly:

Hemingway the writer felt impelled to reveal . . . what Hemingway the private man wanted to obscure. In short, when Hemingway succeeded as the artist, the mask was not impenetrable. Not surprisingly, Hemingway directed his special anger at critics, such as Philip Young, who publicly stripped away the mask to reveal the naked man. (1984, 71)

If in 1933 "A Way You'll Never Be" came out "complete" and "focused," then it must have been (in Carlos Baker's view) a "nightmare" coherence that it embodied for the writer (1969, 228). And if so, Hemingway's declared "amazement" at the sudden emergence of the story from his innermost self, like the sudden emergence of a daffodil from the earth in spring, must be regarded as a concealment. It was one more effort, we must surmise (if we take the Freudian view), to mask from his readers, his critics, *and* himself what was really going on in "A Way You'll Never Be."

But if we take the terms "death," "shell shock," and "compulsive repetition" back to the text of "A Way You'll Never Be," we find that, while it is generally true that Nick's experience of death on the battlefield is what frightens him, the term "death" covers like a blanket all of the detail and specificity both of Nick's fear and of the precise kind of death that he suffers. For between the image of the Austrian soldier who sights down the rifle barrel and shoots him, and the low yellow house by the river, Nick watches *himself* cough "it" onto a rock as the Austrian soldiers rush past him. Which is to say, in his reverie on Paravicini's cot Nick Adams sees himself cough his soul onto a rock on the battlefield where he was wounded and in that moment he sees that it was his soul, his innermost self, coughed out of him and going off and then coming back that left him more frightened than he had ever been. It was the loss of his soul that left him with the image of himself as "yellow," a coward. For the death that Nick suffers he not only lives through but after. It will be later, in "Now I Lay Me," the biographical sequel to "A Way You'll Never Be," that Nick makes consciously explicit the nature of his fear. There he confesses to having lived for a long time with the "knowledge" that his soul would leave him again (as it had on the field of battle) if ever he lay down in the dark and went to sleep. Nick has no such perspective on his wounding prior to the climactic vision of "A Way You'll Never Be." It is this vision linking Nick's cowardice to the loss of his soul that at once specifies Nick's need for the yellow house and constitutes the focus, completeness, and amazement that Hemingway experienced in the published story. For in the mind's grasp of its nature and origin, the fear dissipates.

So we *do* know what is going on in "A Way You'll Never Be." The plot is well ordered and clear because the arrangement of the incidents in the total action is a conscious design of a mind which not only knows but seeks to overcome its own "nuttiness." This is to say that Nick Adams is not mentally deranged or hysterical in a pathological way; he is but mad north-northwest. When he is with Paravicini, or lying on his bunk, he can tell a hawk from a handsaw. And if, as Nick leaves Paravicini to return to Fornaci, he is not yet *fully* conscious that his vagrant soul is his fundamental problem, or even that he has taken a giant step toward overcoming his fear, he is no longer alienated from that part of himself which was given to the hysteria of the recurrent nightmare. Is it purely coincidental that Nick speaks *to* himself for the first time in the final words of the narrative? " 'I'd better get to that damned bicycle,' Nick said *to himself*. 'I don't want to lose the way to Fornaci' " (*SS* 1938, 414; my emphasis).

In 1955, Hemingway told Hotchner that he had tried to write "A Way You'll Never Be" back in the 1920s but had failed several times. In the Hemingway Collection there are five working manuscripts of this story. Two of them are complete drafts, one very close to the published text and the other radically different from it. Ms. 746a, a 32-page holograph almost completely at variance with the published story, we may presume to be one of the attempts that failed back in the 1920s.

A first person narrative, 746a fails primarily because it branches into two separate plots rather than developing two levels of conflict in a single plot and character, as in the published story. It begins as the published story begins, with Nick crossing a field of battle, going through the deserted town of Fossalta, and coming out onto the bank of the Piave where he is challenged by the lieutenant with the red-rimmed eyes. But there the similarity ends. For Nick looks into the young lieutenant's red-rimmed eyes and knows immediately that he is a man "permanently scared." From this moment on, 746a is as much the story of the permanently scared lieutenant as it is of Nick Adams, the first-person narrator.

Of all the characters in Hemingway's fiction, published and unpublished, there is no more perfect embodiment of psychic fixation on war than the red-eyed lieutenant of 746a. Freud himself could not have imagined a more precise or complete characterization of shell shock, paranoia, terror of death, and repetition compulsion. The permanently scared man lacks all perspective on himself and his actions and shows himself incapable of gaining such perspective. Midway through the narrative, for example, as Nick and Paravicini talk, the red-eyed lieutenant appears at the doorway of the command dugout holding at gunpoint two young peasant boys caught in the act of buggery in one of the trenches. The lieutenant illustrates with a gesture what it was the peasant boys had been doing, and he begins explaining to Paravicini that he would have shot them on the spot, but Paravicini interrupts him.

Paravicini sends the two peasant boys along the river bank out of earshot
and turns to the red-eyed lieutenant. "So," Paravicini says to him.

"Now listen closely. Your nerves are undone. You are hysterical. From cause. I understand it is from cause. That has nothing to do with what you tell me, of course. I
understand that. No. Listen. It is very hot weather. There are all sorts of people. Some
of one sort. Some of another. Then too there are vices. Then too there are childishnesses. What they were doing is a childishness. If it were not a childishness it would
be a vice. But you must understand also it is such hot weather and a battalion in the
line does not carry women. Childishnesses spring up or might spring up if not checked.
Man is not a pure animal. There are no pure animals but there is a definite distinction
between childishness and vice. Vice implies corruption. Do I make myself clear?"
    The lieutenant was listening, his face with the uneven stubble of beard was flushed,
his lips not steady, his eyes all wrong. "Yes, signor Maggiore," he said.
    "Good," the major went on in the tone of a lecturer in a popular course at a univer-
sity. "So. We have the heat, the absence of women, the fact that we are not built alike
and the essential childishness. It would be unjust not to mention that those two peasant
boys have made their first attack. They were both very good. I saw them."

But in spite of what he says, the red-eyed lieutenant does not understand
Paravicini. He only hates the major for pointing out his condition to him, and
he hates Nick for having heard it. So Nick not only hears but also sees for
himself how the permanently scared man is. Nick also sees that Paravicini is
very "sound" in what he says to the permanently scared man, and in the red-
eyed lieutenant Nick recognizes a way that he himself might have been. Yet
he suspects now that it is a way that he will never be, and the next major
action of the narrative proves this a fact.
    The Austrians begin shelling the Italian positions not long after Paravicini
sends the two peasant boys and the red-eyed lieutenant back to their positions.
A mortar round comes in and bursts. Then two more come, their sound, to
Nick, the "nastiest" to hear. Then there is a shout for stretcher bearers and
without hesitation both Nick and Paravicini go out of the dugout and Nick goes
up the river bank.

I climbed up the side of the sunken road and in the end of the sunset could see the dark
sausage balloon still up on the far side [of the river] and others far off. One was coming
down. Four men were clustered, bent over, around one of the holes. Two others were
coming running along below the bank of the road. My back was tight waiting for the
next shell. It did not come. Below the river was reflecting the sunset and I looked up it
to the bend and down to where it widened below the town. A farm house [near] the
river that had been shelled to the the ground looked like a pile of chalk.

If Nick is frightened when he leaves the dugout, climbs the river bank, and
stands on its rim, his fear is subordinated to the need he perceives for sizing
up the situation and making a contribution where he might. His back tightens

with anticipation of the next incoming round, but that is perfectly normal and to be expected. In fact, Nick's attention is so fully attuned to the shelling and its results that he is wholly unaware of his exposure on the skyline. Paravicini has to call him down from the bank. And as Nick comes down he sees the red-eyed lieutenant coming along toward him, his left hand hanging limp, blood dripping from the fingers. When the shelling started, the hysterical man had shot himself in the hand. By contrast, Nick's actions demonstrate that his is a way that Nick will never be in actual combat.

So Nick Adams's return to the front in 746a makes it clear that it is not of actual combat that he is afraid. His fear has another source and object than what actually happened or happens on a battlefield. In 746a Nick and Hemingway have no alternative but to face the fact that Nick is afraid of the war in his psyche. This is to say that 746a only clarifies but does not resolve Nick's fear of lying down to sleep in the dark. As for the permanently scared lieutenant, in his self-inflicted wound he purged the full probabilities of his character. With 746a itself he was cast to the bottom of the manuscript trunk, only to reappear in the published story long enough to show his red-rimmed eyes. There was no more substantial role than that for him in the story that suddenly came out focused and complete in 1933, for his hysteria was by then assimilated as a latent possibility into the character of Nick Adams. Thus Hemingway did not, in public, wear what the psychobiographical critic like Kenneth Johnston will certainly concede would have been his most perfect mask in the red-eyed lieutenant.

Hemingway's amazement at the sudden emergence of "A Way You'll Never Be" we can now appreciate as a species of awe, the wonder we experience in something truly beautiful, mysterious, and strange. In light of 746a we see that the story reached its final form because Hemingway could not be satisfied until Nick had not only plumbed the depths and faced but also had grasped intellectually and solved the problem of the nameless fear that drove him to the borders of madness. The 746a draft showed Hemingway that this could not be done in the first person because Nick could not be author of his own experience of nuttiness. Nick had to be free to go to the very heart of darkness, if need be, and that freedom demanded a disinterested narrator. Relieved of the restrictions that telling his own story placed on Nick's desire to face in himself the possibility of permanent scaredness, he was freed not only to report but to enter into and explore as deeply as he must the nightmare vision which, night after night, leaves him soaked with sweat. Thus Nick mines, mills, and refines the ore of his recurrent nightmare; he transmutes its psychic substance into thought—like the alchemist, he changes the baser metals of his life (fear, shame, cowardice) into the gold of understanding. Nick's aim is at once to see what passes for his soul and to possess his soul in the very act of forming it in thought.

On the Piave, then, there was fear, near hysteria, shame, cowardice, and, for a time, nuttiness. Nick and Hemingway admit as much. But permanent scaredness, irreversible shell shock, debilitating paranoia, repetition compulsion, pathological preoccupation with death—these are ways it never was for Nick or Hemingway, neither on the Piave nor anywhere else.

Note

1. I assume that the comparison of daffodils and stories is Hemingway's, not Hotchner's. This is a large assumption, to be sure. For I make it in face of the very influential opinion that Hotchner's *Papa Hemingway* is a yarn spun out of a nascent hero-worship. But I will justify my assumption not with reference to Hotchner, nor even with reference to Hemingway, but with regard to "A Way You'll Never Be."

References

Mss. 638 and 746a are in The Hemingway Collection, the John F. Kennedy Library, Boston.

Baker, Carlos. *Ernest Hemingway: A Life Story*. New York: Scribner, 1969.

Hemingway, Ernest. *The Short Stories of Ernest Hemingway*. New York: Scribner, 1938.

Hoffman, Frederick. "No Beginning and No End: Hemingway and Death." *Essays in Criticism* 3 (1953): 73–84.

Hotchner, A. E. *Papa Hemingway: The Ecstasy & Sorrow*. New York: Quill, 1983.

Johnston, Kenneth G. "Hemingway and Freud: The Tip of the Iceberg." *Journal of Narrative Technique* 14 (Winter 1984): 68–73.

Kenner, Hugh. *A Homemade World: The American Modernist Writers*. New York: Knopf, 1975.

Rovit, Earl. *Ernest Hemingway*. New Haven: College and University Press, 1963.

Young, Philip. *Ernest Hemingway: A Reconsideration*. New York: Harcourt, Brace, 1966.

17

Emotional Disorder and the Order of Things: Nick Adams in Italy

Erik Nakjavani

O Lord, I am working hard in this field, and the field of my labors is myself. I have become a problem to myself, like land which a farmer works with difficulty and at the cost of much sweat. For I am not now investigating the tracts of heavens, or measuring the distance of the stars, or trying to discover how the earth hangs in space. I am investigating myself, my memory, my mind.

Saint Augustine,
The Confessions

The things stand in different truths.

Martin Heidegger,
What Is a Thing?

One of Ernest Hemingway's striking accomplishments in *The Nick Adams Stories (NAS)* that deal with Nick's wounding and convalescence in Italy is his ability to allow Nick's different modes of consciousness to reflect the fear of losing that consciousness. Correspondingly, Hemingway makes Nick's various states of consciousness produce their own pattern of apprehension and narration of the world. This is particularly significant when one considers Nick as a writer-to-be, because, as Joseph M. Flora has pointed out, "Nick Adams is a writer, and the Nick Adams stories have insistently played on this aspect of his being" (1982, 235).

What I propose to do in this chapter is to examine (1) how Nick's diverse modes of consciousness and their images operate as strategies against the threat of the loss of his consciousness, and (2) how they affect the pattern of descriptive narrative discourse in the Chapter VI sketch of *In Our Time ([IOT]* 1925), "Now I Lay Me," "A Way You'll Never Be," and "In Another Country."

Perceptual Images and Non-Reflective Consciousness in the
Chapter VI Sketch of *In Our Time*

In the Chapter VI sketch of *In Our Time,* one finds that Nick is in the war, that he has been hit in the spine, and that he has been dragged clear of machine-gun fire to sit against the wall of a church. In this sketch, Hemingway does no more than obliquely hint at Nick's eventual emotional suffering by giving him a spinal injury. The full extent of the eventual emotional damage done to him remains hidden in the incident of his first wounding. At this stage, one may suggest that the shock to his body reaches his psyche indiscernibly through his subconscious.

That is why immediately after his first injury Nick appears to be calm, lucid, and in possession of his consciousness. Through what Kathryn Zabelle Derounian has called Nick's "restricted viewpoint" (1983, 64), one learns that Nick is looking "straight ahead brilliantly" (*IOT* 63; *NAS* 143). Perhaps one may detect a touch of controlled shock in the brilliant manner of his looking straight ahead. Beyond that, this statement does not seem to convey any other psychological overtone. What is, however, important to note is that Nick does not only look but also equally sees "brilliantly." In the overall context of the sketch, Nick's manner of looking is significant to the extent that it calls forth an act of extraordinarily clear seeing. This significance issues from Nick's status as the center of consciousness of the sketch. A brief analysis of what Nick actually sees makes the centrality of the act of seeing to the sketch quite evident.

Before turning his head to look down at Rinaldi, Nick sees that

the pink wall of the house opposite had fallen out from the roof, and an iron bedstead hung twisted toward the street. Two Austrian dead lay in the rubble in the shade of the house. Up the street were other dead. (*IOT* 63; *NAS* 145)

Nick's range of vision follows a deliberate pattern. There is nothing haphazard about what falls into its fold. Its trajectory moves from the top to the bottom of the house, across to the Austrian dead lying in the shade of the house, and then up the street and more Austrian dead. It traces along its path concrete details of a cluster of well delineated color, profiles, forms and contours in a sort of strict iconic economy. They impart a sense of experienced immediacy and vividness, because they have been well perceived and transformed into a verbal icon through the alchemy of narrative discourse.

In the light of the preceding analysis, it would seem reasonable to assert that immediately after his first wounding Nick's hypersensitive consciousness provides him with an acute sense of exterior reality. If one considers consciousness to be always the "consciousness *of* something," that is to say, of something outside of consciousness, as Edmund Husserl has done in relationship to the concept of phenomenological "intentionality" (1962, 223), then, the world of objects which surrounds man makes up his consciousness and his horizon. If one applies this definition of consciousness to Nick's it becomes evident that Nick's consciousness in this sketch is not only intact but, indeed, remarkably heightened.

It would be helpful to point out here that, following Aron Gurwitsch's definition, I primarily use the term "object" in this chapter in "a strictly descriptive sense" and not "as it is in reality, but, on the contrary, as it appears to the experiencing subject through a given act of consciousness or as it is given to a subject" (1964, 4). It is in this sense that through the interplay of his consciousness and its objects Nick generates so effectively the virtual space and time in the sketch. The created fictional reality then carries over to the consciousness of the reader and registers upon it as a series of etchings, as it were. These so-called etchings are arrested and frozen in the time-space continuum of the here-and-now; that is to say, in the everyday perceptual fashion that the reader as an individual subject encounters and appropriates the world of objects and makes an indissoluble synthesis with it. These etchings—or images, to be more accurate—are purposely deprived of any transcendent or metaphoric dimension. Appropriately, but disturbingly, even the Austrian dead are merely observed as the dead or wholly Other. The dead have already become reified human beings who are relegated to the category of objects that, as a whole, make up the matrix of the world.

So far in this sketch Nick remains on the level of perception, or what Jean-Paul Sartre has referred to in *The Psychology of Imagination* as the "non-reflective consciousness," which puts Nick in direct and immediate touch with the world. He is not in the least in danger of losing consciousness, and justifiably has no fear of it. Quite to the contrary, he is well grounded in the perceptual images of his "non-reflective consciousness," which is characteristic of him in all the other Nick Adams stories. He is still in what one may call the *diurnal* phase of the series of war injuries that he receives. The fear of the loss of consciousness is yet to come to him with the nightfall and the darkness of subsequent woundings.

The Function of Images of the Reflective and the Imaginative Consciousness in "Now I Lay Me"

In the short story "Now I Lay Me," which appeared two years later than the Chapter VI sketch of *In Our Time* (1925) in *Men Without Women* ([*MWW*] 1927), Nick himself is the "narrator-agent," as Carl Ficken has identified him (1975, 108). At the time that the narrated events take place, the memory of the incident of his second wounding is still so intractably lodged in Nick's psyche that it exerts a disabling pressure on his emotions.

Hemingway chooses to give Nick's wounding in "Now I Lay Me" a different setting from that of his previous one, indicating perhaps that Nick has been wounded more than once. Nick tells of having been "blown up at night" (*MWW*

129; *NAS* 144). There is no evidence to believe, however, that the extent of his second physical injury is coextensive with its emotional ramifications. Nick complains of no bodily pain. His body seems to have healed, but his psychic wound still festers. Although he tells his orderly, John, who is worried about Nick's insomnia, "I'll get all right," he hastens to add that "It just takes a while" (*MWW* 136; *NAS* 151).

Nick is fully and accurately aware of his condition, which makes up the kernel of this short story. He states:

I myself did not want to sleep because I had been living for a long time with the knowledge that if I ever shut my eyes in the dark and let myself go, my soul would go out of my body. I had been that way for a long time, ever since I had been blown up at night and felt it go out of me and go off and come back. (*MWW* 129; *NAS* 144)

If one equates what Nick refers to as his "soul" with his consciousness, as it does seem warranted to do in the context of this passage, his obsessive fear, then, can be no more or less than the loss of that consciousness. The shock of the experience of losing and regaining his consciousness after having been "blown up at night" haunts Nick in night-time traumatic flashbacks. But more specifically, through the mediation of the subconscious mechanisms of the psyche, his initial emotional shock has evidently attached itself symbolically to three elements: night, sleep, and death. The symbolic triangular relationship between these subconsciously interrelated phenomena provoke the uncontrollable fear of losing consciousness that Nick suffers from. His antidote for it is a kind of insomnia.

One may begin the analysis of this subconscious triangular relationship of night, sleep, and death with night. No doubt night and darkness stand for diminished consciousness of diurnal exterior reality and the rational security which it offers. Night devours the horizon of the human world and gives the irrational a chance for free play. Night empties the world of the visibility which provides psychic moorings. It can usher in *nocturnal* thoughts, catastrophic anticipations, and the so-called night-terrors. Forced by the void created by darkness to double upon itself at night, to make its own emptiness its object, human consciousness catches a glimpse of its own inevitable final annihilation and death. In this sense, it is revealing that Nick has no fear of sleeping when "it would be light" (*MWW* 131; *NAS* 146) or where he can have "a light" (*MWW* 133; *NAS* 148).

Correlatively, there is a subconscious fear of sleep, which finds its extreme conscious voice in the indirect language of insomnia. Here, again, the fear is that of diminution and disappearance of consciousness in sleep. Sleep, from an experiential point of view, may be considered as a form of temporary death, a death from which one wakes up, as it were.

Finally, death, which designates the summit of this triangular relationship, may be viewed as a permanent loss of consciousness as we know it and experience it. In death the darkness of night and the nothingness of deep sleep become absolute and infinite.

In the extremity of the event of his second wounding, Nick has an intimation of the internal connection between his loss of consciousness and the symbolic triangular correlatives which it suggests. And it is through an understanding of the implications of this intimation that he works out his strategies of maintaining his consciousness. His first strategy is to think about fishing along trout streams known to him from experience. The descriptive narrative discourse of these fishing stories is drawn from Nick's memory. Consequently, it presents images of objects which reach the purity of the conceptual rather than the perceptual images of objects under direct observation. The perceptual image always retains something of the inexhaustible attributes of the material object and its manifold extraneous relationships with other objects. That is why the perceived object ultimately remains in the realm of the opaque. But Nick's "fishing very carefully" in his mind "under all the logs, all the turns of the bank, the deep holes and the clear shallow stretches" (*MWW* 129; *NAS* 144) imparts the purity and the pristine qualities of eidetic images. This eidetic clarity of images carries over to his depiction of other details such as the trees along the streams, the grass, the insects, the worms, the salamanders, and the grasshoppers.

Nick in this story has gone beyond the stage of spontaneous and immediate perception which makes up the woof and warp of the Chapter VI sketch. He has refined the acuity of his images, a process which he further augments in this short story and in "A Way You'll Never Be." As a strategy to hold on to his consciousness, Nick has reached the level of what Sartre has called the "reflective consciousness." Sartre has explained that "to determine the properties of the image as image I must turn to a new act of consciousness: I must *reflect*. Thus the image as image is describable only by an act of second degree in which attention is turned away from the object and directed to the manner that the object is given" (Sartre 1972, 3). Nick by "thinking" about trout streams conjures up images which ensure the existence and the continuity of his consciousness. Because, as Sartre has pointed out, "a reflective consciousness gives us knowledge of absolute certainty," and that "he who becomes aware 'of having an image' by an act of reflection cannot deceive himself" (Sartre 1972, 3). Sartre has provided us with a Cartesian argument of absolute certainty in relationship to the image which clarifies the nature of Nick's efforts in recollection.

In this first descriptive narrative in "Now I Lay Me," the recollected and presented images by Nick evidence both power and paucity. They are powerful in their exactitude and sharpness, which make them resonate in the poetry of their evocations of things past. Their paucity results from a calculated attempt by the narrator to keep them concrete and deprived of any anxiety-provoking symbolic or metaphoric dimensions. This limiting structure of the images in the narrative, allied with their pastoral quality, differentiates them from those still to come in this short story and in "A Way You'll Never Be."

There is further refinement of the images of the "reflective consciousness" by Nick inasmuch as he also presents the reader with what Sartre calls "imaginative consciousness" (Sartre 1972, 14–15). It is through the mediation of the "imaginative consciousness" that Nick is able to go beyond thinking about trout streams which he has actually fished along to creating new ones. "Some nights, too," he recalls, "I made up streams, and some of them were very exciting, and it was like being awake and dreaming" (*MWW* 132; *NAS* 146). The object of the "imaginative consciousness" is an absence, in other words, an image. This consciousness is different from "perceptual consciousness," as Sartre has recognized, inasmuch as it

presents itself to itself as an imaginative consciousness, that is, as a spontaneity which produces and holds on to the object as an image. This is a sort of indefinable counterpart of the fact that the object occurs in nothingness. The consciousness appears to itself as being creative, but without positing that it has created an object. (Sartre 1972, 18)

Nick intuitively grasps the nature of the "imaginative consciousness" when he declares that experiencing it falls in the enchanting magical domain of "being awake and dreaming." Coincidentally, his strategy of maintaining his hold on his consciousness opens up to him the horizon of creativity and its infinite possibilities. In the narrative discourse of these made-up streams Nick has already become a maker of images which emerge out of absence and nothingness: a creator, an artist.

On those nights when Nick experiences a particularly difficult time, he cannot fish. The trout streams dry up in his mind. On such nights he finds it easier to pray. The "imaginative consciousness" now coincides with a kind of religious consciousness with which it shares certain fundamental structures. His prayers serve him as a mnemonic device as he remembers all the people he has ever known and prays for them all. His act of remembrance follows a regressive-progressive pattern. Trying to remember everything that had happened to him before the war, Nick divulges: "I found I could only remember back to the attic in my grandfather's house. Then I would start there and remember this way again, until I reached the war" (*MWW* 131; *NAS* 146).

I find it hard to attribute any Freudian symbolism to the regressive movement of Nick's mind to the attic of his grandfather's house and the memory of the objects it contains: his mother's and father's "wedding cake in a tin can," "jars of snakes and specimens" which with the alcohol that preserved them sunken in the jars "were exposed and turned white" (*MWW* 131; *NAS* 146). For me, they are, once more, images dredged up by Nick's mind to sustain his consciousness. No doubt these images of childhood and early familial life have something troubling and crepuscular about them. This impression is further

reinforced by the fact that Nick is led to such images when his fear and catastrophic anticipation appear to be more acute. In his critique of "Now I Lay
Me," Richard B. Hovey sees the objects which Nick enumerates as Freudian
symbols. He argues that "the tin box symbolizes the female genitals . . . snakes
symbolize the male organ—emphatically so, for a Caucasian, when their white-
ness is recollected" (1975, 185). In the next remembered scene, in which Nick's
mother is "cleaning out . . . the basement" of the new house by burning all
the "stone axes and some skinning knives and tools for making arrow-heads"
(*MWW* 132; *NAS* 147), Hovey once again sees some of the "relics the Freudian
would consider phallic symbols." And in their destruction he discovers "Nick
Adams' first 'wound'—the child's feared wound of emasculation" (1975, 186).

Hovey's remarks are interesting within the confines of Freudian psychoanalytic theory. I would reiterate, however, that these remembered scenes of early
familial life—fraught with tension as they are, as in all the Nick Adams stories—primarily have a supportive function in relationship to Nick's fear of loss
of consciousness. In my opinion, Hovey is much closer to the truth when he
mentions in passing that "Nick's fear of dying is linked with his fear of losing
consciousness," and that this necessitates for him "to keep a rigid hold on his
consciousness" (1975, 182). And this is the crucial point to comprehend and
deepen. Because Nick is totally obsessed with the problem of life and death,
he should be considered an "obsessional" rather than a "hysteric." As Stuart
Schneiderman, elaborating on Serge Leclair's ideas, has made clear, "the question of the obsessional is: Am I dead or alive? The hysteric's question is: Am
I a man or a woman?" (1983, 59). The question of sexuality, as primal as it
undoubtedly is, is not a primary concern for Nick in the short stories that deal
with his woundings and convalescence in Italy. Correspondingly, Nick eventually loses interest in trying to keep awake by thinking about all the girls that
he has ever known and "what kind of wives they would make" (*MWW* 137;
NAS 152). He points out that this strategy only temporarily "killed off trout
fishing and interfered with my prayers," because the girls soon "all blurred
and all became rather the same and I gave up thinking about them altogether"
(*MWW* 137; *NAS* 153). Clearly the fantasies of sex become peripheral to those
of survival in "Now I Lay Me."

It would seem to me more reasonable to think of the dialectical relationship
between Nick's memories of the attic in his grandfather's house and the basement of his parents' first house in terms that Gaston Bachelard has developed
in his *La Poétique de l'espace (The Poetics of Space)* rather than in terms of
Freudian psychoanalysis. In the context of what Bachelard has referred to as
"topo-analysis" (1970, 35–37), he asserts that the vertical structure of the
house establishes a polarity between the attic and the basement. He opposes
what he regards as the "rationality" of the attic to the "irrationality" of the
basement. The attic as the space between the ceiling of rooms and the roof of
the house suggests a protective zone that offers predictable domestic security
within against the unpredictable natural forces without. The attic, therefore,

supports life and becomes allied with it in the subconscious. Few people fear the attic. On the contrary, the basement presents all that is hidden and lurks in the darkness below the body of the house. For the subconscious, it is the part of the house that is buried and, consequently, is grounded in the deep subterranean irrational forces of nature, death, and burial. It resembles the subconscious, in contrast with the attic which may be taken as a symbol of consciousness and rationality.

This polarity between the attic and the basement in Nick's mind is quite demonstrative of his "obsessional" tendencies. There is nothing unduly fraught with anxiety in the memory of his mother's and father's wedding cake. One may even go as far as to suggest that it carries hints of a happier time, that it stands for what it is in reality, a symbol of matrimonial alliance, which has been fertile and to which Nick owes his own existence, the very thing that he so dearly values and is so desperately anxious to save. Equally, there is nothing inordinately fearsome in his recollection of "jars and snakes and other specimens" that his "father had collected as a boy and preserved in alcohol" (*MWW* 131; *NAS* 146). Once again, one may point out that there is a positive element in this recollection inasmuch as it communicates something of the enthusiasms of the father as a boy and his nascent interest in science.

It is only when Nick's memories move down and away from the high and harmonious level of the attic to the intermediate ground level of the "back yard" of his grandfather's house and, later, farther down to the basement of his parents' new house that the elements of fire, destruction, and irremediable loss break loose. The jars of snakes and specimens, preserved simultaneously in the well ordered world of science and the attic, are brought down and set on fire in the courtyard, reducing them to ashes. The initiator of this descending movement of destruction is beyond the reach of Nick's memory, but is undoubtedly his mother. She appears to be relentless in her efforts to create a world of domestic order and cleanliness to replace that of her husband's more scientific one. Her final effort, that of cleaning out the basement of the new house, violates the remaining relics of the symbolically buried past of her husband, his mementos that are deposited there below the ground. It was as if she had opened a tomb and robbed it of its buried sacred objects in order to clean it. In general, one may state that a grave robbed is no longer a grave. An empty grave betrays its own definition. One may also add that a grave robbed is a grave *desecrated* because it clearly attests to an intrusion of the living upon the dead. It sets free all the subconscious fantasies of death, interment and disappearance, on the one hand, and disinterment and a more unsettling redisappearance, on the other. The disappearance of a corpse, the only tangible sign of the being of the dead, is a far more difficult problem for the psyche to come to grips with than death itself. The memory of the destruction by fire of "stone axes and some skinning knives and tools for making arrow-heads and pieces of pottery and many arrow-heads," all primitive man-made tools for protection and sustenance of life, are disturbing to Nick because they elicit in him subconscious fantasies of death, interment, disinterment, and infernal annihilation at a time when he is struggling to keep such fantasies under control.

So the dialectical nature of Nick's memories of the attic and the basement and what each holds and hides of the past can be considered as directly related to the obsessional nature of Nick's personality. Incidentally, that is precisely why the evocations of these memories do not offer any evidence of being entirely satisfactory as an antidote to Nick's problems beyond their utility as an intentional act of the "imaginative consciousness." They do not offer the peace of trout fishing along the remembered or imagined trout streams.

In the context of the language developed in this essay, the strategy which most adequately shows the role played by Nick's "imaginative consciousness" is the one used by Nick at nights when he fails to get beyond "on earth as it is in heaven" in his prayers. On such nights, he explains:

I would try to remember all the animals in the world by name and then the birds and then fishes and then countries and cities and then kinds of food and the names of all the streets I could remember in Chicago. (*MWW* 133; *NAS* 148)

In the preceding passage, the "imaginative consciousness" comes closest in this short story to "conceptual consciousness." The images which it provides attain a high degree of conceptual generality. They stand for universal categories. Even the names of streets are remembered merely as names, like ordinal numbers assigned to particulars. What is interesting about these images in relation to the state of Nick's mind is that he finds in them exactly what he invests in them, no more and no less. These images evoke no other contiguous or subjacent ones. They function as the objects of a consciousness to whose existence they bear witness. They simultaneously offer Nick two internally related advantages: a relatively firm assurance of the existence of his consciousness, and a degree of control over the images of it. The progression of images from the imaginative to the conceptual makes up the narrative discourse within which the stories within the short story "Now I Lay Me" unfold. However, the narrative discourse of the main story itself (from the initial sound that the silkworms eating in the mulberry leaves make to Nick's conversation with John) is constructed through perceptual auditory images, which provide a contrast to the images of the stories contained within it.

Perceptual, Imaginative, Preoneiric, and Oneiric Consciousness in "A Way You'll Never Be"

In "A Way You'll Never Be," Nick is entering what one may call a necropolis. Nick is the center of consciousness in this short story. He transforms into words a succession of images of the dead lying "alone or in clumps in the high grass and along the road" (*Winner Take Nothing [WTN]* 47; *NAS* 154). The instruments of war—"stick bombs, helmets, rifles, intrenching tools, ammunition boxes, star-shell pistols,'' all carefully perceived and accurately rendered—make up the horizon of the dead bodies. Nick's perpetual powers in intensity and accuracy match those he has already manifested in the Chapter VI sketch.

The long sad litany of the dead and the implements of death is finally interrupted by an agitated second lieutenant who abruptly stops Nick. After some sharp protest against his presence on the battlefield, the lieutenant takes Nick to see Captain Paravicini. It is in the conversation with Captain Paravicini, Nick's older friend and the commander of the second battalion, that it becomes clear that Nick is suffering from a head wound, which the captain thinks ''should have been trepanned'' (*WTN* 52; *NAS* 159). Nick, however, claims, ''I'm all right. I can't sleep without a light of some sort. That's all I have now'' (*WTN* 52; *NAS* 159). But soon it becomes clear that Nick's claim of being ''all right'' is tragically hollow. The critical and complex nature of his emotional problems far surpasses that which he suffered from in ''Now I Lay Me.'' Quite perceptive in recognizing the gravity of Nick's condition, Paravicini suggests that Nick lie down on a bunk in the dugout and take a nap. It is when Nick lies down that his mind utterly loses its organizing and regulative sway over his thoughts. They commence to break upon him in quasi-automatic fashion. Soon his mind is awash in disjointed memories of fear on the battlefield, his dependence on alcohol to bolster his courage, his inability to find his grappa during an attack (which he considers to have precipitated his present condition), and the presence of the dead and the wounded.

Once again, as in ''Now I Lay Me,'' these details find their way into the narrative discourse through the mediation of the images of the ''imaginative consciousness.'' Nick's jumbled, freely and swiftly moving memories render the narrative prose more supple than it is in the beginning scenes of the story. Soon, however, there comes a rapid and abrupt shift from Nick's recollections of the battlefield in Italy to his days in Paris before his participation in the war. This shift is drastic and signals the passage from minimally associated and cohesive juxtaposition of memories to free association and discordant juxtapositions:

And there was Gaby Delys, oddly enough, with feathers on; you called me baby doll a year ago tadada you said that I was rather nice to know tadada with feathers on, with feathers off, the great Gaby and my name's Harry Pilcer, too, we used to step out of the far side of the taxis when it got steep going up the hill and he could see that hill every night when he dreamed with Sacré Coeur, blown white, like a soap bubble. (*WTN* 53; *NAS* 161)

Nick reveals that in this recurring flashback of events ''The Paris part came earlier and he was not frightened of it except when she had gone off with some one else and the fear that they might take the same driver twice'' (*WTN* 54; *NAS* 161). The ''Paris part'' appears as what I refer to as preoneiric images or

what Sartre relegates to the category of "hypnogogic images." These are extremely vivid images which, as Sartre has explained, fall into the realm of
"quasi-observation" (Sartre 1972, 53). Sartre has further pointed out that the

hypnogogic image is experienced as being "more true than nature," just as a particularly significant portrait is said to be truer than its model. But it is only an image. But
consciousness affirms nothing concerning its real nature: whether it is constructed of
actual material, whether it is an illusion, or an unusually vivid memory. (Sartre 1972,
53)

E. R. Hagemann (1981, 25–27) and Joseph M. Flora (1982, 130–31) have
both identified the actual counterparts of Gaby Delys (the singer Gabrielle Deslys), Pilcer (the famous dancer Harry Pilcer) and the song "A Broken Doll,"
which Gaby sings in the passage that I have quoted. Even though Nick's personal acquaintance with Deslys and Pilcer is quite doubtful, the passage contains references to two real people and a real song. Nevertheless, the free-
associative or stream-of-consciousness pattern of the passage gives it an unusual surrealistic quality. The hypnogogic—or more precisely, the preoneiric—
images in the passage confer a subtle metaphoric dimension upon it to the
extent that they make evident the precarious state of Nick's mind. It is simply
through the mediation of style that these inherently self-limiting preoneiric images are given a significant metaphoric aspect.

    Soon sleep intrudes upon these images. Nick passes from the preoneiric to
the oneiric stage as he sees the "Sacré Coeur, blown white, like a soap bubble." The preoneiric images, no matter how vivid, are still imperceptibly controlled by the preoneiric consciousness. Once Nick falls asleep, the oneiric
consciousness takes over and divests the images of any conscious control and
invests them with the unlimited range and power of the subconscious. Nick's
immediate fear in the dream world is the presence or absence of his girl (who
is obviously not Gaby), the possibility of her having gone off with someone,
and the less comprehensible "fear that they may take the same driver twice"
(WTN 59; NAS 161). These fears are still loosely connected with preoneiric
images. But without any perceptible transition, Nick falls into deep sleep and
the more fearsome intimations of the subconscious. Nick reports the dream in
oneiric images:

those were the nights the river ran so much wider and stiller than it should and outside
of Fossalta there was a low house painted yellow with willows all around it and a low
stable and there was a canal, and he had been there a thousand times and never seen it,
but there it was every night as plain as the hill, only it frightened him. (WTN 53; NAS
161)

    The first discernible feature of this dream is that it tells a story; it is a nar-
rative. The discourse of the dream and the narrative discourse have much in

common. The dream is, to quote Sartre again, "primarily a story and our interest in it is of the same sort as the naive reader in a novel. It is lived as a fiction and it is only in considering it as a fiction which happens as such that we can understand the sort of reaction that it arouses in the sleeper" (Sartre 1972, 255). The story and its reader or hearer become united in the act of reading or hearing. Similarly, the dream and the dreamer are inseparable in the act of dreaming. Considered from this point of view, Nick's dream is interesting in that it tells a story in a series of adjacent oneiric images that are concrete and are fixed in the spatio-temporal dimension of the dream. As such, these images are descriptive, passive, static, and opaque. But they terrify Nick. It is within the boundaries of Nick's terror of the dream that its images become metaphoric and mediate between him and his subconscious. Insofar as these images terrify Nick, they are animated by him and their significance is communicated to him, as if he were reading a truly frightening story that related to his life in a direct, personal, and yet mysterious way. This dream tells the primordial story of dying and encounter with death as Nick's subconscious makes it its own and recounts it. And it does so with considerable success, through what may be referred to as a series of *silent* metaphors, inasmuch as they have no intrinsic metaphoric structure. The entire cluster of oneiric images in the dream subconsciously intimates death: the yellow house, the wide still river, the boat whose possibility of movement seems to be negated by the total entropy of the universe of death.

This ensemble of images fully discloses that, for Nick, death is the supreme obsession on the plane of the subconscious. Schneiderman has remarked that the obsessional's "ultimate encounter will be death itself; as much as he fears this encounter, he knows that this is the one that counts" (1983, 147). This "ultimate encounter" constitutes Nick's main preoccupation in time of war. If the yellow house is taken as the house of death, one now understands why Nick declared that "That house meant more than anything and every night he had it. . . . only it frightened him" (*WTN* 53; *NAS* 161). The obsessional is simultaneously fascinated and repelled by death.

These crucial oneiric images are interrupted as Nick wakes up and engages in an explanation of his presence in the dugout with an adjutant and launches into a long disquisition on grasshoppers with him. In the forced, meandering, and gratuitous speech on grasshoppers there is a return to the "reflective consciousness" similar to that in "Now I Lay Me." Its images, too, are as sharp as those in the previous story and serve the same affirmative and supportive function for Nick's consciousness as before. One reads, for example, that the larger grasshoppers that fly "have vivid colored wings, some are bright red, others yellow barred with black, but their wings go to pieces in the water and they make a very blowsy bait" (*WTN* 56; *NAS* 164). However, the accumulative effect of these images on Nick's consciousness is not as cohesive and well integrated as in "Now I Lay Me." Correspondingly, the narrated speech, as a whole, is disjointed and attests to Nick's deteriorating state of mind.

"In Another Country": A Return to Perceptual Images and
Non-Reflective Consciousness

In "In Another Country," Nick is going through physical therapy for yet another injury in a hospital in Milan. This time it is a knee wound. However, emotionally he has somewhat regained his balance. No doubt the fear of death still hovers over him. He admits that "I was very much afraid to die, and often lay in bed at night by myself, afraid to die and wondering how I would be when I went back to the front again" (*MWW* 36; *NAS* 171). He realizes the hospital where he is receiving therapy is still both a place of healing *and* dying. He observes that "There were usually funerals starting from the courtyard" of the hospital (*MWW* 33; *NAS* 168). However, the fear of death no longer paralyzes him. At this time, his visual statements evoke a measure of aesthetic appreciation, even sensuality, rather than a feeling of foreboding and anxiety. One reads, for instance, that "The hospital was very old and very beautiful" (*MWW* 33; *NAS* 168). Or that "it was pleasant along the streets looking in the windows," even though what Nick sees is a veritable *nature morte* tableau of eviscerated and dead animals:

There was much game hanging outside the shops, and the snow powdered in the fur of the foxes and the wind blew their tails. The deer hung stiff and heavy and empty, and small birds blew in the wind and the wind turned their feathers. (*MWW* 33; *NAS* 168)

The sobriety of the poetics of this narrative description matches Nick's newly acquired sense of emotional control and steadiness. The images have the weight and the solidity that "perceptual consciousness" confers upon them. They have a certain palpable texture that one would find, say, in a Cézanne still life painting, very rich and very sensuous. Their mystery is now entirely that of the natural world. They are restored to their appropriate external dimension, because Nick is again able to perceive them as such. Death now has taken its permanent existential place in Nick's mind, a phenomenon that, paradoxically, does not deaden but rather intensifies life for him. The constant encounter with it renders his life "authentic," to borrow a term from Martin Heidegger. So now Nick walks along the streets and canals of Milan, crosses its bridges, feels the warmth of roasted chestnuts in his pockets, and enjoys the smoky warmth of the Café Cova. Death is still there as his constant companion, but the awareness of it makes the feeling of the warm roasted chestnuts in his pockets so much more precious. He has learned to look at the world calmly in the inevitable awareness of death, a lesson that has almost cost him his life and sanity.

In the light of what has been said, one may conclude that in the interplay between Nick's consciousness and its objects certain aspects of Nick's emotional life come to the fore. As Sartre has put it in his article on Francis Ponge's poetry, *"L'Homme et les choses"* ("Man and Things"), in *Situations I:*

What we find everywhere, in the inkpot, on the phonograph needle, on the honey on the slice of bread, is ourselves, always us. And this scale of muffled and obscure feelings that we bring to light, we already had—or rather we *were* these feelings. Only they were not visible, they were hiding in the bushes, among the rocks, almost useless. Because man is not put together in himself, but outside of himself, between heaven and earth.[1] (1947, 291)

And that seems to be the story of Nick's falling apart and being put back together again somewhere between fishing along the rivers of Michigan in his mind and walking along the streets of Milan in reality.

Note

1. "Ce que nous trouvons partout, dans l'encrier, sur l'aiguille du phonographe, sur le miel de la tartine, c'est nous-mêmes, toujours nous. Et cette gamme de sentiments sourds et obscure que nous mettons au jour, nous l'avions déja—ou plutôt nous *étions* ces sentiments. Seulement ils ne se laissaient pas voir, ils se cachaient dans les buissons, entre les pierres, presque inutiles. Car l'homme n'est pas ramassé en lui-même, mais dehors, toujours dehors, du ciel à la terre." (The translation is mine.)

References

Bachelard, Gaston. *La Poétique de l'espace.* Paris: Presses Universitaires de France, 1970.

Derounian, Kathryn Zabelle. "An Examination of the Drafts of Hemingway's Chapters 'Nick sat against the wall of the church. . . .' " *Critical Essays on Hemingway's* In Our Time. Ed. Michael S. Reynolds. Boston: G. K. Hall and Co., 1983.

Ficken, Carl. "Point of View in the Nick Adams Stories." *The Short Stories of Ernest Hemingway: Critical Essays.* Ed. Jackson J. Benson. Durham, NC: Duke UP, 1975.

Flora, Joseph M. *Hemingway's Nick Adams Stories.* Baton Rouge: Louisiana UP, 1982.

Gurwitsch, Aron. *The Field of Consciousness.* Pittsburgh: Duquesne UP, 1964.

Hagemann, E. R. "The Feather Dancer in 'A Way You'll Never Be.' " *Hemingway Notes* 6.2 (1981):25–29.

Hemingway, Ernest. *In Our Time.* 1925. New York: Scribner, 1985.

———. *Men Without Women.* 1927. New York: Scribner, 1985.

———. *The Nick Adams Stories.* New York: Scribner, 1972.

———. *Winner Take Nothing.* 1930. New York: Scribner, 1985.

Hovey, Richard B. " 'Now I Lay Me': A Psychological Interpretation." *The Short Stories of Ernest Hemingway: Critical Essays.* Ed. Jackson J. Benson. Durham, NC: Duke UP, 1975.

Husserl, Edmund. *Ideas.* Trans. W. R. Boyce Gibson. New York: Collier Books, 1962.

Sartre, Jean-Paul. *The Psychology of Imagination.* Secaucus, NJ: Citadel Press, 1972.

———. *Situations I.* Paris: Éditions Gallimard, 1947.

Schneiderman, Stuart. *Jacques Lacan: The Death of an Intellectual Hero.* Cambridge, MA: Harvard UP, 1983.

Selected Bibliography

Books by Ernest Hemingway

Across the River and into the Trees. New York: Scribner, 1950.

By-Line: Ernest Hemingway. Selected Articles and Dispatches of Four Decades. Ed. William White. New York: Scribner, 1967.

Complete Short Stories of Ernest Hemingway, The. New York: Scribner, 1987.

Dangerous Summer, The. Introduced by James Michener. New York: Scribner, 1985.

Death in the Afternoon. New York: Scribner, 1932.

88 Poems. Ed. Nicholas Gerogiannis. New York: Harcourt, 1979.

Ernest Hemingway: Selected Letters, 1917–1961. Ed. Carlos Baker. New York: Scribner, 1981.

Farewell to Arms, A. New York: Scribner, 1929.

Fifth Column and Four Stories of the Spanish Civil War, The. New York: Scribner, 1972.

For Whom the Bell Tolls. New York: Scribner, 1940.

Garden of Eden, The. New York: Scribner, 1986.

Green Hills of Africa. New York: Scribner, 1935.

Hemingway: The Wild Years. Ed. and introduced by Gene Z. Hanrahan. New York: Dell Publishing, 1962.

in our time. Paris: Three Mountains Press, 1924.

In Our Time. New York: Boni & Liveright, 1925.

Islands in the Stream. New York: Scribner, 1970.

Men at War. Ed. and introduced by Ernest Hemingway. New York: Crown Publishers, 1942.

Men Without Women. New York: Scribner, 1927.

Moveable Feast, A. New York: Scribner, 1964.

Nick Adams Stories, The. Preface by Philip Young. New York: Scribner, 1972.

Old Man and the Sea, The. New York: Scribner, 1952.

Spanish Earth, The. Introduced by Jasper Wood. Cleveland: J. B. Savage Co., 1938.

Sun Also Rises, The. New York: Scribner, 1926.
To Have and Have Not. New York: Scribner, 1937.
Torrents of Spring, The. New York: Scribner, 1926.
Winner Take Nothing. New York: Scribner, 1933.

Books about Ernest Hemingway

Algren, Nelson. *Notes from a Sea Diary: Hemingway All the Way.* New York: Putnam, 1965.
Arnold, Lloyd R. *High on the Wild with Hemingway.* Caldwell, ID: Caxton Printers, 1968.
Asselineau, Roger, ed. *The Literary Reputation of Hemingway in Europe.* New York: New York UP, 1965.
Astro, Richard, and Jackson J. Benson, eds. *Hemingway in Our Time.* Corvallis, OR: Oregon State UP, 1974.
Atkins, John, *The Art of Ernest Hemingway.* London: Spring Books, 1952.
Baker, Carlos. *Ernest Hemingway: A Life Story.* New York: Scribner, 1969.
——. *Ernest Hemingway: Critiques of Four Major Novels.* New York: Scribner, 1962.
——. *Hemingway: The Writer as Artist.* Princeton, NJ: Princeton UP, 1972.
Benson, Jackson J. *Hemingway: The Writer's Art of Self-Defense.* Minneapolis: U of Minnesota P, 1969.
——, ed. *The Short Stories of Ernest Hemingway: Critical Essays.* Durham, NC: Duke UP, 1975.
Brasch, James D., and Joseph Sigman. *Hemingway's Library: A Composite Record.* New York: Garland, 1981.
Bruccoli, Matthew J. *Scott and Ernest.* New York: Random House, 1978.
Buckley, Peter. *Ernest.* New York: Dial Press, 1978.
Burgess, Anthony. *Ernest Hemingway and His World.* New York: Scribner, 1978.
DeFalco, Joseph. *The Hero in Hemingway's Short Stories.* Pittsburgh: U of Pittsburgh P, 1963.
Donaldson, Scott. *By Force of Will.* New York: Viking, 1977.
Fenton, Charles A. *The Apprenticeship of Ernest Hemingway.* New York: Farrar, Straus, 1954.
Fuentes, Norberto. *Hemingway in Cuba.* Secaucus, NJ: Lyle Stuart, 1984.
Grebstein, Sheldon N. *Hemingway's Craft.* Carbondale, IL: Southern Illinois UP, 1973.
Griffin, Peter. *Along with Youth.* New York: Oxford UP, 1985.
Gurko, Leo. *Ernest Hemingway and the Pursuit of Heroism.* New York: Crowell, 1968.
Hanneman, Audre. *Ernest Hemingway: A Comprehensive Bibliography.* Princeton, NJ: Princeton UP, 1967.
——. *Supplement to Ernest Hemingway: A Comprehensive Bibliography.* Princeton, NJ: Princeton UP, 1975.
Hemingway, Gregory H. *Papa.* Boston: Houghton Mifflin, 1976.
Hemingway, Jack. *Misadventures of a Fly Fisherman.* Dallas: Taylor Publishing, 1986.
Hemingway, Leicester. *My Brother, Ernest Hemingway.* Cleveland and New York: World Publishing, 1962.
Hemingway, Mary Welsh. *How It Was.* New York: Knopf, 1976.
Hotchner, A.E. *Papa Hemingway.* New York: Random House, 1966.

Hovey, Richard B. *Hemingway: The Inward Terrain.* Seattle: U of Washington P, 1968.

Joost, Nicholas. *Ernest Hemingway and the Little Magazines.* Barre, MA: Barre Publishers, 1968.

Kert, Bernice. *The Hemingway Women.* New York: Norton, 1983.

Lewis, Robert W. *Hemingway on Love.* 1965. New York: Haskell House, 1973.

Lynn, Kenneth S. *Hemingway.* New York: Simon and Schuster, 1987.

McCaffery, John K.M., ed. *Ernest Hemingway: The Man and His Work.* New York: Cooper Square Publishers, 1969.

Meyers, Jeffrey. *Hemingway: A Biography.* New York: Harper & Row, 1985.

————, ed. *Hemingway: The Critical Heritage.* London: Routledge & Kegan Paul, 1982.

Montgomery, Constance Cappel. *Hemingway in Michigan.* New York: Fleet, 1966.

Nagel, James, ed. *Ernest Hemingway: The Writer in Context.* Madison, WI: U of Wisconsin P, 1984.

Noble, Donald R., ed. *Hemingway: A Revaluation.* Troy, NY: Whitson, 1983.

Oldsey, Bernard S., ed. *Ernest Hemingway: The Papers of a Writer.* New York: Garland, 1981.

————. *Hemingway's Hidden Craft.* University Park, PA: Pennsylvania State UP, 1979.

Phillips, Gene D. *Hemingway and Film.* New York: Ungar, 1980.

Pivano, Fernanda. *Hemingway.* Milan: Rusconi, 1985.

Raeburn, John. *Fame Became of Him.* Bloomington: Indiana UP, 1984.

Reynolds, Michael S., ed. *Critical Essays on Ernest Hemingway's "In Our Time."* Boston: G.K. Hall, 1983.

————. *Hemingway's First War.* Princeton, NJ: Princeton UP, 1976.

————. *Hemingway's Reading: 1910–1940. An Inventory.* Princeton, NJ: Princeton UP, 1981.

————. *The Young Hemingway.* Oxford: Basil Blackwell, 1986.

Ross, Lillian. *Portrait of Hemingway.* New York: Simon & Schuster, 1961.

Rovit, Earl, and Gerry Brenner. *Ernest Hemingway,* rev. ed. Boston: G.K. Hall, 1986.

Samuelson, Arnold. *With Hemingway.* New York: Random House, 1984.

Sanford, Marcelline Hemingway. *At the Hemingways.* Boston: Atlantic-Little Brown, 1962.

Smith, Paul. *A Reader's Guide to the Short Stories of Ernest Hemingway.* Boston: G.K. Hall, 1989.

Stephens, Robert O. *Hemingway's Non-Fiction.* Chapel Hill, NC: U of North Carolina P, 1968.

Svoboda, Frederic Joseph. *Hemingway & "The Sun Also Rises."* Lawrence, KA: UP of Kansas, 1983.

Wagner, Linda W., ed. *Ernest Hemingway.* East Lansing, MI: Michigan State UP, 1974.

Watts, Emily S. *Ernest Hemingway and the Arts.* Urbana, IL: U of Illinois P, 1971.

Weeks, Robert P., ed. *Hemingway: A Collection of Critical Essays.* Englewood Cliffs, NJ: Prentice Hall, 1962.

Wylder, Delbert E. *Hemingway's Heroes.* Albuquerque, NM: U of New Mexico P, 1969.

Young, Philip. *Ernest Hemingway: A Reconsideration.* University Park, PA: Pennsylvania State UP, 1966.

Index

About the Editor and Contributors

ROBERT W. LEWIS is Professor of English and Editor of *North Dakota Quarterly* at the University of North Dakota (Grand Forks). He received degrees in English from the University of Pittsburgh (BA), Columbia University (MA), and the University of Illinois (PhD), and he has taught at the University of Nebraska (Lincoln) and the University of Texas (Austin) as well as universities in Italy and Egypt where he held Fulbright-Hays professorships in American studies. Currently at work on a Twayne Masterwork Study of *A Farewell to Arms,* he is also the author of *Hemingway on Love* and numerous articles on Hemingway, American Indian literature, and other topics. Professor Lewis has served as president of the Hemingway Society and chair of the board of directors of the Ernest Hemingway Foundation.

JAMES D. BRASCH teaches at McMaster University in Hamilton, Ontario, and is the author (with Joseph Sigman) of *Hemingway's Library: A Composite Record.*

ROBERT E. GAJDUSEK is the author of *Hemingway's Paris* and of similar photography books on Hemingway's Italy and Hemingway's Cuba, which are forthcoming.

BARRY GROSS, who taught in England, Portugal, and Israel, now teaches at Michigan State University and has published widely on twentieth century American literature.

PETER L. HAYS, who teaches at the University of California at Davis, is the author of numerous essays on Hemingway and other modern American writers.

DONALD JUNKINS of the University of Massachusetts, Amherst, is a widely published poet as well as a critic of nineteenth and twentieth century American literature.

EUGENE KANJO teaches at the University of Redlands in California and writes on both nineteenth and twentieth century American literature and film.

FERN KORY is finishing a dissertation on Hemingway at the University of California, Santa Barbara.

ALAN MARGOLIES teaches in the John Jay College of Criminal Justice in New York and has published widely on twentieth century American literature, and especially on the work of Fitzgerald.

LAWRENCE H. MARTIN, JR., teaches at Hampden-Sydney College (Virginia) and writes on twentieth century literature.

LINDA PATTERSON MILLER teaches at Pennsylvania State University (Ogontz) and is at work on a biography of Hemingway's friend of the 1920s, Gerald Murphy.

ERIK NAKJAVANI teaches at the University of Pittsburgh, Bradford, and publishes in comparative literature with a special interest in Hemingway's aesthetics.

CHARLES M. OLIVER of Ohio Northern University edits *The Hemingway Review* and edited *A Moving Picture Feast: A Filmgoer's Hemingway* (Praeger, 1989).

MICHAEL S. REYNOLDS teaches at North Carolina State University (Raleigh) and is the author of *Hemingway's First War: The Making of "A Farewell to Arms,"* and also *The Young Hemingway,* and *Hemingway: The Paris Years* (the first two volumes of his biography).

JOHN PAUL RUSSO teaches at the University of Miami (Florida) and held a Fulbright-Hays grant to Italy in 1987–88.

FRANK SCAFELLA teaches at West Virginia University, organized the program of the Third International Hemingway Conference in Schruns (Austria), and is editing those proceedings for Oxford UP.

PAUL SMITH who teaches at Trinity College (Connecticut) was the founding president of the Hemingway Society and is the author of *A Reader's Guide to the Short Stories of Ernest Hemingway*.

E. ROGER STEPHENSON teaches at Canisius College (Buffalo, NY) and writes on nineteenth and twentieth century American literature.

WITHDRAWN